Irish Blood, English Heart, Ulster Fry

Return Journeys to Ireland

ANNIE CAULFIELD

VIKING
an imprint of
PENGUIN BOOKS

VIKING

Published by the Penguin Group
Penguin Books Ltd, 80 Strand, London WC2R ORL, England
Penguin Group (USA) Inc., 375 Hudson Street, New York, New York 10014, USA
Penguin Group (Canada), 10 Alcorn Avenue, Toronto, Ontario, Canada M4V 3B2
(a division of Pearson Penguin Canada Inc.)
Penguin Ireland, 25 St Stephen's Green, Dublin 2, Ireland (a division of Penguin Books Ltd)
Penguin Group (Australia), 250 Camberwell Road,
Camberwell, Victoria 3124, Australia (a division of Pearson Australia Group Pty Ltd)
Penguin Books India Pvt Ltd, 11 Community Centre,
Panchsheel Park, New Delhi – 110 017, India
Penguin Group (NZ), cnr Airborne and Rosedale Roads, Albany,
Auckland 1310, New Zealand (a division of Pearson New Zealand Ltd)
Penguin Books (South Africa) (Pty) Ltd, 24 Sturdee Avenue,
Rosebank 2196, South Africa

Penguin Books Ltd, Registered Offices: 80 Strand, London WC2R ORL, England

www.penguin.com

First published 2005
1

Set in Monotype Bembo 12pt/14.75pt
Typeset by Palimpsest Book Production Limited, Polmont, Stirlingshire
Printed in Great Britain by Clays Ltd, St Ives plc

A CIP catalogue record for this book is available from the British Library

ISBN 0-670-91445-2

For Martin McNamara – thank you

Contents

Acknowledgements

With all my thanks to the following, in alphabetical but no other order: all of my family right down to the under-cousins; Kevin Anderson; Juliet Burton; William Conacher; Sarah Daniels; Derry City Tours; Ann and Tom Garry; Eleo Gordon; Peter Kavanagh; Eamon Kelly; Jean Kitson; Martin McCrossan; Mary McNamara; Jerry Mallet and family; Paddy Murphy; Jan Nugent; Woodrow Phoenix; Jon Rovira; Micheline Stienberg; Jenny Sykes; Diana Tyler; Mike Walker; Molly and Jasmine Warwick; and the Westway team for their tolerance.

1. George, Don't Do That

The people we were related to seemed to be George Best, Sergeant Lynch in *Z Cars* and Cassius Clay. When these men appeared on television, my mother gave such a knowledgeable running commentary on their state of health and well being, they couldn't possibly be strangers.

My mother also knew them well enough to chide them if they were on television doing something she disapproved of: 'George! You're half asleep!' 'That's enough chat, Cassius, thump him.' 'Bert Lynch, did you not see the poor man wasn't wise?'

Sergeant Bert Lynch, although making occasional errors of judgement, never provoked the hurt, rage and berating of the screen that erupted when George and Cassius finally went too far and she was done with them. George had been silly about girls and drink. Cassius had changed his name and turned − 'Too full of himself, like a maniac.'

Such high-level emotional involvement led me to conclude that not only did my mother know these men, they must be cousins or uncles. We had dozens of cousins and uncles, seldom seen in the flesh, but much talked about. There was a professional footballer, some of them were policemen − none of them had done anything as interesting as turn into maniacs, but I had high hopes of them.

We didn't see our relatives because we'd left them behind in another country. Northern Ireland. George Best and Sergeant Lynch talked like the relatives. They talked like us. Not many people in England did. Cassius Clay was the first black person I'd ever seen. He was something other, like us, so probably belonged to us.

I was four when we moved from Northern Ireland. I was too young to think anything much about leaving, but England was a disappointment. For one thing, talk of England had all been a trick, because we seemed to be in Wales.

Geography was one of many weak areas in my head when I was four years old, but I could tell the words weren't the same: England, Wales. So they needn't think I was fooled.

I'd been hopeful of England because I had worked out that England was where cartoons happened. I knew cartoons didn't happen in Northern Ireland, I could see that looking out the window, so I was sure that they must happen in that other place, the only other place I'd heard of, England. England would be bright coloured, teeming with talking bears, rabbits and exploding cats. Looking out the window in England would be as good as watching television.

But North Wales looked like Northern Ireland. And cartoons, my father informed me as I wept on our new kitchen floor, happened in a place that was 'not real'. Whatever that meant. Not only had we pitched up in a profoundly disappointing place, I had to start school among unintelligible children and learn songs in a whole new language. Songs about birds sitting on the roof of a house. Maybe it was just the one song that took a very long time to learn, or there's a whole sub-section of traditional Welsh music devoted to the bird-on-house-plague that afflicted the place in some traditional-music-composing era. What-ever the reason, to this day I know the Welsh for 'the bird is on the roof of the house'. I can't say it's stood me in good stead.

We lived on an RAF base full of stranded English officers and their families – no real consolation for the sudden onset of school and the lack of cartoon animals outside the windows. My interest in the place rallied when new neighbours moved in. Black Americans. I immediately started stalking them.

Despite me, the new neighbours became very friendly with my mother. Something about my mother's rapid bonding with this family fuelled my suspicion that Cassius Clay was one of us.

My mother and I started using American words for things – *candies, the movies, the trunk of the car* . . . The Americans gleefully copied my mother's reverse-angle English: 'Would you not have a cup of tea?' We were always calling in and out of each other's houses, swapping dishes of food and not behaving like the other officers' politely boxed-in families.

Too soon, the Americans moved away. This was worse than the whole trick about cartoons. Something of a drama queen of a child, I was again disappointed to learn that lying on the kitchen floor and weeping loudly didn't change the harsh realities of life.

I persisted with the floor tantrums anyway, just to have something to do, now the Americans were gone. Close to the moment when I was going to drive her to have her own floor tantrums, my mother had a reprieve. We had replacement neighbours. New Americans. We were heading round with home-baked soda bread and welcomes right away . . .

I balked at the sight of them and howled with rage. My mother had lied. These weren't real Americans. They were putting on the accent but I could do that. Did they think I wouldn't notice they were the wrong colour?

As she apologized to the shocked couple from Texas and hauled me wailing home to bed, my mother told me that most Americans were white. I couldn't understand why she was siding with the neighbours in the plot against me. But there it was, leaving Northern Ireland meant your father started raving about things being 'not real', and your own mother turned against you.

The diversion to Wales lasted only six months, then we settled in London, England proper. By the time I was six, I'd grown hard and cynical and knew there was no point bothering myself with great expectations of the new country.

My accent began to change; my younger brother and sister started speaking and sounded like they'd always been in England. It worried me that they didn't have much to say other than 'mine!' Usually about something that was mine. But the siblings were small and could always be ignored. It was more worrying to discover that my job, as a child, was to keep learning things, with no resting in front of cartoons when I felt I knew quite enough about the world. And the things I had to learn changed all the time – just when I'd got done with shoelace tying, there was telling the time and plaiting my own hair. To add to the difficulty, I learnt that very little information could be trusted. Especially information that came from my parents. For example, as soon as I started to learn the book-reading business, I found stories that led me to suspect real Americans were probably not black or white, but red.

As for the English, I'd learnt, so far, that they were the ones you needed to be like. Especially at school. Never mind multiculturalism, the dominant culture was white and cockney, jeering at parents whose accents were African, Greek, Italian, Eastern European, too obviously from the officers' married quarters . . . or not recognized as Irish.

'Your mum's German,' the boy who sat behind me kept insisting. There were worse things to be than a suspected German. This boy behind me, Glen Walker, had an older brother with a shaved head who talked about something called 'paki-bashing'.

I was nearly seven, I was flexible, I could float like a butterfly and avoid anyone bashing me. If only my parents would flex too. Not only did they insist on maintaining their unrecognized, guttural accent, my mother slapped me for saying 'paki' and, determined to show we were as good as anybody, she dressed us with a rigid elegance only the Queen bothered with in London. Dresses, coats and hats to match. I'd leave the house hoping to die.

'You're German and you're posh,' Glen Walker said on the way to school.

I wasn't sure what posh meant. I suspected it might be worse than the traitorous implications of German.

The way we dressed didn't seem to be from the same era as the miniskirts in the streets around us. Several times I'd mentioned wanting a miniskirt myself, but my mother dismissed the style as 'immodest'.

Our seventeen-year-old baby-sitter wore a minuscule miniskirt. She was vaguely related to an RAF neighbour. This had confused my mother because, as she later muttered, 'It was obvious the sort of her from those skirts.'

I liked the baby-sitter, she let us get out of bed in the night and smoke cigarettes with her. She also hung around with a boy at the end of the road who she told us she 'snogged'. I knew to say nothing about the cigarettes, but didn't know my mother would be so outraged by inquiries about the meaning of 'snogged', that the baby-sitter would be permanently replaced by a dour woman recommended by the parish priest.

My mother's involvement with priests, and my father's lack of involvement, didn't seem spiritually significant to me as a child. I thought it was a man thing, fuelling my creeping

suspicion that if you grew up to be a man, life was generally better: you had your breakfast cooked, you asked people
to bring you clean shirts and you didn't have to go to mass.
Or catechism. Or benediction, or the stations of the cross
– or any of the hours of endless boredom being a Catholic
involved.

Having an accent also seemed to be something to do with
being a Catholic. The priest was Italian and most of the
congregation talked like my mother. No, not quite like her.

'From the South of Ireland,' she'd say of a fellow parish-
ioner, as if they had some kind of handicap it wasn't polite
to notice.

Which was a funny thing, because my father's family lived
in this South of Ireland place. And they had a sweetshop.
What could be wrong with that?

All my father's family lived there except for his mother.
She lived in North Belfast in a big old house full of lodgers.
We'd pay short visits to her because the lodgers took up
most of the room and she didn't like us to discuss them, let
alone speak to them. We'd stay long enough for me to notice
that she went to mass. I didn't know if her husband had got
to skive mass like my father did. Her husband was dead.

He had been a soldier, she'd told me, so I imagined some
kind of heroic war death. If I kept asking her about it, looking for heroic tales, she changed the subject to complain of
the big old house he'd left her to manage, with its back
garden that would grow nothing but nettles.

She did seem to manage, because she had money, fold-
ing paper money that she gave away to her grandchildren
with endearing generosity. She'd hand out generous tokens
because she couldn't come any closer. She was mysterious,
clever and bleak.

I'd complain to myself that she was all very interesting

but not even trying to be the cuddly kind of creature story-books said a grandma should be. Sometimes she talked of leaving Belfast and going back to her people in the South; I encouraged this, of course, because I'd heard about the sweetshop. Surrounded by sweets, she was bound to get cuddly.

Belfast Grandma, as we called her, was part of an annual pilgrimage back to the North. After Belfast, squashed in a small red Hillman, fighting and vomiting, we travelled on to my mother's parents in County Tyrone. They lived on what everyone in our family called 'Granny's farm'. This was an intermittently cuddly Granny. She was a tall, charis-matic, playful and forthright woman, who could probably have persuaded people that Tyrone was 'Granny's County' because she had a gift for making people delighted to be alive if they'd pleased her and feel dead grey in the heart if she dismissed them as an annoyance.

Granny was really a tenant in the farmhouse, or rather my grandfather was, with some low-rent arrangement because he was vaguely related to the landowner. We didn't know or care about these indicators of economic status when we were children. We had free run of all the farmyard, the orchard and surrounding fields. The only taboo was the pig sheds, because, my grandfather said, 'They'd trample a child to a pulp.' The pigs were stinking, squealing, disgusting things, so no one was tempted to find out what it might be like to be a pulp.

Otherwise we were in child paradise; straw bales to climb on; stray cats to chase; unripe fruit to test; slightly scary farm hands to follow about until they'd show us where there was a dead rat and make us retreat screaming, until we thought we'd quite like to be scared some more.

Granny sang Frank Sinatra songs, kept hens and baked.

My grandfather grew vegetables, had a dog called Fury and watched television. Again, here was a man who never seemed to have anything to do with priests. When he went out on Sundays, dressed in his finest, he appeared to be going somewhere less boring than mass. He'd return cheerful, with fruit pastilles for the children, and the mysterious answer to questions on his whereabouts that he'd been 'to see a man about a dog'.

It obviously wasn't his own dog, as he'd left Fury at home. And if he was trying to acquire a new dog, he was taking his time about it.

Once he came home from a Sunday excursion and showed us how to strangle a chicken. This wasn't cuddly, but it was an impressive entertainment.

He never repeated the legendary extrovert act of my mother's childhood – banging two saucepan lids together to stop a baby uncle crying. It stopped the howling uncle so successfully that he started clapping his hands together, imitating the saucepan sound: 'Bim pa! Bim pa!' So memorable was this event that, from that day on, everyone called my grandfather 'Bimpa' and lived in hope of another such outburst of uncharacteristic frivolity.

Bimpa skived priest involvement to do other things but he had turned his Protestant life upside down for priests. He was not only a Protestant by birth, he was in the Royal Ulster Constabulary, as Protestant an organization as it could manage to be. To marry a Catholic he'd had to cause uproar among his colleagues and family – he'd had to convert. He did it, for love. Then, apart from weddings and christenings, he seemed to feel he'd done enough for the priests – they'd got his life, they weren't getting all his Sundays as well.

As if fearful he'd escape back out of the faith, Granny

packed Bimpa's home with statues of the Virgin Mary and pictures of the sanguineous Sacred Heart. My father, as a lackadaisical agnostic, obviously didn't need so much hemming-in with threatening icons of what he was up against, because we'd no such rampant religious accessorizing in our house. And my mother had too much belief in tasteful home furnishings to allow enormous plaster Infants of Prague in the hallways – despite my floor-flinging insistence that we should get some, or the devil would have us.

'Where did you get all this about the devil in your head from?' my mother asked – a fairly disingenuous sort of question to a child brought up a Catholic. But in fairness my mother had always muttered more darkly about 'immodesty' and 'idleness' than about the devil himself.

I expect it would have been the cousins who put all this about the devil in my head.

The cousins were the rogue beasts of the farm holidays. One set in particular. The loud, fearless offspring of my mother's eldest brother, Joe. These children multiplied every year, were good at everything and referred to us as 'the English cousins'.

It soon became clear that being English meant we always fell in the mud on any adventure, cried and bruised the most easily and had the imaginations of stones.

Sporadically, in small hunting packs, the cousins might appear for an afternoon at Granny's, but the real onslaughts came when the family drove up through Derry, crossed the border and converged on the Donegal coast, in the town of Buncrana.

We'd stay in a sedate guest house. Uncle Joe rented a glorious ramshackle Georgian house that rapidly filled to the ceiling with his children and their friends, once they'd burst out of small, hot cars.

Perhaps there was a phase in the sixties where small red cars were a sign of something. We had our small red Hillman; Uncle Joe and his wife Helen had a bright red Volkswagen Beetle each. Somewhere in these Beetles they'd put eight children; two grandparents; a dog; groceries; bedding; towels; clothes; buckets; spades; beach balls – and usually assorted extra children belonging to neighbours or other relatives.

Once everyone had run about their house refusing to share rooms with brothers who bit, or sisters who'd stolen a cardigan, imagining where a ghost might be, or a secret passage full of dead nuns, someone would shout: 'You children get out of the house!'

My parents would sit drinking tea and playing cards with the other adults, paying no attention to pleas that it was raining, or we wanted to watch television – we were driven out to roam the town and beaches with the cousins.

Being children from a danger-seething city, we weren't used to being left to our own devices from dawn to way after dusk. There were only three of us English weaklings, so any opinion we might have about time to go home had little influence. We didn't like it when it was getting dark; we tired quickly and most bizarrely, in the eyes of our uncle's independent children, we wanted to see our parents.

This most frightening family of cousins were fast-moving natural leaders, with athletic strength and sarcastic wit. Their favourite place was the scrappy fairground on the sea front, haunted by the kind of leather-jacketed young men that baby-sitters would snog and children who looked like the kind who went to the other school in North London, kids who had all their parents in prison and would raid our school with sticks.

The cousins would always defend us if fairground children mimicked our English accents. Stones would be thrown, insults screamed and jumpers pulled. But left looking at us when there was no outside threat to us, the cousins found us very poor specimens.

Our main interests were television and food, with my sister and I making an occasional reckless diversion to play with dolls. The cousins did things like swim in the Atlantic every day, regardless of the weather – frequently bad in Donegal – just because they wanted to be able to finish their holiday saying they'd swum every day. Say it truthfully. They were big on truthfully whereas we . . . Well, some kind of shadiness must have crept into us over the water because we saw no harm in a lie about a thing like that. So what if they skipped the day when hailstones swept out of the mountains? Who would know? They didn't follow the twisted logic of this. They always had to climb the highest, jump the furthest, spin fastest on the waltzers and even pray the longest at mass. They seemed to be born with a sense they couldn't rest easy, that there was a long competitive haul ahead and you had to be strong enough for it. Somehow we were raised to feel that we'd already made it, we had a middle-class English life, and it would probably carry on that way. We didn't think there was any problem that couldn't be solved by crying and telling our parents.

Cousin fear made me quite glad when the Buncrana days ended and we could return to Granny's exclusive attention back over the border on the farm. She'd fuss over us warmly, although attempts at rebellion were crushed with shaming references to the cousins' admirable extrovert qualities and religious fervour. Apparently she'd do the same to them – why couldn't they sit quietly, dress neatly, talk elegantly? To us the cousins were eager, brave angels; to them, we were little foreign gentry. Granny kept us all in line with our desperation to be her favourites.

The little foreign gentry had their holiday cut short in the late 1960s. There were people on the television throwing things, breaking windows and yelling in Strabane, a sleepy market town, three miles down the road. A few more miles down the road, in Derry, there were cars on fire, people flinging flaming milk bottles, men with bleeding heads reeling into doorways . . .

Bimpa, Granny and my parents stared at the television.

Bimpa gave out about someone called Bernadette Devlin, who was shouting at the camera.

The television showed Belfast – fire and blood – then back to a car on fire in the evening streets of Strabane.

The next morning I went up to Strabane with Granny – she said there was a prescription to collect, but she wanted to hear the news first hand. On the main street, the man with the chemist shop was sweeping up broken glass and putting wooden boards on his windows. He said that there'd be no stopping them now. Whoever they were. He too seemed to blame Bernadette Devlin.

'That stupid loudmouth wee girl. Haven't we always got on fine here?' he said to Granny. She didn't answer.

'Mind the glass,' she said to me. As she walked away, stiffened.

In a few days there were other things on television. Men in suits talking, talking . . . Then pictures of British soldiers spreading out over the bridge into the city of Derry. My mother pointed at the screen when it showed pictures of a barricaded side-street and said, 'Would you look at the Bogside.'

The Bogside, like Bernadette, was somehow responsible for what was going wrong. So, apparently, were the soldiers – my father said several times that they were 'a big mistake'.

Peculiar, because wasn't someone in the RAF almost the

same as a soldier? Maybe he should be down on the bridge instead of watching television at Granny's.

Bimpa was shouting at someone else on the television now . . . Now a fat man called Paisley was to blame. There were more pictures of cars on fire in Derry, soldiers running and boys were throwing stones in the Bogside. Near the chemist shop in Strabane, more boys were on television, running away from something.

'That'll be Duncan the Orangeman with his windows broken again,' Granny remarked flatly.

It turned out my father wasn't supposed to be on the bridge with the soldiers but he wasn't supposed to be on holiday any more either. We had to leave early and had a week in a hotel in Clacton-on-Sea to calm us down after the upset. I wasn't too upset. There was a shiny new fairground and no cousins to make us swim when it was raining.

I didn't know that this early exodus from the summer holiday was the real leaving of Northern Ireland for us, the one that made the difference. There were no more long summer months on Granny's farm near Strabane, passing through Derry to Buncrana. The place names in the geography of our holiday roamings had taken on meanings way beyond family connections.

Strabane seemed to add prefixes to its name: 'Volatile Border Town Strabane', or 'Heavily Nationalist Strabane'.

Derry and Belfast seemed to be full of death. Buncrana became a haven for IRA men to rest and hide themselves in.

My father wasn't allowed to go back unless it was on 'strict personal business'. If someone was sick or dying, not if he felt like a holiday.

My parents' accent was suddenly very familiar to people in London. No more being mistaken for Germans. Everyone in England knew what a Northern Irish accent sounded like. It sounded like a threat.

I learnt that the words Catholic and Protestant were about something more elusive than who had to go to mass and who got to skive.

I noticed my mother would never watch the news; my father would watch, then come into the kitchen to tell her what had happened in Northern Ireland that day.

'God,' she'd say quietly.

The events that had interrupted our holiday became a dark anxiety in the background to my mother's life. Not so much for my father, not directly. Belfast Grandma had retreated south to the sweetshop. She lived over it, in a tall house in Tipperary, with her sister and two brothers. They formed an eccentric ménage of people who all seemed to get on each other's nerves; they were irritated but they were safe.

My father didn't sit at ease in front of the news. Now he talked to the television. He grieved over Belfast streets he recognized, where houses burnt and people wept to camera. He cursed politicians and pundits who voiced opinions on Northern Ireland. Whatever they were saying, I understood it was more seriously offensive than Cassius Clay changing his name, or George Best doing something silly with a girl.

If my mother, by accident or the suddenness of a news flash, caught sight of a familiar location in a report of a shooting, bombing or riot, she'd freeze. She'd close her eyes and wait for it to be over.

Geography. The world goes round, people move around and before they know it, time has passed and the place they left may no longer be a place they can go back to. Even a small place like Northern Ireland doesn't sit quiet on the map; it disgraces itself, draws as much attention to itself as huge places like America and confuses people who've never even been there when they think about it. I showed a friend of mine a large-scale map of Northern Ireland. He touched it and looked surprised.

'Oh,' he said. 'It's all seasides and lakes.'

I said of course it was. The seasides and lakes were the things I remembered the most.

'It's not the geography I imagine,' my friend said. 'You know, from the news, you think it's all streets. Urban.'

I didn't know how much more knowledgeable I was about Northern Ireland – and I had relations there, dozens of them.

I did know another thing about the geography. Northern Ireland was a really small country. And the odds, as years of news turned into decades, that death and injury wouldn't strike close to my family seemed to become very poor indeed.

I remembered seasides. Lakes, summer farmland and rolling gorse-covered mountains. I knew cousins, aunts and uncles who were funny, smart, easy-going – displaying none of the characteristics of Northern Irish people discussed by politicians and news pundits. I didn't think I was wrong. I didn't think the news was wrong – not the basic facts of bombs, burnt houses, dead people, and then the painful wrangling of something called a peace process. But the two views of the country didn't seem to make a full picture.

I wanted to go back to see where news and memory met or diverged and to see what on earth sort of place it was I thought I came from.

'Well, I'm sure this is a project to be encouraged,' my uncle Joe said when I called. 'But there's a drastic crisis in a golf match on television, distracting me from my normally heartfelt enthusiasm for long-lost nieces. You'll get a more sensible conversation if I call your aunt Helen to the phone . . .'

2. Location, Location . . .

'Imagine if Laurence Llewelyn-Bowen bought that house and said, "You need to knock it all through and have a big living room, and that thing has just got to go, paint it over and put in a big picture window."'

Mikey and I squealed at the idea. We knew how to entertain each other, had struck up a rapport within minutes. He was one of my cousin Veronica's children; on our last meeting he'd thrown a toy at me, but that was probably a three-year-old's notion of rapport. At fifteen he was emerging gloriously himself, interested in fashion, style, a career as a celebrity hairdresser – and to the devil of dullness with Northern Irish politics.

That Laurence Llewelyn-Bowen would be buying a house on a Loyalist estate in Portadown was as unlikely as his surviving the first brushstroke of painting over 'that thing' – a giant mural on the gable end of a house commemorating deceased local charmer Billy Wright.

Billy Wright faced the road, it was impossible to avoid seeing him, just as it would have been impossible for Mikey to grow up in this area and not know who the man was. Never mind that Mikey would rather have seen a mural of Beyonce and would have been overjoyed to see someone as flamboyant as Llewelyn-Bowen move into the neighbourhood – Billy Wright had been the local celebrity he'd had to grow up with.

Billy Wright's nickname was 'King Rat'. He'd been assassinated in the Maze prison in 1997 by the INLA. Some said it was by another Loyalist faction — whatever, he was dead now. Previously his career had included rabble-rousing at Orange marches through Catholic areas of Portadown; leadership of the hard-line Loyalist Volunteer Force; intimidation of softer-spirited local Protestants; drug-dealing and organizing the assassination of local Republicans. There is much evidence to suggest that Billy Wright considered anyone of the Catholic faith to be a Republican and dealt death indiscriminately.

Never mind him, my aunt Helen was in trouble in the back of the car.

'I just pulled this to see what it was and it won't go back now. Is it broken? I think it's broken.'

We pulled over so Mikey and I could attend to the emergency. I'd hired a car with such a ridiculous number of fancy features that you only had to touch a button and all manner of unexpectedness sprang out of dashboards and seatbacks. My aunt had found that at a press of a lever she had a tray table and cup holder in front of her, but the unexpected ensemble refused to spring back from whence it had sprung. It took the three of us shoving to put it back in place.

'I love this car,' Mikey said as we continued our journey. 'It knows automatically when to turn the headlights on. It knows when it's raining. And look at these . . .'

Under our feet were secret compartments. Lifting a tag in the carpet revealed an odd-shaped space in which to hide things — I don't know what — your lunch, your wallet . . . ?

'Very handy for smuggling,' Mikey said.

'Yes,' I said. 'If we pick up any drugs or guns on the journey, we'll put them in there.'

Mikey looked at me, a pretence of shock.

'Guns and drugs? I was thinking eggs.'

My aunt laughed. 'God bless you child for your innocence.'

Later, this story was passed around the family to great amusement – the wild ideas of the cousin from England and the more likely reality. Drugs and guns would be way outside my family's understanding, but impish, innocent smuggling was such common practice only the very holy and law-abiding regarded it as an offence.

What went on in innocent smuggling varied. These days, you would probably bring petrol or farm produce from the South to the North. When we'd crossed the border in my childhood we'd taken groceries and dairy produce from the North to the South because, as Granny said, 'You can understand why an English thing like cornflakes would be more expensive in the South, but that the butter they sell in the North comes from the South to be packed and gets sent back to the South costing more, well there's a hen's logic in that.'

So Granny involved us in small crimes on our holidays, passing by a police and customs hut in a lather of excitement, as the couple of men on duty stopped the car and asked if we'd anything to declare. On hot days I'd panic – what if the butter was melting, dripping out of the boot of the car, and we all had to go to gaol for ever?

Luckily we were never made to pay for these crimes.

Crossing the border had been easy in Granny's day, now it was easy again. In the Troubles, the roads were gun, concrete and metal sheet blocked. You weren't so much worried about your butter melting as a British soldier holding you too long in conversation. You didn't want to be sitting there, talking about where in London you were from with a lonely teenager from Tottenham, when you knew border posts were targets. You didn't even have to be that edgy; talking to a boy with a gun, other armed boys behind him, when you were just trying to visit your relatives, was seldom a comfortable moment.

All over the roads in Northern Ireland, the boys with guns would appear from nowhere and ask you where you were going. Jarring your nerves and wasting your time. You'd have the scary thought that the one who'd stopped you might be the soldier who'd just lost his head with the tension of patrolling Northern Ireland and misunderstand some sudden movement you made for your driving licence . . .

Aunt Helen ran a constant restrained resistance to this. Some morning in the late eighties we'd been stopped by soldiers – we were on a two-mile journey to visit a cousin who'd just had a baby, possibly Mikey had been the baby . . . The young soldier asked Aunt Helen where she was going and where she'd come from.

'Will it really mean anything to you,' she sighed, 'if I tell you the name of the wee townland I've left and the wee townland I'm going to? Will you see them in your mind's eye?'

The soldier looked like he'd cry with his actual eyes.

'I have to ask while we note your number plate.'

'Do you have a grandmother?' my aunt asked him.

He nodded, glancing to see where his companions were.

'Does she drive?'

'No.'

'I expect she takes a bus then, takes a bus to wherever she's going about her business, the sort of harmless business a grandmother like her and myself would be going about.'

'I have to ask,' the soldier said. 'It's my job.'

'Well, a job's a job, I daresay.'

Aunt Helen sighed and told him where she was going.

He said, 'Right then, off you go, sorry to trouble you.'

'I'm very sorry about it as well,' my aunt said politely. Then she made an impatient 'tut' as she sped out of his hearing. 'They're only wee boys. I do feel sorry for them, but still . . . How would he like his granny stopped by a gun?'

She did this sort of thing all the time, no matter how much of a hurry she was in, she had to let at least one soldier a day know how annoyed she was to see him.

The soldiers' absence felt like something had relaxed all over the country. It wasn't about the politics, it was about how their presence made the place feel. Made ordinary people, as they went about their business, feel like criminals.

Of course, I have already confessed my family were criminals, guilty of many egg-smuggling-type crimes. And possible unconfessed damage to the interior of a hire car. The tray table thing kept popping out, we'd definitely done something to it, but we had to press on with our adventure.

'We'll glue it up and say nothing,' my aunt suggested as we arrived at our destination. She had, after all, lived as a Catholic in the hinterland of Portadown, known as 'the Orange Citadel', for several decades and had learnt to discriminate calmly when it came to the subject of what should be worried about and what shouldn't.

Aunt Helen settled herself in her friend's kitchen, introduced me and chatted a while about how much I looked like my mother and, pleasingly, she concluded her observations about me saying, 'I've found she has that same magic way about her that her mother has and her mother had before her.'

Her friend took a long stare at me. I tried to look as though I had a magic way about me but suspected my aunt had oversold me.

'Now,' Aunt Helen said, 'I'll stay here and talk local gossip with Kathleen while you two go down the yard and talk to the men about the eels.' She looked at Kathleen. 'As I said to you, Kathleen, Annie does a bit of writing, so the eels might be a story for her. Go on, Mikey, go with her, it'll be more interesting for you than our gossip.'

I could tell by Mikey's face he didn't think going down the yard to the shores of Lough Neagh, with an icy February wind whipping off the water, would be guaranteed more interesting than gossip.

Not that gossip was accurate for what Aunt Helen did. She seldom stopped talking or asking people questions about themselves, but it was always jubilant: 'Where did you get those beautiful curtains, they remind me of the curtains I was thinking of for the front room only mine had more of a blue thread through them, I think yours are nicer, lovely against your wallpaper, is that new wallpaper?'

Never anything bad about anyone who wasn't in the room, never a word allowed into the conversation that wasn't a positive reinforcement of everyone in the room. She'd hold her hand up if you tried to tell her something she feared would be scandal-mongering: 'Now, if this is gossip, you know I don't want it.' Around her you learnt the difference between gossip and gossip. The way she orchestrated her constant need to converse and yet avoid the bad type of gossip was a skill I'd have tried to cultivate myself, if I hadn't been so fond of hearing bad words about others.

Shivering in our fashionable outfits, Mikey and I made our way down the scrubby grass of the yard.

'Will they know who we are?' Mikey had asked as we went out of the back door.

'Say you're with me,' Aunt Helen told him. 'Go on, the pair of you. Come back and tell me what you've found out.'

'Hmm,' Mikey said, begrudgingly resigning himself to the assignment. 'I expect they'll tell us everything, what with Miss Magic asking.'

'I think it's only fair that she said that about me,' I said.

'You know she says things like that about everybody,' Mikey crushed me.

Lough Neagh ahead of us looked grey, bleak and not at all the sunny shimmering type of lake I remembered as a feature of the countryside.

Mikey suddenly seemed a bit shy. He was so sharp I'd forget he was only just fifteen.

'So,' he said awkwardly, 'you must be used to investigating things.'

'Investigating? I don't know.'

'You must have investigated things before, to write books. What'll we do? Just go up and say, tell us about the eels?'

I panicked as a dog in a cage barked at us and Mikey realized I might not be entirely a proper grown-up and on top of the situation.

'Do you want to go back?' he asked hopefully.

'No, no.' I stepped sideways away from the dog. 'We'll get chatting a bit first.' I took a steadying breath, trying to sound urbane and James-Bond-like, to calm my younger relative. 'Then ease our way into the eel investigation.'

Mikey nodded, happy to see we were putting distance between ourselves and the barking dog. 'It's like a zoo out here, have you ever seen the like?'

Not really. Although more aviary than zoo. The long stretch of yard leading down to the lake shores was full of bird cages, bird sheds and loose-strutting, peculiar-looking birds.

The first man, Ed, was in a long, low shed full of birds I did recognize – pigeons. We introduced ourselves and he showed us eggs that were about to hatch, temperature gauges, baby pigeons feeding . . . I wished I could think of intelligent pigeon questions to ask but I'd never been called upon to be interested in them before.

In addition to the pigeons, Ed had all manner of rare hens, including tiny, jet-black Bantams, like little feathery jewels. The birds were for competition. He pointed with pride to his potential prize-winners, then with sadness to a slightly distorted baby black bantam.

'This one's gone a bit wrong in the breeding,' he said. 'You have to breed them closely related, so you get these genetic freaks.'

The poor freak suddenly made a throaty complaint and darted off behind a bush, as if ashamed in front of the visitors.

I felt we'd made a good show of interest in the fowl collection. It was time for me and my investigative assistant to get to the point.

'I was told you were an eel fisherman.'

'Not me,' Ed said gruffly, turning his attention to a piece of shed that needed hammering. There was an embarrassing pause. Mikey looked at me, imagining I'd know what to do next.

'I see,' I muttered feebly. Any notions Mikey had that I was good at leading an investigation flew off across the lake and gusted away on the cold wind.

Ed nodded to a dark-haired younger man coming up from the direction of the water. 'Damien's the one for the eel fishing. I went once but I couldn't be bothered with it again.'

Well, if fishing for eels was anything like eating them . . . Once I took a bite out of a jellied eel and that was more than enough. No amount of rapturous talk about fresh eels fried in butter from Damien would convince me to bite one again.

'Ask him if he eats them himself,' Ed grinned when Damien had finished the eel-eating eulogy.

'I don't,' Damien admitted. 'People who live round here

seldom eat them these days. They were food when people hadn't two pennies to rub together. Now they're just work.'

But people in the Netherlands, Scandinavia and fancy London restaurants were going crazy to eat eels – 700 tons a year crazy for Lough Neagh eels. And this craziness, like a lot of things in Northern Ireland, meant politics slithered about in the history of what would have seemed the simplest of trades.

I was getting into my investigative stride and did have a vaguely informed question: 'I heard it was always the same families who fished for eels. That they pass the licence on.'

Damien nodded. 'Since the early seventies, that's when they set up that system. So the locals could be the ones to benefit. People say that's unfair, but there's only so many eels in the lake. Less now, the lake's getting polluted and the water level's been dropping. That could take years to sort out.'

Prior to 1960, the predominantly Catholic fishermen had plied a small livelihood from eel fishing. It hadn't looked like being a great money spinner, so nobody bothered with them. A 1960 court ruling suddenly entitled the private company owning the fishing rights to the whole of Lough Neagh to buy all the catch, at a price they decided. So the fishermen couldn't shop around for the best price – an independent way of life had suddenly become a job, unlikely to have a fair rate of pay. Many of the fishermen took to fishing illegally, bumping up the statistics of Catholics with criminal records.

With the help of the local priest, the Lough fishermen formed a union and managed to buy a 20 percent shareholding in the company with the fishing rights. By 1971 the union had bought all the rights and become a co-operative, comprised of families who had traditionally fished for eels on the Lough. By the eighties, with these families being mostly Catholic, there was talk of discrimination against Protestants. But, as Damien said, this talk had rumbled on but not come to a crisis, 'Because it's not all that attractive as work. You don't work long hours for your money but it's tedious work.'

The eel fishermen would go out at night to lay the eel traces, putting a hook on the line at even intervals. I asked Damien if it was soothing to be out on the water in the darkness.

'Not soothing, not so much. It's intensive. You're concentrating on the hooks so you don't hurt yourself and the boat is moving all the time.' He shrugged. 'But it's a short burst of hard work, then it's done. Same thing in the dawn, hauling them in. In a matter of hours your money's made.'

I asked him how big an eel could get, because I had some schoolbook vision of giant rearing beasts with electric tails and shark's teeth.

'Oh, as big as two or three feet.'

I didn't think we were talking about the same type of eels.

Damien was busy now, helping Ed put the finishing touches to a new house for weird hens. Mikey had wandered off up the garden in search of the genetically mutated black bantam, the incest survivor as he called it.

I had a new question. It had come into my head entwined with my schoolbook vision of eels, so I had a suspicion it was an embarrassing question. I was glad Mikey wouldn't be near enough to hear it.

'I was just thinking of something I remember from school. Don't all eels have their spawning grounds in the Sargasso Sea?'

'The where?' Ed looked at me as if I was a little genetically mutated.

'Yes,' Damien said, though looking dubious. 'I heard that. Somewhere like Mexico. And they have to swim for thousands of miles.'

'Well,' Ed retorted, 'if they get to Lough Neagh from Mexico, fair play to them.'

Damien and I looked at each other, both troubled by the fragment of information we shared but couldn't substantiate.

A rumpus up the garden changed the subject.

'He's in the dog's pen!' Mikey was yelling. 'The little incest one's in the dog's pen!'

The big hunting dog was growling at the distorted bantam but backing away.

'They'll be all right,' Ed said. 'The dog knows to leave the fowl alone.'

'The lion and the lamb,' Mikey said brightly, coming back over to us.

Ed smiled at him. 'Well, it won't be the dog that kills it, but that poor thing won't live long.'

'What a shame,' Mikey said. 'It knows it's doomed and meanwhile all its brothers and sisters will go on to glory, winning prizes . . .' He undercut his romantic view of bantam angst, asking, 'So are they worth a lot?'

'Depends what you mean by a lot. They're not from Mexico but they are from France, those wee black ones. They're rare enough.'

'Anyway, they're gorgeous,' Mikey gushed.

And Ed smiled more broadly. 'You could say that. You could indeed.'

Very few places in Northern Ireland were far from the countryside; very few Northern Irish people were completely urban. People fished for eels and kept small hens, even if they did something else for a living. Ed and Damien were electricians. Mikey's own father was a schoolteacher, forever busy on the family farm in his spare time, or helping a neighbour with lambing, or a market garden harvest.

Incidentally, and fair play to them, Lough Neagh eels, like all eels, did try to make their way to the Sargasso Sea to lay their eggs. The Sargasso Sea was closer to Bermuda than Mexico, so pleasant enough for an eel who could make it, I imagine. The baby eels, elvers, would drift back in the Gulf Stream for a couple of years until they pitched up in the lakes and rivers of Europe. This fantastic natural process was rather slow, so to meet the demands of crazy people who liked to eat them, tons of eels were raised on farms locally. Your Lough Neagh eel could have been everywhere, or nowhere.

The almost unbelievable lives of eels may have turned out to be true, but my aunt Helen told other tales about Lough Neagh that I couldn't confirm as fact. She said the Lough was formed by the giant Finn McCool, who lost his temper with a Scottish rival and picked up a clump of earth to throw at him. He threw short, and the earth clump landed in the Irish Sea, forming the Isle of Man. The vast hollow where the clump had been soon filled with rainwater to form the Lough.

Fairy people were supposed to live under the Lough. There were tales of fishermen seeing lights and being lured down to wondrous magic cities below the water . . .

'Oh, I don't think that's true,' Mikey said.

'Really?' My aunt feigned offence. 'Well, young grandson, this is the largest freshwater lake in the British Isles, so don't you think it would have been churlish to leave it without a few legends attached to it?'

Several minutes passed explaining the word churlish to Mikey.

'Oh, I wish I'd never said it,' my aunt complained as we

bickered over possible meanings. 'It's not even a word I normally use. It must have been something I picked up from my English niece.'

'Anyway, English niece,' Mikey tapped my notebook, 'largest freshwater lake, write that down. Using only very long words of course.'

We were giggly all the way home, all the way past Billy Wright and into the warm glow of Mikey's home, where Aunt Helen had other grandchildren needing to be fussed over, to compensate for Mikey getting an exclusive afternoon excursion.

Mikey and his brothers and sisters were the children of my cousin Veronica. We decided the official word for this was 'under-cousins' – and that I was an 'over-cousin'.

Veronica's husband, John – my cousin-in-law? – presented us with bowls of home-made soup to 'take the chill of the lake off us'. Then he rushed out to do something on the farm, tutor a child in difficulties at school, coach the local Gaelic football juniors or continue his struggle to organize cross-community sporting events. Veronica and my aunt went to visit a sick neighbour. Under-cousins and their friends gathered to cross-examine me about writing books. Mikey acted as chairperson.

'Are there crimes in the books?' a burly unrelated child asked me.

'Not really. It's just about Northern Ireland, what it's like.'

'Daddy says you wrote a book about Africa.' Mikey's seven-year-old sister Mary sat next to me. 'Are there animals in it? Any lions or tigers or elephants?'

'Some. There were some elephants, I think, but it wasn't really about them.'

'There are no tigers in Africa.' Mikey the chairman waved a hand as if to disqualify Mary from the round of questioning.

'If I don't ask how will I find out?' she retorted pertly.

Mikey's ten-year-old brother Jack had been hanging back from the inquiring scrum. He was a gruff, sporty little boy, usually accompanied by an obedient train of followers.

'You're not writing about the Troubles are you?' he asked suddenly.

'No,' I said. 'I think enough people have done that.'

'Good,' said Jack. 'Thank Christ for that.' Then he looked at me closely. 'You promise it's not about the Troubles?'

'Promise.'

'Thank Christ,' he said, retreating to the back benches again.

'Stop swearing,' Mary said.

'Fuck off,' Jack said, delighted with himself.

'Anyway, she's writing about interesting people she meets,' said Mikey. 'So obviously it will be mostly about me, who else is there?'

Jack looked at him as if he was something that had just swum up from the Sargasso Sea. 'You have to do something to be put in a book. You're fifteen, you haven't done anything yet.'

'Doesn't matter,' Mikey said. 'I'm just typical of my generation. I want to be fabulous and famous and I don't want to have to do anything for it.' He flounced off to another room to watch the final of *I'm a Celebrity, Get Me Out of Here*. A title that obviously summed up his feelings about life so far.

'He has to do something, doesn't he?' Jack asked with a frown.

'Not necessarily,' I shrugged, thinking that being so splendidly himself was probably enough for someone to have achieved at fifteen in rural Armagh.

Ploughing a lone furrow ran in the family. Mikey's father,

John, tried hard to set up projects to encourage co-operation between the local communities. Sport was his thing, so that's what he tried. He wanted the Gaelic Athletic Association to allow their premises to be used for these mixed events, provided he could get these events to happen at all. He'd had one meeting – twenty Catholics attended and two Protestants. The Protestants he'd invited.

'It's very frustrating,' he told me. 'When they saw the two Protestants, the Catholics said, "You see, they're not interested." But I said to them, "Did you invite the Protestant over the road from you?" And of course they hadn't. None of them had done what I'd asked them, to invite a Protestant they knew. Because they do know each other, Annie. They pass each other in the street every day. They know who's going to be approachable, and who would be out of the question. But no. People don't want to stick their necks out. It's all very well muttering that the Protestants in this area have been in the wrong, a lot of them know that, so it's up to us to say, "We know you're not all the same, let's change things." But it'll be up to me to keep going round inviting Protestants personally. People say they're scared of intimidation from fellow Catholics, it's not that. They're embarrassed they'd ask a Protestant who'd say no, as if embarrassment ever hurt anyone. People get themselves scared talking about intimidation more than they ever actually experienced it. We can't live like that any more. All we're talking about is kids playing a few inter-community games of basketball.'

He'd picked basketball because it had no sectarian connotations, it was a foreign game played by everyone. But even so, his successes were tiny. And the Gaelic Athletic Association weren't helping much. 'Wringing a concession from them to use their grounds is like pulling teeth. A lot of attitude of "Why should we make the first move?" But somebody has to.'

John wanted to keep trying to make first moves, because, he said, 'I don't want all this around my children. My eldest son who's away at university, he said to me after some incident at Drumcree, just down the road, that he wasn't going to have anything more to do with Protestants. I asked him how he'd buy anything in a shop, get on a bus . . . I told him, whatever's happened you can't decide to ignore two-thirds of the people around you. Anyway, it was just a momentary thing. He's long since realized there are more interesting things to do with life than build up a hatred. Thank God. Because if one of my children did choose to get caught up it would break my heart. The only end to that road is death or prison.'

I told him his children seemed singularly uninterested in sectarianism, the Troubles . . . Jack didn't even want to hear about it and didn't want over-cousins writing about it.

'Hmm. Well, you'll have to see,' John said looking at me in his quiet, earnest way. 'Maybe the thing you say you don't want to write about will be the very thing you do write about.'

'I wanted to write a cheerful sort of book,' I said.

John thought about this more than I deserved. 'I expect it depends what happens to you just before you write it.'

He pointed to a large house at a crossroads. 'I wanted to buy that a few years ago. Have it for my tutoring business. But it would have been ashes the day after I'd paid for it.'

'Ashes?'

'My money would have been the wrong colour. The person selling to Catholics is in trouble and the Catholics won't be left to live quietly with what they've bought. That's why I built the extension on our own house for the tutoring business, just to get on with things regardless.'

'So things aren't getting better?'

'Some things are, some things aren't. And . . .' He smiled. 'How I feel about the way things are going depends on what I've seen on any particular day. You're going along opti- mistically then something brings you up short.'

3. Shrapnel Jam

Optimism dominated the next day. A bright winter sun shone, as Mikey, my aunt and I drove through the gnarled plantations of apple trees surrounding the village of Loughgall. We were going to look at antique shops and find a nice tea-room.

'There's people round here have made fortunes from apples,' my aunt said. 'Fruit in general. Strawberries in summer. Pears. Blackcurrants. All manner of fruit but mainly apples.'

We talked a bit about the price of apples, how apple-growing, long and lucratively established in the area, was under threat with the entry of Poland into the European market. Those Poles, with their vast apple orchards and their inevitable price undercutting.

'Maybe they won't be as nice as Irish apples,' Mikey suggested.

'They'll be cheap apples,' Aunt Mary said. 'That's all most people want from an apple.'

Loughgall was chocolate-box cute. Pretty-coloured houses lined the village main street, and there were cute, or intriguing, objects for us to point out to each other in the antique shops. None of them cheap, but what you'd want from an apple you might not want from an antique. You'd want to keep an antique, know its history. Perhaps it came from one of the fine mansion houses around the village. Houses like Loughgall Manor, with its 300-year-old yew tree walk and ornamental lake. Houses built by the seventeenth-century settlers from Worcestershire who established the apple orchards of sharp cooking Bramleys.

Until my freezer-dipping generation came, a good apple pie and the ability to cook one was essential in a Northern Irish kitchen. My aunt would get up in the night if she thought there weren't enough pies nestling in airtight tins in the kitchen below. My transplanted mother could still come close to weeping if she'd turned out a mediocre apple pie. So a blasé attitude to cooking-apple quality was all loose talk from my aunt – a bad apple would make a bad pie and all would be lost.

Loughgall also had Sloan's House, where the Orange Order was founded by Protestant farmers in 1795. This pretty, immaculate village, surrounded by apple blossom in the spring, with shiny copper kettles in the ruched curtained windows of its beeswax-smelling antique shops, could provoke thoughts to bring you up short. But we were having a pleasant day and I'd made my promise to Jack. It was time for tea and a discussion with Aunt Helen about how I drank too much coffee and it was bad for me.

'I'm not saying never have coffee. Just take tea instead occasionally.'

I said I didn't really like tea but maybe I'd have a herbal tea.

'Oh.' She pulled a face. 'You can't drink that. Whatever kind they say it is, there's only two kinds. The kind that tastes like air freshener and the kind that tastes like glue.'

We drove home past the Diamond, where the battle was fought between Protestants and Catholics in 1795 that led to the founding of the Orange Order and the flight of many Catholics from Armagh to the West of Ireland . . . Every corner seemed to have a story relating to the Troubles.

On the corner to turn back into Aunt Helen's road, it

was hard to see if a ten-ton truck was going to round the bend and hit us. A man opposite was fixing his garden fence and had a clear view of the road.

'He might wave us out,' Mikey grumbled.

'Him?' My aunt snorted. 'Thirty years at the end of our road and he'd not wave so much as wave hello, let alone wave you out. He can see it's me in the car. That's what his problem is. And it's how he is, but it's that kind of wee sectarian thing that really annoys me.'

I swung the car over the road fast, sending up a flurry of black crows from a hedgerow, like burnt paper from a bonfire.

'Serve the man right if a huge pile-up skids into his lawn,' I said, as I gritted my teeth and pressed hard on the accelerator.

'Oh, she does get cross,' Mikey squeaked excitedly, once he was sure he'd survived. 'And anyway, you're not allowed to tell her about things like that. She's promised Jack she won't write about the Troubles.'

'Has she?' My aunt smiled. 'Well I expect she'll not get far in life if she ignores a promise made to young Jack.'

'Fine for her. I have to live with him. You say you'll do something and you don't do it he'll nag and nag . . . You should have heard him about the PlayStation . . .'

I did understand how Under-cousin Jack felt — not about the PlayStation, I've forgotten what that domestic drama entailed. But the Troubles . . . The irritating boredom of it all. I'd been older than Jack when the tedium of the Troubles had struck me — a teenager, busy with blue eye-shadow, platform shoes and seeing the sort of boys who worked on fairgrounds in a new and admiring light.

By the time I'd left school, Northern Ireland seemed very far away, I'd almost lost touch with the cousins, uncles and aunts. However, there were reports relayed to me, in my mother's most reproachful tones. The cousins were all over-achieving, with proper jobs – doctors, teachers, university lecturers, bankers, civil engineers. And they all seemed to become adults immediately – getting married, buying houses – while I still had spiky green hair and wasn't sure what to do with myself. I could afford to dither and rebel. I was almost entirely English.

But I couldn't avoid feelings that would well up and surprise me. There was not only the constant news about Northern Ireland. There were the bombs in London and there were the dramas . . . Film, television and theatre loved the Troubles. I hated these dramas. I hated the radio phone-ins after some mainland bomb, where English people would talk endlessly about 'the problem with the Irish'. You'd have thought all we did and all we thought about was something to do with the Troubles.

In a documentary interview, I remember a man from Belfast saying that living with the Troubles was 'like trying to ignore an elephant in the living room'. Was this true? Was it as big as an elephant? And anyway, weren't there other rooms in the house? It seemed to me there were people, particularly in my family, who'd learnt that if an elephant did get in, it was still possible to lock the living-room door and live in other parts of the house. Even if you sometimes felt a bit restricted, or disturbed by trumpetings and crash-ings in the night.

Through the seventies and eighties, I didn't see my relatives often but I knew they were humorous, cultured, accom-plished, hard-working . . . They somehow managed to restrain themselves from what, in England's documentaries and dramas, you'd think must be an innate urge to destruc-tion and self-destruction among the Northern Irish.

The public image of the country had made life difficult for people with the distinctive accent. My mother talked of 'double takes' in shops when she asked for service too loudly.

My local shop in London was run by Gerard, a chatty man from Derry. He told me an Englishwoman had stood at the counter berating him after a bombing in England.

'She stood there in my shop, going on about this bomb when she heard my accent . . .' Easy-going Gerard frowned hard at the memory. 'And she demanded to know why the Irish hated the English so much. I just said to her, "Mrs, go look at your war memorials and see how many of us died for England."'

Around that time he'd been on a train in London talking to his daughter.

'We'd been getting quite noisy, laughing about things that had happened back in Derry at my brother's wedding.'

At the end of the journey, a young man who'd been sitting opposite said to him, in a strong Belfast accent, 'I just want to say, you've inspired me. I've not been here long and I've felt very self-conscious about my accent, what with all the bombs. But I've done nothing, why should I keep my voice down?'

None of this botheration for me; I had an English accent that I was working hard to make more fashionably Estuarine. Quite often, I pretended I was from somewhere else, or people immediately wanted to talk politics. At college, I'd let slip where I was from to some really irritating student from Dublin and he tried to get me into a political discussion. A Republican pose seemed to me the way he made an identity for himself at the big swamping English college. He told me if my family included no political activists, it was because they were middle-class. He said pacifism was also taking a side in Northern Ireland – the side of self-interest. His lack of self-interest led him back to Dublin and a career as a bank manager, so my instincts he was phoney were possibly right.

My family had definitely shifted itself into the middle classes, but pacifism had cost them more than it gained them. Instead of keeping to their tribe, many of my relatives had tried to engage in cross-community activities and politics. They were very dismissive of the threats, from all sides, but there had been recurring threats – hate mail, strange cars following them home at night, intimidating whispers in public places. Nothing had done them any physical harm, but they'd put themselves in the way of harm.

To his dying day, my grandfather, Bimpa, had sighed bitterly over the intransigent and self-interested among his fellow Protestants and what they'd forced the Catholics to do. The Catholics he'd married into. A love conquering all, fine and dandy kind of marriage – but a poor career move for an RUC sergeant. He was never promoted after his marriage and took early retirement.

A similar thing had happened on my father's side of the family.

A Protestant from Lurgan, Grandfather Caulfield had been an officer in the British army, then a civil servant. Suddenly, in his fifties, he lost his heart and some might say his head – but he'd had enough of bachelor life. He married a Catholic girl, from the South. He isolated himself from his family, his colleagues in the Protestant-dominated civil service and the rumour was that his solace was gambling and chain-smoking – lung cancer killed him when my father was twelve.

There were sadder things about Grandfather Caulfield than the effects of sectarianism. He'd probably been a bachelor too long and didn't know that even if someone marries you, they don't always love you. Grandma told my mother she'd been charmed by him, and had met him when she was thirty-two and thinking herself lucky to be proposed to but . . .

When he'd been in the army, my grandfather lost half his foot on a World War One battlefield. Grandma kept the shrapnel from his foot in a jamjar on her mantelpiece. I remember my sister looking at it when she was barely tall enough to reach it and asking what kind of jam had been in the jar. Everyone laughed and no one knew the answer. But I think my sister was right to ask. If Grandma had loved him, she'd have carefully chosen what she kept the shrapnel in.

Poor Belfast Grandma. Sectarianism hadn't been the cause of all her troubles, but it hadn't helped.

Her family, down in Tipperary, had been shocked by her all round. First, in her late twenties, she'd run away to work in the Co-op in Belfast; then she'd married someone who seemed almost English. Hers was a family so enthusiastically Republican the women had run around with guns in the Irish Civil War. Her mother, reputedly formidable, had been incandescent with rage and full of never-darken-my-doors-type talk about the marriage. After Grandma was widowed, she did open the doors again, but always behaved as though Grandma was a disgraced sinner she'd had to forgive. No wonder Belfast Grandma wasn't cuddly.

These were common enough stories in Northern Ireland. Not only were mixed marriages more frequent than might be imagined, there were still mixed communities and hundreds of busy people like John with their cross-community projects in areas where people had stopped mixing. There were constant stories of how, when it came down to it, some very unlikely people made exception to their sectarian rules.

Aunt Helen told me about some cousins of hers who were known to be 'connected'.

'They were all very big in Sinn Fein, and you know, some of them beyond that. The sort of people where it wouldn't do to inquire too closely what the men in the family might be doing after dark.'

The father in this 'connected' farming family was dying. Everyone in the area had known him, an affable, helpful man, who'd always be the first to lend a tractor to pull someone's car out of a ditch and all that kind of rural decency. One of the people he'd known since childhood, just around, just to talk about the weather with, was Ian Paisley. So despite the way their lives had diverged, Paisley came to pay his respects to the man on his deathbed. All other friends and the family left the room – their father wanted to see Paisley, but they didn't.

Who knows what this staunch old Republican had to say to his long-time acquaintance, Reverend Ian, but unfortunately they were his last words. Paisley emerged ashen-faced from the father's room and took the lady of the house to one side.

'He's gone,' he whispered.

She whispered back, 'Ian, slip out now so I can be the one to discover he's gone, because no one's going to believe you didn't suffocate him.'

Paisley had taken this with a quiet laugh and slipped his bulk out of the door with unusual discretion.

Less strange but more touching was the story of the family who lived directly opposite Aunt Helen and Uncle Joe. There were no houses for hundreds of yards around, but these two houses faced each other. The full Catholic house of Joe and Helen and the Protestant couple opposite.

'The old couple were very serious Loyalists,' Uncle Joe

told me. 'We were on nodding terms but never more than that. Their son, David, grew up with our ones, playing in the fields together, and a much more toing and froing situation developed.'

The old couple moved away to a bungalow by the sea. David married and brought up his children to have an affable relationship with the Catholic neighbours. Their youngest girl had great difficulty at school and it occurred to David there were two retired teachers living opposite. In fact, Aunt Helen was what is now referred to as a special needs teacher, although she always said, 'I'd say I taught the backward children, because that's what they were called then.'

Backward or needy, nevertheless the little girl Rachel came on leaps and bounds with evening and weekend tutoring in Aunt Helen's front room. There was some reciprocal arrangement with David, an electrician, and everyone was quite happy with the skills barter and the contact.

Uncle Joe was astounded to receive a letter of thanks from the grandparents, the old couple who'd barely managed more than a civil nod for years.

'I knew the old boy, so I knew what it cost him to write and thank me for anything. I wrote back and said what a delight the child was, indeed, how delightful his whole family was. And that was the end of that, no Christmas card from them but a bit of something had shifted.'

David and his wife had done more than shift. Around the 12th of July, Rachel was very excited to see that every house in Portadown had a flag flying – a Union Jack, a flag of the Orange Order, a cross of Saint George . . .

'Can anyone have a flag?' she asked.

'Oh yes,' her mother told her. 'Anyone who can afford to buy one.'

'But we don't have one,' Rachel frowned.

'Well, that's because Joe and Helen don't have one and it wouldn't be nice for us to put one up if they don't have one.'

Rachel puzzled over this a moment and obviously decided it was an economic problem.

'I know, next year, we'll buy two flags and give one to Joe and Helen.'

Uncle Joe laughed remembering the story: 'So there you are, and it's not so much the story that tells you something, but that David rushed over to tell me this funny thing Rachel had said. I knew we were fine with them, that he felt he could tell me that.'

4. The Heavens Are Closed

'Oh, this isn't busy. When I was younger I barely had time to bless myself but now I just have these few wee things I have to do.'

Aunt Helen's few things would have been a full-time job to anyone else. When she was younger she had her eight children, her work as a teacher, community ventures, socializing and devout religious observations . . . In the nicest possible way, she was like the Terminator: she just kept coming whatever you threw at her.

Today she had a group of fellow pensioners she took on a weekly treat – 'the girls', she called them, although she was the youngest at seventy-four.

'You'd be welcome to join us, but space is limited, they'd end up wanting to be in your novelty car, not my old thing, and the whole excursion would get very scattered and be no manner of treat for you. Did you say you had places to see? A pity your uncle will be no use to you today . . .'

Uncle Joe had a sacred commitment in his calendar – a golf day. I wasn't tempted to join him, even as a spectator, although I had read about every course in the province. Ask the Northern Irish Tourist Board what the country's greatest asset was and your mail box would be stuffed with golf holiday brochures. There were scrappy seaside courses and lush championship-level courses. There were over ninety golf courses in Northern Ireland; the baggage carousels at Northern Irish airports were a constant log jam of awkward golf bags coming from Tokyo, Madrid, Toronto, Helsinki,

Capetown . . . Packs of happy men roamed hotel lobbies wearing one glove, looking like some international convention of absent-minded house-breakers. It took a severe amount of trouble to put off golfers – they had always visited Northern Ireland and known there was more to the place than fighting. So whatever it was they did out in their bunkers with the bent sticks that was so compelling, they'd been good for the country.

I had bigger prizes to hunt than golf trophies. Just outside Dungannon there was a tiny village called Castlecaulfield, with a ruined castle beside it. Toby Caulfield built the castle in 1619 when he was sent from Oxfordshire to keep the Donnelys down. His boss, Lord Mountjoy, named the region Charlemont, from his own Christian name. The Caulfields became the earls of Charlemont, then took assorted routes into Irish life. Or went back to England as soon as they could.

People assume Caulfield is a Protestant name; unless they're Catholics from the South called Caulfield. I once crashed a car in Dublin and the large supervising policeman insisted Caulfield was a County Mayo name. As I'd caused the crash, I didn't like to argue – and Caulfields were likely to be from anywhere, of any creed. They had hundreds of years as the powerful earls of Charlemont, switching religion through marriage and conversion, or not. Even if they didn't convert, they had a reputation for being tolerant of Catholicism, especially after the eighteenth-century penal laws were passed forbidding Catholics to vote, join the armed forces or buy land.

The penal laws also made it illegal to educate a child in the Catholic faith – hence the improvised 'hedge schools' for Catholic children and the continuing obsession with education among the Catholic community today.

The earls of Charlemont backed Henry Grattan in the formation of the United Volunteers, a militia intended to replace British soldiers who were fighting the American Civil War. Although the United Volunteers declared themselves loyal to George III, they took up the American revolutionary cry of 'no taxation without representation', campaigning for economic equality for Ireland and an independent Irish legislature. When the Act of Union abolished the Irish parliament, the earls of Charlemont refused to sign. As punishment, the Irish earls were punitively taxed and had most of their property confiscated by the British Crown.

Castle Caulfield wasn't much of a prize these days, but the Municipal Gallery in Dublin once belonged to the Caulfields. I'd cast my eye around when I was last in Dublin – a bit of panelling here, a bathroom there . . . I could see the gallery making a very nice house for me and I'd been considering suing to get it back.

Castle Caulfield was at the back of a modern housing estate and, apart from the gatehouse, was mostly just overgrown humps. Not a very imposing sort of ancestral home. The house had been burnt by nationalists in the 1920s, as had the other Charlemont home in the area, Castle Roxborough. In 1921 a building contractor had bought the ruin at Castlecaulfield and sold off most of the stone. The locals hadn't felt very sentimental about the Caulfields at the time.

I asked the woman in the village shop if she knew why the village was named, just in case she'd any evidence to help me get the Municipal Gallery back.

'Well there is a castle down that way,' she said. 'But I only moved here from Coleraine five years ago, I've never bothered with it myself.'

I bought some sweets from her, even though she'd lazily missed her chance to be involved in redressing one of the

great wrongs of Irish history . . . Then again, the earls of
Charlemont had probably done quite well out of Ireland
and only refused to sign the Act of Union out of greedi-
ness to maintain their independent colonial power, not
concern for the poor peasantry. It was just possible that if I
decided to make a scene, the Dublin government would
argue the gallery belonged to the Irish, not descendants of
invading English lords, and I'd end up feeling very foolish.

Disinherited, I drove up to Lurgan on a quest for a more
recent ancestor. My Caulfield grandfather was buried there.
As I'd never known him and what I did know about him
seemed sad, I wanted to check he wasn't in some terrible
neglected or desecrated place.

My father seldom visited Northern Ireland now and
Grandfather Caulfield had few people left to care about him.
Those Caulfields that were left, distant cousins, owned the
plot and belonged to a branch of Protestantism called the
Ebeneezer Tabernacle – a no-frills religion that didn't believe
in gravestones. They were old people, so my parents had
decided there was no point upsetting them and sneaking in
a gravestone for my poor grandfather, all alone, his Catholic
wife buried miles away with her family in Tipperary.

I had phoned these distant relatives, my grandfather's
cousins. They'd been very friendly and eager to meet, but
I'd called at a time when every one of them was stricken
with serious old people ailments, one just out of hospital,
one about to go in . . . There were a couple of younger
sons, both abroad on business. I was sad not to meet them
because any scrap of information about my long-dead grandfather would have been welcome. Belfast Grandma had talked
about him very little, my father only had childhood memories of him. There was the shrapnel. A photograph of him
looking dapper, hat tipped over one eye, and a letter from

some neighbours sent after his death saying, 'His courtesy and charm will be missed.'

A snarl-up of heavy lorries surrounded me as I drove into Lurgan. At the same moment a snowstorm came down out of blinding sunlight. I was sure I'd crash and end up in the unmarked Caulfield plot myself. But the snow and the traffic disappeared as suddenly as they'd arrived – I could see clearly enough to fling the car into a parking space.

Lurgan had been a prosperous linen town, and was now a busy shopping and market town. The poet, painter and polemicist George Russell (AE) was born in Lurgan, as was the Quaker scholar James Logan, who had helped found Pennsylvania.

Of more interest to me, my guidebook informed me that the famous greyhound Master McGrath had been from Lurgan, owned by Lord Lurgan. In the town-centre parish church there was a stained glass window depicting this three-time winner of the Waterloo Cup, and Master McGrath was at the top of Lurgan's coat of arms. All strange and interesting, because down in Tipperary, one of the 'must see' items on holidays to Belfast Grandma was a statue at the roadside of Master McGrath. Maybe we'd been told it was from the same town in the North as our grandfather, but I don't remember listening to such tales – we'd just liked to stop and look at a big statue of a dog.

The Shankill Park Protestant graveyard was off the main road and reached through a vast warren of a council estate. An estate with a tricolour flying from every other house. Typically English misjudging Northern Ireland, I worried I might find the graveyard vandalized, gates padlocked . . . It was fine. It had a wrought-iron fence no higher than an average graveyard fence and the gate was open.

It was a beautiful little place, well tended with leafing

shrubs and dignified yew trees. The grass was rich green and birds were singing. There were graves dating right back to 1760. A large fancy tomb in the middle was for the Brownlows, the English family who'd run everything in the district when English families did. Lord Brownlow had been very active in encouraging planters to come from England and Scotland to take up cheap land leases to develop Ireland's linen industry. Around this area of the country, several things were named after him, including a burnt-out, lawless estate in the nearby new town of Craigavon. The wretched Brownlow estate was a hive of UDA drug-dealing and intimidation. Probably not the legacy Lord Brownlow would have wanted for himself.

All along one side of the graveyard was an area of neatly cropped grass — it looked as though unmarked people might be in there, but I realized I wasn't going to have a psychic revelation to help me find my grandfather. My father had said to ask at the gatehouse to be shown the grave.

'There's an old boy in there knows where everyone is.'

There was no old boy now. A friendly young woman in the gatehouse told me she had a map of where all the plots were, but I'd need to get the plot number. Presumably the old boy had died and taken some of his knowledge with him.

I asked the woman if she knew of people being buried with no headstones for religious reasons, thinking this might narrow the field.

'Oh, there's lots with no headstones for lots of reasons. Sometimes, if they're very old graves, the headstones are just lost. Then . . .' she pointed to the long blank grass area, 'there's all those. That's a plot the Salvation Army bought for victims of the famine. So there's an awful lot unmarked.'

She smiled sympathetically when I said I was looking for

my grandfather. She was particularly sympathetic because the wind had just caught one of my eyes, making it water. To stop what must have looked like a weeping Englishwoman on her doorstep, she said gently, 'All you need to do is go to Craigavon Town Hall, and they'll have the plot number in their registry. Then I can show you on the map.'

I thanked her and decided not to bother with the Town Hall. I didn't need to see what exact patch of ground he was in; I'd seen he was all right, in a pretty and well-tended place. I walked back up through the streets of tricolours and decided being surrounded by them was probably right for him too, a Catholic girl being the love of his life.

In a newsagent's I saw a postcard with a drawing of the greyhound Master McGrath. I bought it to remind myself of the strange connection. Turning up in Lurgan and Tipperary, the famous greyhound seemed to have so much to do with my grandparents, I was starting to think of him as a deceased family pet.

I drove down to Armagh, city of saints and scholars. I started with the saintly end of town, by accident really, because I was looking for a teashop my aunt Helen had recommended – couldn't find it, but couldn't miss the imposing Catholic cathedral. Maybe this had been her plan – she knew I'd only be going into a teashop demanding coffee, when really I should be paying more attention to my health and my soul.

The cathedral nearly made me feel religious, if not like giving up caffeine. There was a steep approach and then a swoop of steps up to a high-spired frontage. It was the kind of ecclesiastical architecture that boomed 'Sinner!' at any small humans below. I expected a thunderbolt to pick me off as I climbed and climbed to reach the statues of arch-bishops at the entrance level.

I made it. I respectfully familiarized myself with the arch-bishops while catching my breath. One was archbishop when building began in 1849, the other was archbishop when the cathedral was completed in 1873. Work on the interior went on long afterwards and the dazzle of stained glass, mosaics, paintings and marble had been recently restored and further embellished. It was such a sensual feast I had to be careful not to get over-stimulated and reel back down the long flight of steps.

Uncle Joe felt there was no need for such a fuss and bother of decorativeness. It wasn't so much that he thought people should be there for God not the architecture, but that the lavish interior had been provided largely by collections, raffles, bazaars and donations from the local Catholics. And again, the re-embellishment had been paid for by taking up collections from Catholics and gifts from the Vatican. He believed the money could have been better spent solving the ground-level problems of the Catholic Church – compen-sation for the victims of abuse was one of his suggestions. Or sending it out to the thousands of people dying of AIDS in Africa. I agreed with him. Mostly. But there was some-thing about the celebratory extravagance of Armagh Catholic cathedral that I wanted to exist. I did like to see a bit of joy in a religion, as well as the trying to be good business. I liked a bit of height and spirage to make me amazed that people cared so much about God they'd put all that work into showing they cared.

'There's also building contractors,' Uncle Joe reminded me. 'They'd care a lot about a place like that.'

Building contractors were busy on Saint Patrick's Anglican cathedral, so it was closed to visitors. At the core of this cathedral was a fifth-century church, founded by Saint Patrick himself. The Catholic cathedral was also called Saint

Patrick's . . . And there's going to be plenty more of Saint Patrick in this chapter, so if you've got something against him, I apologize, but it really can't be helped.

I visited Saint Patrick's Trian in the centre of town, thinking it said 'Train' and was some kind of holy novelty ride – saints on strings would jump out saying 'boo!'; skeleton nuns would trail ghostly tendrils of ragged veils across my face; puppet monks would swing across my path on ropes wailing piteously . . . It seemed like a hilarious idea. But it wasn't the idea. The Trian was a heritage centre, with a restaurant, tasteful shops, exhibitions and lecture halls. The name Trian came from one of the ancient divisions of Armagh – it was divided into three sections. The heritage centre also had three sections: *The Armagh Story*, *The Story of Saint Patrick* and *The Land of Lilliput*, an exhibition about *Gulliver's Travels*. Swift had written a considerable amount of this book while staying near Armagh.

The woman at the main desk told me there was a bargain ticket if I took in all three exhibitions. With freezing weather outside, no aunt or under-cousins to keep me company, I thought I might as well fill the day and take the bargain ticket.

'Lilliput's just starting. I'll phone up and let her know she's got one more,' the desk lady said.

In my haste to buy a bargain, I hadn't considered that something called *The Land of Lilliput* might not be a very scholarly and dignified exhibit. I entered a brightly coloured room where a dozen children were dressing themselves in garish approximations of medieval costumes. They were excited, I was embarrassed. I don't know why, seeing as I started into the building hoping for some kind of saintly ghost train. I think I just felt caught – surrounded by giggling children, I realized that I was in Armagh, city of saints and scholars, looking for a laugh, and I should be trying harder to be appropriate.

'Ah,' I said to any grown-up who might help me. 'They sold me a ticket, but I don't have a child . . .'

A nice middle-aged woman in a uniform, 'her', presumably, introduced herself as Deirdre and said, 'Maybe they could have noticed that downstairs and explained.' She smiled reassuringly. 'But don't worry, it is quite interesting to see how the exhibition's laid out. It's very innovative.'

I said I didn't mind, as long as I didn't have to dress up.

'No,' she said. 'You don't have to. And I promise I'll answer any serious questions about Swift you might have.' In a self-effacing tone she added, 'I'm actually quite a student of his work.'

Deirdre then clapped her hands, cheerily trilling, 'Come along, children!' And led us through to the Land of Lilliput.

It was quite spectacular, a twenty-foot model Gulliver pinioned, with dozens of Lilliputians swarming over him – all poking, carrying, squabbling in a frenzy of lively detail. The children loved it, had their photos taken and we moved on to the next part of what I now saw on my ticket was 'a child-centred interactive experience'.

The next section used puppets, holograms and films to take us through excerpts of *Gulliver's Travels*. It was very soothing to spend time in a darkened room being told a story with holograms, puppets etc. I could have stayed all afternoon, but the lights came back on and the children and I blinked out of the fantasy to find Deirdre again.

While separating sometimes petulantly reluctant children from their costumes, Deirdre gamely answered my questions about Swift's connections with Armagh.

'Ah, you see, in Swift's day, Armagh was a big ecclesiastical centre, so he'd several associates in the area.' She broke off to stare down a small boy who was refusing to hand over a hat. She faltered; he scampered away hat in hand.

'Bring that back here . . . !' She sighed and realized she didn't care. 'Anyway, you know what might be more interesting for you. Just round the corner is the Robinson Library, the first public library in Ireland outside Dublin. It has a copy of *Gulliver's Travels* in Swift's own hand corrections. You can see his own mark upon the page.'

Then, perhaps because I didn't look as sufficiently interested in seeing Swift's own hand as a sane person should be, she suddenly added, 'Did you know that, when he died, Swift left his money to found a lunatic asylum in Dublin? Because, he said, "No country needed it more".'

A new crowd of children were pouring in. Deirdre flashed into a big smile and said, 'Welcome to the Land of Lilliput,' as she tried to separate two little girls brawling over a pink nylon medieval frock. I could see how doing this all day might make your mind run to where you could find a good lunatic asylum in a hurry.

Next, Saint Patrick. No puppets, but there were taped commentaries and actors in touch-screen re-enactments of his life. The exhibition was called *Saint Patrick's Testament* because it was centred round writings on the saint found in the ninth-century manuscript *The Book of Armagh*.

The actors in the screens told of the saint's life in a chatty, intimate manner. Saint Patrick was a Briton, sold into slavery to the Romans, became holy in Rome, returned to Ireland, converted the Celts, chased snakes . . . All this disputed detail did have a core of truth. In the fifth century a holy man named Patrick did choose Armagh to be the site of his church and around it grew colleges, schools . . . By the eighth century, Armagh had become an ecclesiastical and scholarly centre. This centre of learning and prayer was ravaged and disrupted at the time of King William's wars, but in Georgian times, Archbishop Robinson came to the city and worked hard to re-establish it as a capital of Christianity and learning.

Using the best imported architects and the warm-coloured local limestone, Robinson commissioned a palace and the public library – as well as restoring older schools and churches.

Robinson, star of the *Armagh Story*, another section of the exhibition, was a good man on the churches and libraries but maybe not a lot of fun. The green central mall in Armagh was once a race course. The large balconies on the surrounding houses were to provide first-floor reception rooms with a good view of the races. Robinson put a stop to the races and declared the mall should be a promenade for contemplative scholars.

My head, unused to scholarly contemplation, had started haemorrhaging with the history of Armagh and Saint Patrick – especially Saint Patrick. I'm sure he was very holy and influential, but after the kidnapping into slavery, his life was not the high-concept, action-filled, dragon-killing saint's life of a Saint George type – he didn't even go interestingly nuts like a lot of ancient saints. And he was in no way the green beer-drinking party animal you'd expect if you associated him with the Saint Patrick's day parades in New York and Dublin. Credit to him that he seemed a man who would have firmly bolted his monastery against such parades but I couldn't find him interesting.

There was something in Armagh that I had always found strange and intriguing. The Armagh Observatory and Planetarium. Of course, now I had the educating benefit of the Saint Patrick's Trian experience, it all made sense – Armagh had been a centre of scholarship at a time when astronomy was a growth area in the sciences. Robinson, a keen amateur astronomer, had founded the observatory in 1790 and it had attracted many famous star-gazers over the centuries.

Patrick Moore, the *Sky at Night* man, was the first director of the new Observatory and Planetarium, opened in 1968. I wasn't sure how many of Robinson's old charts and instruments I wanted to study, but I fancied a look through a big telescope. It was the middle of the day, but if they promised me I'd get to see something good, I could always come back later.

The main glass doors of the Observatory were open. Inside there were all kinds of boxes and bags piled on the floor, as if they were moving out, or a burglary was in progress.

A young woman with a very pointy face came out of an office door and looked at me accusingly. I stepped away from the boxes.

'We're not open until two o'clock,' she said. I was about to grunt acknowledgement of this and leave, when she added, 'There's not that much to see anyway.'

No? The whole sky didn't count then?

She was too scarily pointy to be facetious with, so I asked what happened at two o'clock.

'Look,' she said. 'We've had a lot of problems with funding here lately, so there's no proper planetarium show. Nothing.'

'No telescopes or anything?'

'Yes, there's telescopes.' She was so irritated with me now, because obviously whatever had happened to their funding it was me that had done it. 'You can come back later and look at them but there will probably be a lot of school groups in, you know, children,' she added with a look of bitter distaste.

Yes, I did know children, I'd just survived interactive Lilliput with them and they weren't so bad. Maybe I should tell her there was a very good lunatic asylum in Dublin, if the children tipped her over the edge she seemed very close to . . . But far too frightened of her, I just mumbled, 'Thanks, I'll come back later.'

'It's not what it should be here, just remember that,' she said, again with the underlying accusation that she knew fine well it was me who'd done it.

I wouldn't be back. I'd tried to enter into the scholarly spirit of Armagh, knowing I'd never make it into the saints' club, but I'd been shown I wasn't welcome there either. No wonder. As I sat in the car to write down some notes about Saint Patrick, and all I was supposed to have learnt an hour ago, I realized the only thing that had wedged itself in the mesh of my sieve brain was that the 17th of March, Saint Patrick's day, hooted and tooted and dyed green all over the Irish Diaspora, was the day of his death. I found that rather depressing.

The sky was clouding over, it was getting even colder and everything was starting to feel bleak. Maybe because now I'd started to find all my aunts and cousins and under-cousins, I was missing their company. Maybe I shouldn't have started the day at a lost grandfather's graveside. I thought of abandoning sightseeing and heading home, but it was only one o'clock. It would seem wimpishly early to say I'd had enough. I realized I'd not heeded Aunt Helen's advice, that sightseeing was best conducted with tea breaks at regular intervals. I made my way over to Robinson's Palace, where there was the second establishment on my aunt's list of excellent Armagh tea-rooms.

They were welcoming in the tea-rooms and restored my faith in what I'd come to regard as one of the immediate comforts of Northern Ireland – the friendliness. It seems

like a galloping great Pat O'Brien of a cliché to talk about
friendliness in Ireland, but it was there in crock of goldloads
in the North. A shy, genuine desire to make someone who
seemed a bit lost find a place and settle themselves. My
relations who hadn't seen me for years had done it to me,
strangers at the airport had done it to me – not only direct-
ing me to what I wanted, but making sure it did turn out
to be what I really wanted when I found it – be it a taxi
stand or a place at the family fireside.

An almost superstitious feeling had welled up in me the
minute I'd walked into the arrivals lounge – I was surrounded
by people with Northern Irish accents, so everything would
be fine. I knew where the superstition had come from. My
mother would voice it when we got off the boat – it was
usually a boat journey when we were kids. Someone would
speak to her on the Belfast quayside, and she'd just beam
with an all-body smile: 'Ah, Northern Irish accents,' she'd
say and it was a signal to relax, we were on holiday, we were
home safe.

The throaty rumble of the accent was hard to imitate.
My mother and I brooked no pretenders. On an evening
when we'd time on our hands, we had compiled a list of
actors who'd got it wrong. Some you'd have thought would
know better and some you wouldn't: Val Kilmer, Jonathan
Pryce, Richard Gere, Tommy Lee Jones, Mickey Rourke
. . . They'd all tried and wandered pitiably all over the Celtic
soundscape.

In fairness to them, a leading British dialect coach told
me the accent was notoriously difficult to learn because:
'The vowel system is not in the everyday canon. It might
be easier for open-eared Scottish people to get it than
Americans, English or even other Irish people. It works on
a very centralized vowel system phonetically speaking.'

I didn't know what that meant, but surely a famous Hollywood actor could afford to have it explained to them.

They were probably busy people. If they got the vowels right, they still had the sentence constructions. Full of left-over Gaelic word order, it could be so easy to get tangled, get stresses in the wrong places . . . Instead of saying, 'I am,' people said, 'I would be the kind of person who . . .' Instead of offering you a lift they'd say, 'Would you not like a lift?' And if they were making a list, they'd say, 'I'm after making a list, so I am.' It was no accent for people to just make a grab at and hope to get away with.

I couldn't do it either, my mother said I sounded terrible: 'I can't believe you can't hear it. You veer around to all extremes in the one sentence. And you've every reason to be good at it, not like these poor creatures on our list.'

I don't know what we were planning to do with the list. Blackmail? Offer my mother's coaching services for the next time they wanted to try it? I've no idea. But we have our list, we'll use it one day.

Thawed out, I thought I'd better have a look round the fine buildings of Robinson's Palace. This was made pleasant by an actual guide rather than tapes and touch-screens.

Robinson had certainly been a stylish fellow. The private chapel was so delicately and simply decorated it was time-less. The walls were clad in a soft pink stone known as Armagh marble, actually the local limestone polished up, and to my eye a subtler, pleasanter stone than marble. Completed in 1786, the chapel, as my guide informed me, was consid-ered to be one of the finest examples of Georgian neo-classical architecture in Ireland.

'That means it's Greek-looking,' she added helpfully.

The palace itself was being used as council offices, so not

open to the public. But we could inspect the old kitchens. Then we echoed along the low, 43-metre-long servants' tunnel, leading from the kitchens and servants' quarters to the palace. This was known as 'The Whistling Tunnel' because the servants had to whistle as they carried food along it to show they weren't eating.

Just as she was chattily filling my head with such historical trivia, my guide abandoned me.

'Now here in the stable block there's a "Day in the Life" exhibition. Just press a button on the wall as you go into each room and the whole thing springs to life, showing you how people lived in Robinson's day.'

Again I was alone with technology. Taped voices accompanied each room full of wax people – the stable boy, the lady of the house, a dinner party, the kitchens . . . And there was a model of Robinson himself, looking out over a beautifully painted backcloth of rural Armagh, conversing with a rather know-all young man called Arthur Young.

Arthur Young was an English agricultural reformer. As I listened to the tape of him, expounding on where the Irish peasant farmers were going wrong in the way they farmed flax, I felt, despite the posh Caulfield hackles I had, some kind of ancient Irish peasant hackles were rising on the back of my neck. Just something about that 'the trouble with the Irish' tone of Arthur Young's voice, whatever the merits of his agricultural theories, hurried me home to the relatives as snow came down like a judgement on somebody.

Me probably, for having all the historical splendours of Armagh to see and getting a bit fed up with them.

Cars in the drive at my uncle's didn't mean anyone was home. One belonged to a cousin who was working abroad, one was an old car of my aunt's that needed selling . . .

There were no lights on in the dusk gloom of the house, so I presumed I was home alone.

Years of being surrounded by people, pets and uproar had given my uncle Joe an ability to sit motionless in his chair reading a book, hearing nothing, seeing nothing else but the words in front of him. Not even noticing it was getting dark until all light had gone.

Usually there was a give-away cloud of pipe smoke from the chair to signal he was there and still alive – on this evening he must have been between pipes. I went into the kitchen, made a cup of tea, emerged with it and was very startled to hear an amused, lugubrious voice from his chair.

'One cup of tea. Well now, Miss Caulfield, isn't that the trouble with being brought up in England? It gives a person a very selfish disposition.'

I forgave him and made him a cup of tea. After all, he'd done me a favour, I'd been looking for an excuse for my self-absorption for years.

'Your cousin Siobhan phoned,' he said when he'd had the tea and smoked a pipe. 'If you can dig your way out of the snow here tomorrow, she's suggesting lodging you for a couple of days while she's off work to take you to the seaside. Isn't the seaside some important component of your book?'

'Very important.'

'Well, yes. From Timbuktu to Toraigh, we'd all be in a bad way if there was no seaside.'

I'd no idea if that was an actual expression or just something he said to amuse himself.

To amuse himself further he asked, 'And then you're going to leave us for Belfast, is that right?'

'I'll be back.'

'You'll be very welcome. Only, if you get taken hostage, make sure it's on the Falls Road, we might know some people there could help you, but I'm not sure about our contacts on the Shankill.'

I knew he was joking, but then I wavered. 'Do people get taken hostage?'

He laughed. 'I was just trying to add some spice to your travels. But if anyone does kidnap you, they wouldn't want to have to answer to me.'

Then, having fondly teased his naive niece into a nervous breakdown, he went off to watch golf on television because, monotonous as the game was, on television the true glory of its monotony really shone out.

5. Dogs Can Sing and Dogs Can Disappear

'Let's go. There's an old naked man in that room up there, he's seen us.'

'Naked? Where?'

'The right-hand bedroom. Quick, he's coming to the window.'

'He's not naked. He's got a vest on.'

'He'll still think we're filming him.'

'He's opening the window.'

'Run!'

My cousin Siobhan and I ran squealing round the corner and didn't stop till we got to the car.

'I don't think we actually have to get out of town,' Siobhan said as I grabbed the passenger door handle. 'I think he'll only go so far in his vest.'

'No,' I said. 'But let's get up the high street, mingle with the crowd. Just in case he's a real nutter who would come out in his vest, with a gun.'

We'd only been in Buncrana ten minutes and already we were children again, running squealing from some nonsense, getting the possible consequences hysterically out of proportion, close to collapse on the pavement with too much laughing.

Maybe there was just something in the air of Buncrana for us, too much ozone. Especially for a city girl like me.

We'd not been trying to traumatize elderly locals, just taking pictures of the old Buncrana holiday home.

'I hope we've not brought on a heart attack or something.'

Siobhan reviewed the pictures in the digital camera with concern. 'He might have a vest on but I expect it was a bit scary for him.'

We'd no time to let conscience hold us up. Our next stalking operation was to the guest house where my family had stayed.

The drive was overgrown but there was an ugly new sign out front, indicating the guest house was still open for business. Siobhan looked at the building and wailed.

'It looks terrible.'

'It is February,' I said. 'I expect they have a holiday in winter or something.'

'But it's not the same place at all. It's ruined.'

It had been our guest house, I didn't see why Siobhan was so disappointed. But it had symbolized something in her memory.

'It was where I imagined royal people would stay,' she said. 'I'd think, my cousins from England stay there, so they must be a bit royal.'

'Siobhan, as a child did you think all English people were a bit royal?'

'I hoped they might be, especially if they were cousins,' she admitted.

'I thought everyone with a Northern Irish accent was a relation,' I said. 'Especially if they were famous.'

'I think there was always a lot going on when we were children,' Siobhan concluded. 'Comings and goings of people we only vaguely knew, it's not our fault we got the wrong end of every stick. Oh, look at this guest house, it's ruined.'

I remembered a much more elegant grey Georgian house than the place we were looking at. A landlady sprang to memory. She'd a shiny Irish setter, an elegant, regal kind of dog. Everything had been just so inside, polished and full of Englishmen in tweed hats going fishing . . .

Dilapidation of the building and grounds wasn't the disappointment so much, it was the obvious dilapidation of taste. The place had been painted a deep orange with peach trim. Not a political orange. Just part of a Donegal madness for painting houses in toytown colours. We'd seen purple trimmed with pink houses; blue and yellow houses; red houses and forty shades of green houses. Siobhan knew of no explanation for this but had definitely observed it was on the increase. Perhaps in the Mediterranean all these brightly coloured houses would have looked right, but in Donegal, particularly on a snowy February day, they smacked of a bleak desperation. They reminded me of ageing faces over made up. Houses in this landscape had to be plain grey, or white, if they didn't want to look tawdry and slatternly, and that was that.

We peered in the windows of the once correctly grey guest house. No one around. The wide staircase had its tone lowered with a swirly beige and brown seventies carpet. And you could tell, even through the net trimmed window, that the inside of the house would smell of damp and vinegar.

'Definitely new management,' Siobhan said crossly, a childhood icon of glamour wiped from her memory.

The perceived glamour of our little English family had been a major topic of conversation on our return adventure into Donegal. My sister and I having shop-bought clothes had tormented Siobhan as a small child.

'To me that was so posh. My mother would buy some material and give it to a wee woman in the town to make up into dresses for us. In those days, hand-made clothes was the cheap way. And not only did I never get clothes with a shop label in them, like you and Jo had, I was the youngest. All my dresses had been worn by three other sisters first.'

I said I did seem to remember my sister getting hand-me-downs.

'Not all the time. I definitely don't think so. I remember your mother sent over some dresses of Jo's for me to have. Beautiful dresses with shop labels. They were hanging in my wardrobe and I said to Mummy, do you think Annie had these before Jo? And she said definitely not, no.'

I said her mother was probably just trying to big up the third-hand dresses as mere second-hand dresses. My sister definitely appeared in our family photos in dresses I'd been in. And if she had to have an unnecessary number of new dresses, it was because I was a considerably fatter child.

'Oh no,' said Siobhan. 'Don't say that. She was an extremely thin child. And now I'd say you were both extremely thin.'

Siobhan, unless she had something wrong with her eyes, would have seen that Jo was previously thinner and still thinner – but Siobhan had a long day ahead with me, returning to childhood, so she probably sensed it was best to head off descent into any dark pits of sibling rivalry.

Cousin rivalry pits, although not dark, did seem to be murky in both our memories. I remembered parcels of clothes coming from her mother and feeling that if we had to have clothes sent to us, we must be very poor, practically some kind of orphans.

What was sent to us, from Granny and from aunts, were hand-knitted items. Because they knew my mother always said life was too short for knitting. She recently confessed she'd said this in a sour grapes kind of way, because she just couldn't do it.

'Don't you remember the jumpers I made you? I got it

into my head that if I was to be any kind of a mother I would knit for my children. I made each of you a jumper and when I put them on you, each one of you looked like a cat in a stocking.'

I suggested that maybe it had taken her so long to make the jumpers we'd all grown a bit by the time we got them.

'Grown a bit, nothing. Unless when I measured you for your jumper you had one arm six inches higher than the other.'

So apart from occasional care packages from Ireland, we had to have shop-bought knitwear – one person's posh is another person's mother strangling herself in loving attempts with wool.

With courage that came close to the bravery of my mother's determined knitting, Siobhan and I decided we had to go back down the road where we'd traumatized the old man in his vest. If we didn't do it, we'd miss out on an important childhood landmark opposite their old house.

'Let's go into the street from the other end, so we won't be so easily recognizable,' Siobhan said, shoving her camera in her shoulder bag. One of the useful things about my cousins was that you could leave them on a desert island and they'd think of something to say to amuse themselves.

Our landmark was an immense cream-coloured church – all pillars and porticoes. Another of the Mediterranean notions of Donegal, set amid grey local stone and snow-bitten cold. And it didn't end there: beside the church was a gaudy fake rock grotto to Our Lady, surrounded by benches, as if Buncrana had the kind of weather suited to outdoor worship.

Siobhan and I wondered whether Our Lady had actually appeared in Buncrana.

'A bit convenient if she'd have appeared down the side of the Catholic church like this,' I said.

'They'd have built round her, don't you think?' Siobhan was younger than me but she was smarter.

Anyway, it was certain that if the grotto was built where there'd been an actual apparition, with possibly attendant miracles, we'd have all made a great deal more fuss about it, been bringing dolls and pets down for a cure, and not just used the grotto path as a short cut down to the beach.

I don't remember Buncrana town beach being beautiful. It always had a slightly neglected air about it, a sense that there was someone in the town planning department who hated the beach and wanted it to look as unattractive as possible. There'd been permanent piles of construction material beside the swing park and areas were forever being fenced off, apparently for no better reason than to add ugly fencing to the vista.

There'd been no improvement. The little funfair was gone, probably for good, because a factory had been built at the end of the promenade. Great for the last spree of Buncrana's textile industry; not so pretty on a beach front.

Some time in the seventies, I remembered *Fruit of the Loom* T-shirts being very popular all over Europe. This American multinational brought work to Donegal and Derry for twelve years – nobody much cared that their factories looked less than charming at the seaside. They cared more when *Fruit of the Loom* got into arguments about unionization with their Irish manufacturing plants. The company pulled most of their manufacturing out of Buncrana and Derry, moving to Morocco and the Far East, where non-unionized labour would work for less.

Tourism in Donegal was increasing, but it was seasonal, and hundreds of jobs making T-shirts was a more useful thing to see beside the seaside than mere seaside.

Actually it wasn't the sea you could see at Buncrana. It

was Lough Swilly, deepest sea estuary in Europe. This meant that, although frequently rained on, Buncrana beach was sheltered. Not so the spectacularly beautiful beaches my uncle Joe liked to seek out, further up the peninsula, on the Atlantic coast. Beaches of sweeping sand dunes and waves that came out of nowhere, smashing paddling children into tears at the water's edge.

'My father loves driving around the Donegal countryside, that's why we'd go to those obscure beaches,' Siobhan said. 'He'd say, "I hear *Death Drowning Blizzard Beach* is the best in Donegal." But it was only a excuse to drive for miles.'

I did recall long drives through the mountains in small cars, being kept amused by spotting dozens of little grottoes to Our Lady set at remote roadsides. Most of these statues were weather-beaten but never untended; they'd have jamjars of wild flowers in front of them, or incongruously bright sprays of garden blooms at chipped holy feet.

Donegal had kept much of its magical remoteness and still had a considerable Gaelic-speaking population, despite streams of people coming in from Dublin and the North, buying second homes, or completely relocating, to spend the future surrounded by stunning scenery and a simpler way of life. This influx had caused some decrease in simplicity and intermittently the scenery was marred by frighteningly inappropriate architecture. Not only the houses painted the colours of clowns' trousers, but extravagant structures thrown into the landscape, to show that the owners were very fancy folk. Fancy folk who couldn't see their split levels, colossal water features and glassed-in decks just looked wrong.

We drove toward the interior of the Inishowen Peninsula and were pleased to find it was still possible to drive for miles and not see another car. There were still tiny farms on hillsides, tumbling down into the rocks around them, or possibly growing out of them, they seemed so ancient and rooted.

'I bet there's old people in those houses who see no reason to care that the rest of the world exists,' I said, feeling wistful about how right those old people might be. The rest of the world had nothing to compare to the craggy, gorse-covered face of Donegal.

'You might think that,' Siobhan said, 'but my father told me he'd been out walking in these kind of Donegal wilds and seen an old man cutting turf. My father was betting to himself the man would be a native Gaelic-speaker, with all manner of fine old mountain wisdom. He sat down to smoke, hoping for a chance of striking up conversation with the man. My father's Gaelic's very good indeed and the thought of a chat with a remote old mountainy man would be just a joy to him. Anyway, a wave of a cigarette packet brought the man over. "That's lucky, I'd come out without mine," the man said, in an American accent. Turns out, he wasn't some ancient turf-cutter left over from the nineteenth century. He cut turf for his own fire in the wee farm cottage he'd inherited from his parents. He'd come back from a life spent working as a hotel manager in New York. He looked out over the mountains and said to my father: "You dream of coming back to this in New York." My father said he understood and asked, "Did you ask yourself why you ever left?" "Oh no, I know that," the man says. "It's a piece of heaven but there's no eating in it."'

'Don't tell me it's all Americans up there, don't tell me that.'

Siobhan smiled. 'Just trying to save you from disappointment.'

Before tourism and returning money, Donegal had fishing, turf-cutting and subsistence levels of farming. This is why it was only recently occurring to locals that the patches of new building and development could be controlled to be less fearsome-looking. If all the scenery was scarred and marred by incomers and their schemes, one of Donegal's assets, the beauty of the place, would be lost. Meanwhile, every second son in Donegal was a surveyor and estate agent and money was finally being made without having to cross the Atlantic to find it.

The tiny country roads Siobhan and I were exploring were proving to be too much for us. It had been snowing heavily for a couple of days, now the snow was melting into mud in some patches, or hiding ice in others. We decided to abandon the old remote routes to the Atlantic beaches and head for a cup of coffee somewhere overdeveloped.

'Anyway,' I said as we turned back, 'we would get to one of those beaches and we'd be all alone on remote sand dunes and be set upon by the crazed ghost of one of your disappeared dogs.'

'Not ghost necessarily. A dog still alive but full of rage and bitterness. He'd smell we were the family that abandoned him and tear us to shreds.'

The shred-tearing might have been unlikely. My cousins always had Jack Russells – tough dogs but, no matter how cross, probably not beyond us to fight one off.

The Jack Russells would survive well with the family until holiday time. Then, despite all instructions to keep hold of them, keep an eye on them, they'd go off into the dunes after rabbits, be lost for hours and have to be declared dead down a rabbit hole by my uncle. He'd keep the search going as long as possible because the caterwauling grief that would erupt from his own children, their cousins and associates, at the moment he had to declare a dog death would be an unbearable turn of events for a soft-hearted man.

One summer he had a reprieve from this annual dog tragedy, saved by a Jack Russell called Sam. Sam had been kept on his lead, kept an eye on . . . Cousin Maggie diligently had Sam's lead hooked round her foot while she tried to get changed for swimming. Changing was never easy with Atlantic winds whipping up stinging sand and whisking away towels. Sam was pulling and pulling to get away but suddenly he discovered he didn't just have the perverse and stubborn type of brain common to Jack Russells – he discovered himself to be a dog that could make plans. He moved closer to Maggie, he sat still and waited until she lifted her foot. He'd worked out that the closer he was, the looser the lead was. So all he had to do when she lifted her foot was shake his head to pull the loop of the lead and he was a free dog, off across the rabbit-rich sand dunes.

What Jack Russells didn't know was that if they went down a rabbit hole after a rabbit, they couldn't necessarily get out again. We would try not to listen to Cousin Raymond, who was a bit too good at describing either the slow, bewildered suffocation of a dog roaming the underworld, or the sudden choking of a dog as a sand dune collapsed around him.

We searched and called for hours. 'Sam! Sam!' we cried plaintively. We peered down rabbit holes, we began to weep in unison. It was getting dark and my uncle had to announce the search at a sad end. Maggie cried the hardest, blaming herself for the death of Sam. Some of her siblings blamed her too, and there was fighting as well as grief, while adults tried to pack us flailing and sobbing into small red cars.

As compensation, my father rashly announced that he would take everyone to the ice-cream shop on Buncrana high street for Knickerbocker Glories.

'You see, that was posh,' Siobhan recalled. 'We'd never heard of Knickerbocker Glories.'

I assured her that our London childhood hadn't been wall-to-wall Knickerbocker Glories either.

'I think my father just said the first exciting-sounding thing that came into his head. We were all in such a state, he knew just saying "ice cream" wouldn't do it, so he blurted out something wildly lavish he remembered from the *Beano*.'

I did recall him looking slightly baffled as he realized he'd three Formica tables full of tear-stained children eating huge glasses of coloured ice cream and glacé cherries. At least fifteen of us, gorging on the shop's top-priced item. He'd paid up cheerily with a very large note, but seemed evasive when I'd suggested we might still be sad about Sam the next night and maybe we'd need the Knickerbocker Glory cure again.

Luckily for his holiday spending allowance, there was no need for another such extravagance. The next morning we went back to the beach and, standing there barking, shameless, his lead lost somewhere in his overnight debauchery, was Sam. Sam fine and dandy and not even emotionally scarred.

After that, Sam survived for years. My cousins' family had found the dog that was smart enough for them, the dog they could count on.

Siobhan thought the coffee shop on Buncrana high street was where the palace of Knickerbocker Glories had been. The sweetshop also looked familiar. The high street had definitely expanded, far more shops and bars, some of them so flashy they would have sneered to serve a Knickerbocker Glory. Even though the working people of Derry were more likely to go for a week in Spain than on the traditional trip to Buncrana, it was still a thriving seaside town. There were always people from the North, like my family, who didn't see that Spain had anything but the weather on Donegal. Spain also didn't have the contrast, the startling moments when the sun did shine on Donegal and display the place as spectacular.

Today when the sun came out, Donegal looked like Switzerland. Snow-covered mountains glinting in winter white light. We took a detour to a local beauty spot, Father Hegarty's Rock.

Buncrana's recent reputation as a home from home for Republican fighters tied in with a quarrelsome history. In the eighteenth century it had been the site of an English garrison and was the location of Wolf Tone's arrest during the 1798 rising. The stories of Buncrana's part in the struggles of Ireland against the English were not part of our childhood holiday landscape – except for Father Hegarty.

When Catholic priests were persecuted, Father Hegarty had stood up for his faith but had to flee when English soldiers came to put a full stop to his rebelliousness. They'd chased him up to the headland, now known as Father Hegarty's Rock, and slashed his head off with a sword. It had bounced back down the cliff path fourteen times.

This was where we came into the story. Taking the walk up to Father Hegarty's Rock with Granny, to say a little prayer for the poor man, was made more interesting by looking for the fourteen dents made by the bouncing head. We'd scatter around the path finding dents, waiting for Granny to examine them and pronounce them as yes, head-shaped, or disappointingly only a place where the rain had moved a stone. Once, to everyone's envy, Maggie had pointed out a small boulder and said there was a bloodstain on it. Granny had agreed it could well have been blood, adding a new strand of goriness to the adventure – bits of mashed litter examined to see if they were spilt brains, a piece of animal fur poked at with a stick to see if it was a scrap of scalp . . . Part of Granny's charm had been knowing exactly how to keep children excited for hours – give them some kind of morbid quest and they'd be no trouble at all.

Granny's robust attitude to gore sat a little strangely with her poise and properness. Siobhan had spent much more time with her than I had, and although I remembered you could win high praise from Granny for being well turned out, with brushed hair and shiny shoes, I didn't remember references to Miss Bamford's Academy for Young Ladies.

'Oh, you must remember,' Siobhan urged. 'She'd say, "You look just like a young lady from Miss Bamford's Academy for Young Ladies." Or she'd tell you off and say, "Siobhan, no one would ever do such a thing at Miss Bamford's Academy for Young Ladies."'

Where Granny came from, in the hills of County Tyrone, there were one-room village schools, surrounded by sheep. There really didn't seem to be a place for such an exotic establishment.

'You never know,' Siobhan suggested. 'Maybe there was a Miss Bamford who thought the daughters of country farm-ers needed to be refined, you know, just out of her sheer madness. They were all up there in the hills, walking with books on their head, pouring tea into china cups correctly and saying "how now brown cow".'

We giggled over Miss Bamford for some time, deciding it was probably some made-up place of Granny's. After all, she could keep children busy for hours looking for a dead priest's head dents. She'd have been capable of concocting Miss Bamford's as some sort of Saint Trinian's in reverse – an imag-inary standard of fine behaviour for us all to aspire to.

I asked one of my uncles if he'd ever heard of this hedge finishing school. He'd said, 'Finishing school? People in those hills were as finished as they'd ever be by the time they were ten years old.'

But Tyrone country life wasn't as frill-free as he thought.

'That was a real place,' my mother laughed when consulted. 'It was in Lifford, just over the border from Strabane. Your granny and her sister Rose, for some reason, were sent to this academy for young ladies. Maybe it was because they were the two youngest of five girls and it was decided that they'd be sent in a different direction in life . . . I don't know. But they were sent off from the wee farm on the hills to board in this establishment. I think they did learn a lot of grooming and deportment, poetry and music appreciation, that kind of thing. Mainly, though, it was a secretarial college. They'd learn all these peripheral things but the main idea was to be a better class of secretary. Granny hadn't the slightest interest in the shorthand and typing, she loved the music and poetry side of it. But Auntie Rose had been mad for the shorthand typing. She got all kinds of distinctions and applied for a job in the big department store in Strabane as secretary to the manager. Unfortunately there was a young lad, Dekkie Doherty, who worked in the store, who was from our village. He was, well, you'd sort of say the village idiot but he was also a bit likely to make a grab at young girls in places they shouldn't be grabbed. And my grandfather said that no daughter of his was working in the same establishment as Dekkie Doherty. And that was that, Auntie Rose wasn't allowed to take the job.'

Auntie Rose and her Miss Bamford ways I knew very well. Thwarted in Strabane, she'd married a railway worker and moved to Croydon. Visiting her was a constant pressure of hand-washing, sitting up straight and being told that

women who wore trousers were 'fast'. All this had felt strange
in a two-up two-down railway cottage with an outside toilet,
and I'd gone through a phase of feeling there was something slightly Miss Havisham about her – although she had
a quiet and devoted husband in an armchair in the corner
of the living room. But I'd been on the right lines – it wasn't
being jilted at the altar that had made her stuck in time; it
was being denied the romance of the secretarial expectations Miss Bamford had promised her.

Granny, Auntie Rose and certainly Miss Bamford herself
would have been appalled to see Siobhan and me becoming raucously hysterical on the Greencastle car ferry back
across to the North, trying to decide how to do away with
ourselves quickly if the ferry sank, so we wouldn't have to
fall into the freezing stir of dark grey water all around us.
Siobhan grabbed a handful of plastic carrier bags from the
back seat, tipping the shopping out and yelling over the
throb of the ferry engine: 'We'll stick our heads in these,
and it'll all be over quickly.'
 Siobhan had diverted to do something as grown-up as
grocery shopping because she had a husband, two children
and a life I'd imagined might have rendered her more sensible than me. But she couldn't claim the return to Buncrana
with me had disrupted her normal steadiness of mind – back
home in Castlerock she had her husband and two children
but she also had a dog that sang. You only had to go near
the piano in the living room and the huge golden Labrador
would leap on to his performing perch on a window seat,
wagging his tail. You could disappoint him and play some
Chopin or you could get the best out of him with 'Chopsticks'
or 'Lavender's Blue'. It was sort of madness-inducing after it
went on for more than a minute, but the dog did bark loudly

and in rhythm with the music. The more the dog barked, the more forcefully Siobhan's children would bang the piano. It felt like the most noise and the craziest noise I had ever endured in my life. Luckily their house was a good distance from any neighbours, because if the Osbournes had lived next door they'd have had to get up a petition.

Siobhan's house, right on the sea front, all huge rooms and bay windows, did make me think about what the word for doing away with your cousins might be. I could lure her, her family and the singing dog out to sea and leave them there, forge a will bequeathing the house to me, the lovely cousin from England . . .

No, not really a foolproof plan.

Until quite recently, vast numbers of rooms and proximity to the sea didn't add to the value of a property in Northern Ireland — because it was in Northern Ireland. So, as compensation for living there, anyone with a half-decent salary could live very well indeed.

Receding fears of violence had sent Northern Irish property prices rising steeply, but it was still a place where it didn't take that much money to have a quality of life unimaginable on the same salary in London. There was a steady stream of returnees in their thirties who'd left to go to university in England, Canada, even Australia, stayed on to build a career — and now just wanted to come home. Middle-class couples with young children were buying up big houses and resettling the countryside. Siobhan and her husband had tried London for seven years: 'I keep telling the kids we lived in a flat as big as the kitchen we have now and they don't believe me. They've got lovely little schools here, the sea, relatives a few miles away . . .'

'What about you? Do you miss the bright lights or do you prefer it back here?'

'It's just more comfortable to be somewhere you understand. Where everyone talks like you. Don't you feel it yourself, a sense of coming home?'

I didn't know. I felt very carried away with the thought of a cheap big house by the sea. But I suspect it was more the series of warm, hilarious reunions with uncles, aunts and cousins that was making me feel I'd returned to something I knew well. I certainly didn't feel I was in a place I understood. I understood my cousins, but not the place.

And we'd just been to Buncrana. Who wasn't going to feel nostalgic about the location of childhood holidays? Even though we English cousins had been the slightly odd, trailing-behind trio of our family at play.

The flashy hours of winter sun had abandoned us when we left Donegal. Rain came down in a bitter cold wind as Siobhan showed me the homeward sights: 'On your left now, you're passing Magilligan, prison on the sea. They've got a wide range of prisoners in there, I don't know how many politicals but otherwise it's burglars, paedophiles, the usual. Except they've started putting asylum-seekers in there. I think that's awful, sticking them out here in the middle of nowhere, no bus service for their families, nowhere to stay. Anyway, the more foreigners come here the better, mix us up a bit. That's something I miss being back here. Everywhere you go, everyone's white, white . . .'

Magilligan couldn't have been anything but a prison. And there wasn't much else to observe but the size of it, in such a small country.

Past the prison there were miles of flat, bleak beach. Siobhan said this was an area where they spoke a language known as 'Ulster Scots'. I'd read about this. A minority language, spoken mainly by older farmers and fishermen. It was getting all kinds of grants and reappraisals. Apparently there were 1,500 people who spoke it exclusively, but thousands more who had knowledge of this ancient form of Scots English. It had a new name, 'Ullans'. It came from lowland Scotland with the settlers in the early seventeenth century and was similar to the lowland Scots in Robert Burns poems.

Ullans had been dismissed as a dialect of English until Britain signed the European Charter for Regional and Minority Languages, and it became a recognized regional European language. Ulster Scots had been looked down on as a poor folk's way of talking, but now campaigns were running to describe it as a language that had been discriminated against. The idea was that Ullans should have the same status as an indigenous language in Ireland as Gaelic.

There were irritable claims from Ullans campaigners that words claimed for Gaelic – like the widely used 'craic', meaning fun, geniality – was Ullans, not Gaelic. It was the kind of Northern Irish rankle that made me feel very 'oh, get over it'.

But I defer to Siobhan's more tolerant viewpoint: 'Catholics have all the romanticism, all the claims to traditional things here. There's very old things on the other side too. I've heard people round here talk it. It's good if it doesn't die out.'

Yes, good, I argued, but it was a shame it had to be stirred into the pot of things to fight about.

'Some people might stir it in,' Siobhan said, 'but things don't always go that way. It's more like an anoracky thing for academics.'

We took a swerve off the route home to look at the famous Downhill Palace. The remains of a gaunt mansion on a windswept headland had a sign at its neo-classical gates, telling us to leave the car and walk to the ruins, but sleet was coming down in the wind and we couldn't cope. Cheekily we bounced the car right up to the back of the ruins.

The palace had been built for Bishop Hervey in the 1770s. It had once held libraries and a two-storey picture gallery, but a nineteenth-century fire had damaged the interior. Gradually the building had deteriorated into the kind of cliff-perched ruin you wouldn't want to be in after dark for fear of Dracula.

Closer to the cliff's edge was the well-preserved Mussenden Temple, a domed rotunda the bishop had used as a summer library and place of worship.

'People can have weddings here now,' Siobhan told me. 'Imagine, on a summer's day, it would be gorgeous.'

If you could ever stop the clifftop breezes getting up your frock and blowing away the bridesmaids.

The temple was an elegant little piece of strangeness. It was inspired by the Temple of Vesta at Tivoli and dedicated to a young cousin of the bishop, who died before it was completed. Apparently the inscription round the dome translated as: 'It is agreeable to watch from land someone else involved in a great struggle while the winds whip up the waves out at sea.'

Siobhan and I had struggles of our own as we darted out of the car to take pictures of the temple: sleet lashed us, a herd of sheep was staring at us, and a man in a tractor was approaching, shouting something at us.

'I don't know what he's saying, but let's get out of here,' Siobhan yelped over the winds.

We made it to the car, manoeuvred noisily and escaped a man who was probably just a friendly farmer wondering if we needed help.

'I was brought up in the country,' Siobhan said. 'I know

when someone's telling me to get out of it and when they're friendly.'

'Maybe he's someone who the bishop watched drown at sea and he comes up to haunt anyone who goes near the temple.'

'Don't be silly,' Siobhan said. 'He was in a tractor. If he was a drowned ghost, he'd come shivering up covered in seaweed and barnacles.'

We spent the evening in Siobhan's local pub because she'd promised me as new blood to her pub quiz team. It was the sort of cosy old pub you'd see in a tourist board promotion of Ireland. Full of smiling, weather-beaten old boys and fresh-faced young girls coming in from the cold clad in thick knit jumpers, all greeting each other because they all knew each other and drank branded stout together.

Siobhan had told me their area was called mixed, but was predominately Protestant. I noticed a few small, framed certificates on the pub wall, like Rotary Club certificates, detailing money raised for charity by the local branch of the Orange Order.

'My friend who captains our team takes the quiz very seriously,' Siobhan warned me. 'So try your best.'

I did, but was a little put out when the friend overruled me on a football question and I turned out to be right. I was wrong about so many other things after that I couldn't get up a justifiable sulk.

There was a question about how a new pope was declared elected, which surprised me; Siobhan had to remind me not to jump to conclusions, people in a middle-class Protestant pub were not going to start screaming and laying about themselves with bowlers just because someone mentioned the Pope.

'You've got to be here more. Each little environment around the country is different. I've lived in London, I know how it's made to look worse than it is.'

'Made to?'

'Not on purpose. Jesus, have you come over here thinking everything's a conspiracy? If nothing's happening, that's not news, is it? You don't see the pub quiz, you see a blown-up pub. Now, think, what's the next line of this song?'

We were on a very tricky music round. Some tables were surrounded by people humming and stumbling over the second line to an Adam and the Ants song. At other tables, older competitors were getting cranky, but they'd had an easy run of it with Charles Aznavour and the Beatles.

'Do any of us know this?' Siobhan asked. 'Or should I run home and get my dog to help us out?'

6. One Way of Looking at Belfast

The Belfast Europa hotel had been bombed thirty-three times. For many years it was the only major hotel in the city centre. It was where journalists used to stay, hence the thirty-three bombs – convenient for the journalists as they didn't have to leave the bar to get news; convenient for the bombers as they were guaranteed to make the news.

I'd expected something more imposing, a battered but dignified establishment in a solid central avenue of Belfast. It was central, right beside the bus station. It had a gaudy seaside-night-club-looking frontage, with an excess of pink neon even seaside night clubs haven't used since the seventies.

The reception area was a little more impressive – high marble, over plush seats, and a sweeping curve of staircase leading to what a journalist had described to me as: 'Nothing special rooms. Worth a couple of nights though, for the history.'

I'd arrived from Portadown feeling very dishevelled. There'd been snowy squalls on the road, making me pull at my hair with driving stress and generally rub my make-up all round my face, as I tried to figure out what might be in the road two feet ahead of me. I'd dropped my backpack in a puddle as I carried it into the Europa and I was wearing a warm but very old anorak that always made me look a little Care in the Community.

Still, if they were used to journalists, they were used to dishevelment and Care in the Community.

I asked the receptionist, all grooming and manicuring to

a Miss Bamford's Academy level of perfection, if she had a room for two nights. She looked at me and distaste flickered into her eyes. She consulted the computer for what felt like an unnecessarily long time. Smartly dressed businessmen were gathering around the desk with questions for the girl. She turned to me, smileless.

'We have a room,' she said. And then added, not quietly enough, 'But you know it's a hundred and sixty pounds a night here.' This was when she finally smiled. Pityingly.

I knew then what the danger in the Europa hotel would be for me. Not bombs. The danger would be that I'd throw down my credit card to spite my face – 'Only a hundred and sixty pounds, I'll take three . . .'

Common sense bellowed down the shouts of my pride. But the businessmen were all listening in now, I had to save face somehow. I remembered I owed a lot of emails.

'That's fine,' I said calmly to the receptionist. 'You do have internet facilities in the rooms?'

'No,' she said.

Phew.

'But there is an internet café just two doors down.'

I made a face as though I was considering the matter. 'You have a gym, though,' I said, trying to make her worried I might be someone famous in disguise, in dire need of a work-out before a starring role in a multi-million-dollar movie. I made a sneery face that I felt implied all this.

'I'm afraid not. There is one two blocks north.'

'Two blocks north,' I echoed disdainfully.

'They don't have a car park either,' a businessman interrupted. Possibly he was a salesman used to a life of bluffing and wanted to help me out, possibly he was just disgruntled with the hotel. As well he might be.

'No car park? I'm sorry, that's no use to me at all.' I

gave the receptionist back her pitying smile and then marched out, trailing my muddy rucksack, dishevelled dignity intact.

I spotted an anonymous hotel just down the road and was relieved to discover I could have the thrill of staying very near to the Europa for less than a quarter of its inflated prices.

'It's because the Clintons stayed there, they've got all up themselves,' the very different kind of receptionist in the second hotel told me when I complained of their neighbour. 'I mean, there's nothing in there worth that kind of money. And did you know it was bombed about thirty times in the Troubles? They'd have to pay me to stay there.'

A bath and noticing the sun was out made me feel less grouchy about Belfast. I went for a stroll along the road, found the Grand Opera House. Designed by Frank Matcham, it had all the curly, gilded, fancy frills and painted cherubs a Matcham theatre should have. There were posters up for a play that pronounced: 'Hilarious', 'Back for an extended run'. The play was a *History of The Troubles According to My Da*. It sounded interesting. It was sold out. The box office clerk suggested I book tickets for a show coming in the following month: 'It's the same kind of thing, you know, a quirky personal view of Northern Ireland.'

I declined the tickets and went out feeling a little crest-fallen to have discovered I was in the middle of researching a quirky, personal cliché of a book.

I'd started now, so I'd have to go on with it. I had my bus map, I had my street map and knew exactly what house to look at to see where George Best was born.

It was a basic-looking house, in a street of houses that looked the same, on an estate that all looked the same. There were tattered Union Jacks outside a couple of houses and vacant lots full of litter. If I was making a documentary about George, I'd have filmed the two boys kicking a football in a nearby cul de sac, with a boarded-up house on the corner. See how far George travelled in life . . . But then . . .

Eamon, my footballing uncle, was the first person I'd heard express any sympathy for the back-on-the-drink-despite-the-new-liver George Best.

'They took him away from the cosy wee world of East Belfast far too young and in all those years no one fought him to the ground to make him sort his head out. Did you read his autobiography? He doesn't realize it, but every word in it tells you he's had nothing but misery in his heart since he was a wee boy. Pele said Best was the greatest footballer he'd ever seen – imagine knowing that about yourself and still not being able to find any peace?' Eamon sighed. 'People think professional footballers are spoilt, but it's a very stressful life. A couple of bad days, an injury and that's it, you're finished.'

Eamon had been an international. He left because of injury and had taken up teaching. He reckoned he'd had the best of both worlds – could point to his clippings and caps and know he'd been good enough; could point to his big happy family, his teaching achievements and know he'd had a proper life as well.

'George was definitely amazing. That's a gift from God. But you should look at Danny Blanchflower. He was from Belfast. Captained Spurs when they won the double, was footballer of the year twice. He got injured and went into managing Northern Ireland – but he was a footballer with a university degree; he wrote about football and campaigned to stop footballers being exploited. Before his campaign they got paid next to nothing. There's an all-rounder, a role model.

Anyone tells you footballers are thick, tell them about Danny
Blanchflower.'

And not about George, who'd started in a little street in
East Belfast where I began to feel self-conscious. A man was
watching me from his garden gate. Disturbingly, he was
pretending to be polishing the garden gnome in his hands
while keeping his eye on me. I was still wearing the anorak
that had aroused suspicion in the Europa; perhaps this neighbourhood had been endlessly hassled by scruffy, anoracked
characters, stealing gnomes from gardens near George Best's
old house. I wouldn't touch his gnomes; I didn't want a
souvenir. Poor George. If only he had been related to us,
he'd have had Uncle Eamon to talk to and it could all have
been happier for him.

It was getting dark and cold. No sign of a bus for half
an hour. I wondered if I should have left the hunt for George
until morning.

A bus with a destination and number I didn't recognize
pulled up at the stop. I'd memorized the numbers I'd need
for the city centre, in case something bad happened up in the
remote reaches of East Belfast. The driver opened the door.

'Where were you wanting to go?' he asked, as if he'd
caught me graffiting the bus shelter.

'City centre?'

'I go there. Get in.'

'You weren't on the timetable,' I said as I paid him.

For the first time he stopped scowling at me. 'I'm a new
route. I come as a big surprise to everyone.'

He winked at me. 'What, do you think I'm trying to
kidnap you?'

Uncle Joe hadn't said anything about what to do if
kidnapped by a bus driver in East Belfast, so no, I hadn't
been thinking that.

'I was just thinking a London bus driver would never do this.'

The driver laughed. 'If I was as busy as those boys, you think I'd bother?'

I sat in the empty bus and saw his point.

The bus system in Belfast was still underused because buses were often attacked during the Troubles – pelted with stones, petrol bombs or hijacked for use in barricades. Taxis became the preferred form of transport. The cabs often operated as service taxis, waiting until they were full of people going in the same direction. They could be as cheap as buses and could dart around trouble spots to get people home.

There were complicated things to remember about the cabs in the Troubles: as a general rule, the black cabs, like London cabs, were the Catholic ones. They'd go to Catholic areas and were rumoured to be a form of pension scheme for retired IRA men. Ordinary cars went to Protestant areas and had Protestant drivers. Maybe their drivers were retired paramilitaries as well, but these days I think there were just a lot of middle-aged men driving cabs of all kinds because there were no other jobs for them.

Guided black cab tours were the latest thing being advertised in the expansive new Tourist Information Office. You could go on a black cab tour of the attractive Antrim coast, up to Giant's Causeway, ending your day sampling product at the Bushmills whiskey factory. You could take taxi tours round the blue plaques of Belfast to see how many famous people had lived there. Or, you could take what some guides referred to as a 'Conflict Tour'. Other guides took a more oblique approach in their leaflets and offered 'a tour of the political murals in the Falls and Shankill areas, with an explanation of the recent history of the city'.

'What next?' Uncle Eamon had laughed at the leaflet.

'Re-enactment of riots, tourists running about with paint-ball guns firing green or orange? Black cab tours. I don't believe people want to do that.'

I did want to do it, of course, but felt wrong for want-ing it. It seemed too soon. It seemed too cynical that some-thing recently a matter of life and death was now an entertainment. It was everything that had irritated me about all those plays, all those films and thriller series where the province was so dramatically useful, so fascinating for audi-ences living in nice calm places. But I also mistrusted my feeling about the showing of the Troubles to the world – perhaps I didn't want them to be shown to me.

Besides, if sites of violence were becoming tourist attrac-tions, rather than sites of violence, didn't that mean the Troubles were really ending?

The guide on my tour, Peter, said he didn't feel they were ending. He felt they were changing. Locations that were dangerous had changed, the ways the paramilitaries operated, and who they were, had changed. He said there were new problems: 'Those former paramilitaries and rabble-rousers might be talking peace but they've left behind them some very sick and bitter people. There's people who are traumatized and people who've just become bullies and criminals all over this city.'

As a tour guide Peter was very interesting but not cheering.

Evidence of the sick and bitter remnants had been on the news the night before my tour. A teenage boy's suicide in the Ardoyne area of Belfast. He'd climbed the scaffolding on the tower of Holy Cross church and hanged himself. He was one of twelve teenage boys who'd committed suicide in this area of Belfast in the first month of the year.

The Ardoyne had become a stronghold of the extreme nationalist group the INLA. The boy who'd killed himself, and his friend who'd killed himself the week before, had been terrified of the next thing the INLA might do to them. With justification. The eighteen-year-old friend had been shot in the legs by the INLA when he was sixteen. He'd done something dumb like sell drugs, steal a car, maybe he'd mugged someone.

Last night's suicide had been abducted by the paramilitaries the previous year, buried down a manhole for a day, to teach him a lesson for some kind of infringement of INLA local bylaws. According to his mother, he'd been full of paranoiac depression since then. He'd been terrified if he saw anyone talking on a mobile phone in the street, thinking this was a signal someone was being ordered to do something to him. His mother said the INLA controlled everything and everyone in the Ardoyne; no one would inform the police about anything because the punishment would be unimaginable.

With this in my mind when Peter picked me up, I felt bothered all over again about doing the tour.

Peter was younger than he'd sounded on the phone, in his early thirties with a fresh-faced look belying the packet of cigarettes on the dashboard. As we set out, he said, 'Now I just wanted to check what it is you're interested in. You did say you wanted the more political side?'

I said I felt weird about it, what with things like the suicides in the Ardoyne still going on, but it was the political side.

He gave me a sort of forgiving nod. 'That's what most people are interested in. It's what they've heard about Belfast and they want to try and understand it.'

He started the engine. 'I can take you up to the Ardoyne if you like, the Holy Cross school is up there. You know about that.'

The news reports and television drama about the Catholic children who'd been spat at, stoned and threatened while walking through a Protestant area to their school had gripped attention in Britain for a time. I knew it. It was one of the things that people used to dismiss the Northern Irish as incomprehensible.

Peter said the Ardoyne had the highest suicide rate in the United Kingdom.

'I read something in the papers this morning saying that teenage boys get into a copycat pattern with committing suicide. So this might not be the end of it. Then you have to remember that the suicide rate for young men is exceptionally high anyway. Apparently in America a teenager commits suicide every two hours.' He made an awkward smile. 'I looked this up on the internet last night because I had a feeling, you know, that teenagers did this, you know, killed themselves more than you'd think. On the site I found for the Samaritans it says for men under thirty-five it's about five hundred in England a year. But that's the whole of England, not this one little area of Belfast.'

I said the suicides and the news of how the INLA still control the place had shocked me.

'It's bad if you have to live in certain areas. Generally people can go about their business in Belfast in a way they didn't used to. There's new shops opening. New hotels, new restaurants. Look at that Waterfront Hall. That's all glass. There's more good news than bad in Belfast for the last five years, there really is.'

'And it's so beautiful,' I said, so he wouldn't start to conclude I was only impressed by bad news. 'All the old buildings. And from most places in the city you can see the mountains.'

I had been brought up watching news reports that didn't

show the real look and feel of Belfast — a city of colossal architecture, with a long waterfront, nestling in mountains.

We turned into the broad, scruffy Shankill Road, with mountains on the horizon. Peter pointed out the Glasgow Rangers supporters club and a shuttered building where IRA gunmen had burst in and killed the shopkeepers. I noticed almost every shop in the road was locked and shuttered.

'So have all these shops closed down now?' I asked.

Peter laughed. 'No. They're not open yet. It's only ten past eight. They'll start opening after nine, once they've got the kids to school.'

So easy to mis-see in Belfast.

We turned off into a housing estate, ugly sixties architecture, litter and neglect. There were similar estates all over Britain.

'Public housing,' Peter called it.

We stopped to look at what made the estate Northern Irish, a political mural. Some schoolchildren passing glanced at us and moved on.

'Do people mind you doing this?'

'At first they thought it was strange, but when I explained myself they didn't mind. They want people to take an interest. And I have this van now instead of the black cab, just so I'm not making any kind of statement.'

Although advertised as a black cab tour, we were touring in a comfortable new people mover.

Peter asked if I wanted to get out and take a picture of the first mural. I said no, because taking pictures seemed a step too much towards misery tourism for me. And I didn't like the murals, regardless of content.

It was inevitable that whatever happened, the murals were going to be preserved for tourists to look at, with a lot of patronizing flannel written about the artistry in them. I didn't think these things were art. Mostly, they were like kerbstones of Northern Irish streets, painted red, white and blue, or in the shades of the Irish tricolour, to show how the people who lived there were supposed to feel. Belfast had a world-class university, increasing numbers of modern art galleries . . . The city had far more brains and talent than I ever saw in a political mural.

We were looking at a clumsy black and white mural on a gable wall titled 'Sinn Fein Contribution To The Peace Process'. There were four panels showing IRA men training FARC guerrillas in Colombia; smuggling arms from Florida; the IRA breaking into police files at Castlereagh; and Sinn Fein spying on their colleagues at Stormont. There was a central portrait of Gerry Adams, one side of him a suited man with a briefcase, the other side a man in uniform with a gun.

'You see, he's half a politician, half paramilitary,' Peter explained.

'Half a politician is better than a whole paramilitary,' I said.

Peter didn't say anything.

The next mural was the face of a UDA man who'd been killed by the UFF.

'Don't ask me to explain the difference,' Peter said grimly. 'It's all territorial stuff going on with these Protestant paramilitaries now. All to do with money. Drugs and protection rackets. Apparently some of them live in Spain now. Control things from there, in the sun.'

He waved a hand at the painted kerbstones: 'More red, white and blue here than in London I expect.'

We passed a mural of King Billy prancing on his horse victoriously. Peter checked I knew who he was. He slowed and said wearily as we passed another brightly painted man on a horse, 'Here, they've even got Cromwell. That's going back a long way, isn't it?'

I agreed. I'd taken King Billy for granted, but Cromwell . . . Although it was fair enough, Catholics still told tales of his wickedness to the Irish. Everyone had long memories.

Deciding we'd dwelt too long on the negative, Peter drove on, saying, 'The people round the Shankill have suffered a lot: drive-by shootings, assassinations, petrol bombs – but look at these new housing estates here.' We drove into more modern public housing. 'You see how nice they are? Despite it all, people take real pride in their homes.'

Pride and some kind of notion to make the estate look like Tyrolean chalets, with carved wooden shutters and geranium-stuffed window boxes. There were acres of rose trellises, pokerwork panels and burgeoning hanging baskets. Anything that could be stuck on to the outside of a house to make a desperate bid for glamour had been slapped on to these houses.

'You can imagine they're just as nice inside,' Peter said. 'Everything like a new pin.'

Despite all the housework going on to show how life was normal, the massive Peace Wall was still up between the Shankill and the Falls. And a new layer of fencing had recently been added to the top, as boys had been throwing stones over it. The metal gates between the Shankill and the Falls were open, but the police closed them at night. Otherwise, Peter said, boys gathered around them and caused trouble.

This wasn't necessarily some schoolboy vandalism – in Ireland 'boys' referred to men up to at least the age of fifty.

On the Falls Road side, the houses were closer to the wall, gardens backing on to it. They had grilles of wire mesh over the gardens, stretching up to the roof of the house. This protected them from petrol bombs and stones.

'You can believe me that each one of those gardens is perfectly tended,' Peter said.

Living neatly was obviously part of the key to sanity. Every window I could see in was spangly clean, with white white nets or elaborately ruched blinds. Miss Bamford could have held out a finger, trailed it round every surface in every house and not found a speck of dust to tut over.

Peter lit a cigarette as he led me into a small Garden of Remembrance on the Falls side of the wall.

'On the Protestant side there are more murals but on the Catholic side they have more of these Gardens of Remembrance. I'll show you the Catholic murals later, but they're fewer and more grouped together.'

I asked if it was something to do with the nature of the Catholic religion, that they paid more elaborate attention to the dead.

Peter dragged on his cigarette and narrowed his eyes, considering me. 'I don't think that's true. The Protestants have murals to the dead, the Catholics have gardens. They both romanticize the dead.'

I was considering Peter too, trying to figure him out, but he seemed carefully neutral – I suppose he had to be in his job. But the more we talked, the more frankly and angrily pacifist he revealed himself to be.

The frosty morning was warming up with bright sunlight. The Garden of Remembrance had perfectly pruned shrubs and new wooden benches. There were plaques fastened to the wall commemorating the dead. On one plaque there was a list of 'Volunteers', IRA activists. The plaque with names not prefixed by 'Vol.' had a list three times as long. Peter pointed this out to me.

'There are more civilians than IRA men.' He drew a last long smoke of his cigarette. 'Most of the people killed in all this are innocent.'

As we turned back to the car, he said, 'I doubt that wall will come down any time soon. The media might like to see it come down, they might see it as a positive thing. But it's not like the Berlin wall. The people in Berlin didn't want that wall. The people here want this.'

A wall you couldn't see through or see over.

On another wall was a grouping of Catholic murals. There was a painting of plastic bullets, explaining that there was a new kind, even more dangerous. Critical of all sides, Peter pointed out, 'Any of those things are dangerous. If a plastic bullet hits you in the wrong place, it can kill you.'

There was a painting of an RUC officer and an identical officer of the reformed PSNI – Police Service of Northern Ireland. Peter said Catholics didn't believe anything had changed, and Catholics still wouldn't join the police force.

'They'd have to leave their neighbourhood. They'd have to move to a mixed area. There's still a lot of intimidation.'

I had Catholic relatives in the police. They'd joined because they believed some Catholics had to, to try and change things. They lived in mixed areas and believed that things had changed, a little.

Many of the Catholic murals related Irish struggles to other causes – the Palestinians, the Basques, the Catalans, the Palestinians again. There was a painting of a young Turkish hunger striker – the explanation under her portrait said she was inspired by Bobby Sands.

A mural commemorating Bobby Sands himself provoked something in Peter. He looked at the mural with distaste and said nothing for a long time. Then he told me something I'd never heard before: 'You know the families of the hunger strikers could have signed a form to get their son off the strike, have them intravenously fed, but they wouldn't do it. Some people say the families were intimidated, but it was more subtle than that, they were made to feel it would be such a shame on the family to sign those papers. That their son would never forgive them and their neighbours would never look at them again.' He looked almost tearful. 'But if it was my son dying I'd have signed it. Imagine, people wouldn't sign a piece of paper to stop their child dying.'

Peter seemed so distressed I could only do what he was doing, stare at Bobby Sands and think about it.

When I was a student people in London went on marches supporting the hunger strikers – not me. Whatever post-punk phase I was in seemed more interesting. Somehow I chanced into a party given by left-wing playwrights – one of the playwrights was reading a smuggled letter written on toilet paper by one of the hunger strikers. I wanted to punch her in the face. There was something so ghoulish, in a comfortable Chelsea home, this earnest woman holding a piece of toilet paper scrawled on by someone who was dying . . . Maybe I just didn't want to admit that rather than chopping off my hair and tinting it pink, I could be interested in something to do with where I came from. Maybe I was right to be annoyed that these middle-aged, middle-class playwrights loved the fact that someone was dying for Catholic Ireland. There was something demeaning about being taken up as a cause. It made us seem more dispensable than any kind of discrimination – Irish Catholics were only notable if they managed to kill themselves in some interesting way. Our courageous ability to self-destruct was even more charming than our abilities with pipes and tin whistles.

I don't remember why I'd been at the party, possibly a college tutor had taken me . . . I'd left mid-reading and gone to drink Snakebite in a pub in Shepherd's Bush. My youth might have been mindless, but at least no one was telling me, or my parents, I'd be most useful to society if I was dead.

We turned away from Bobby Sands' giant painted face. I said, 'It is an incredible thing to do, to starve yourself to death in this day and age.'

Peter shrugged, he'd obviously had enough of thinking about it. 'Well, something gets into the culture and they all do it.'

I was getting a feeling that Peter was working as a tour guide in a city he really couldn't stand. Perhaps he just couldn't stand doing this particular tour. But business wasn't bad, whatever he thought about it.

'I'm strangely busy for February. But Belfast gets a lot of visitors now.' Peter and I paddled out of deep waters into a nice little pool of small talk. 'There's the cheap flights thing. And Belfast's cheap. Foreigners generally, far more foreigners who feel it would be all right to take a look.'

'There's a lot to look at.' I pointed at a spire on the horizon. 'I can't believe how many churches there are.'

'Three hundred churches,' he said.

We turned away from the spire and towards the square tower of Holy Cross church. Scaffolding climbing one wall of it.

'There's where the lad hanged himself.'

There were a lot of ways a teenager could have chosen to kill himself. But hanging from church scaffolding? The boy wanted his death to cry out.

The Ardoyne was mostly not 'bleak', 'grim' or 'strife-battered', as I saw it described in London newspapers a few

days later. The reports on the suicides and the INLA intimidation were full of clichés. And I realized that film made
about Holy Cross school had completely ignored the geography of the area. It didn't look the same as the ugly estates
in the film. This was an area of tree-lined streets. There
were large red-brick mansions and attractive detached houses.
The Holy Cross school, the suicides – these things were
more complex and unsettling because they were happening
in places that looked pleasant.

Peter showed me where the Catholic section of the road
became the Protestant section the Catholics had to walk
along to reach Holy Cross school. A tree-bordered road,
with the Catholic school on one side and the Protestant
school directly opposite.

I asked why all hell had suddenly broken loose – hadn't
the school always been where it was?

'I don't know. The demographic changes and people get
stranded. There was some change in the Protestant groups
around here, some more extreme elements moved up this
way. So there's a little Catholic area back there that's got cut
off from its school. Then something bad happens, some
intimidation of Protestants. For instance, the Protestant old
people go all the way down to the Shankill to collect their
pensions, when there's a nearer post office in that Catholic
enclave, but they feel scared in there. So something happens
one way and gets paid back another way. And if there's
extreme elements around, they push people into reacting to
something they were already furious about anyway.'

Peter then drove round to the main road, showing me
what would have been the long way round for the Catholic
children to walk to school, avoiding the angry Protestants.

'There's a main road,' I said. 'But it's not an impossibly
long walk. It's not that much longer.'

'No, and if their parents were having to walk with them anyway . . .'

He paused a moment then decided to tell me what he honestly thought. 'The IRA put pressure on Catholic parents to keep insisting they walk their children the short route because they knew there was massive PR value in the pictures of Protestants spitting at Catholic children.'

It certainly had been a PR gift. I didn't want to believe what Peter said, but it didn't surprise me: 'Well, they say the Republicans are great masters of spin.'

He enthusiastically agreed. 'Yes, like I was saying about the hunger strikers. People get manipulated. It's hateful.'

I realized that whoever was spitting, whoever was manipulating, what I hated was the gift given to people with contempt for the Northern Irish – look at them, look at what they're doing now . . .

Heading back past Protestant-muralled Sandy Row, Peter pointed out how close it was to the centre of Belfast. 'The thing is with Belfast being so small, if trouble starts, it's soon in the middle of the town and brings it to a standstill.'

I still wanted to know where he was coming from. And how much was he saying things because my accent had led him to believe I was English. It was so hard to hear what people were telling you in Northern Ireland and not wonder what their agenda was. I told him that my family were Catholic and we'd left in the sixties because my father joined the British Air Force. I thought this exposed me as a bit of everything, unlikely to react to whatever he was.

'Oh, yes,' he said. 'A lot of people did say, "We've got an opportunity, we're leaving." A lot of people left. It's still an under-populated city.'

Again he'd evaded me. I wasn't nearly savvy enough about all the subtle signs and whispers that had to be read from people in Northern Ireland to ask the right careful questions to get a fix on their position.

I did know I could have taken another cab and been told the recent history in a completely different way. I didn't know what to do with Peter's opinions but comb through them for facts. I was constantly gouging around in my own opinions and finding lumps of things I wasn't sure I'd thought, or inherited, or been hyped into believing. It was definitely one of the character traits of people from Northern Ireland – knowing that not only do people not tell the truth, but what they think is the truth may not be true. It made for a very cynical disposition.

On the news that night there was a story from the Ardoyne to make even the cynical feel a tug at their heart. A big INLA arms cache had been found in a minicab office in the area and the information had come from a local informant. The boy who'd killed himself on Holy Cross church had made something change.

The Falls Road was murals, Remembrance Gardens, grilles over gardens and full of disturbing thoughts, or, it was the place I visited a few mornings later when I went to look for Belfast Grandma's old house.

I'd overestimated my skills as a map-reader and my strength of leg. The walk started well, Belfast looking very Sunday morning, with shop shutters closed and church doors open. I had to go west, then north, and with a bit of effort I'd make it in about half an hour.

An hour later, I was in the Falls Road, passing the murals and too far west, nowhere near north enough.

Two old ladies with small Scottie dogs were talking outside a newsagent.

A man with a black eye staggered towards me and asked

me for some money to get home, I muttered something into my map and kept walking. Another staggering man with a black eye came past me and didn't ask for money. Perhaps they'd been fighting each other and the second one had got away with the first one's wallet . . . Maybe they'd both come out of the pub I was passing, the pavement in front of it smelling of disinfectant. I kept going in case more black-eyed men staggered out.

A group of teenage boys headed towards me, exuberant, and one of them shouted a confirmation of what I was thinking.

'Mornin'! We're still drunk from the night before!' Then he held his arms open wide. 'But we're giving out free hugs.'

I said that was very nice but I didn't need a hug.

'You can see she doesn't,' his friend said. 'She needs directions.'

'Here. I know Belfast very well.' The hugging one grabbed my map. 'Where are you going?'

'Thorndale Avenue.'

'Where?'

'It's off the Antrim Road.'

He frowned at me, confused. 'So you're lost then?'

One of his friends grabbed the map. 'Give us that. You can't even read.'

The friend squinted at the map. 'Where off the Antrim Road? That's a long road and miles from here.'

'It's miles,' the hugging one confirmed. 'You'll need a taxi. We'll find you a taxi.'

Out of nowhere, one of the old women with Scottie dogs pushed her way into the middle of the boys, demanding, 'Is this wee girl lost? Would you not think to help her instead of standing around?'

'We're helping, we've got her map,' a boy protested.

'What would you know about maps? Where is it you want, dear?'

'Thorndale Avenue.'

'Oh, I know Thorndale Avenue.'

'My grandmother used to live there,' I said. I was suddenly inspired by a wild notion that if the lady was old she might turn out to have known my grandmother . . .

Belfast was small but not that small.

The boys were losing interest now. One of them handed back the map and said, 'She knows everywhere, she used to be a nurse.'

I was sure this had a logic and thanked them as they drifted off, shouting that they were going down the town to find some girls to hug.

'Wee skitters,' the old lady said. 'Now, dear, Thorndale Avenue. I know it very well. Did you know Mary McAleese was born there?'

I didn't.

'So you're not a relative of hers then?'

'Not as far as I know.'

At least I wasn't the only one out on the streets with far-fetched notions in the back of my mind.

'No. I just thought I'd ask. It would have been a thrill if you were, wouldn't it? You'll not have been there in a while?'

'Not since the late sixties.'

She looked at me with deep concern. 'Well, dear, you do know you'll find it's changed a lot. It won't be the street you remember I'm sure.'

I said I didn't mind.

'If you're sure, then. You'll need a taxi.' She spun round and waved to a man parked in a side-street.

'Jim, come and take this wee girl to Thorndale Avenue!' she roared in a voice twice her size.

She tutted over me as she put me in the car. 'Imagine you didn't know about Mary McAleese. You'll need to know something good about the street when you see it now.'

I thanked her and braced myself to find the avenue pretty much burnt to the ground.

It had been a genteel street of large red-brick houses, in an area so quiet we'd been confidently allowed to go off unsupervised into parks and, more interestingly, into a nearby scrap metal yard. A child-friendly proprietor had let us play for hours in the shell of a sports car.

Jim the taxi driver took a wrong turn and went down a street into New Lodge, where I had a feeling the scrap yard had been. New Lodge was painted with murals demanding truth and justice for the New Lodge Six, shot by the British army in 1973.

Possibly they'd been shot from the abandoned barbed-wire-covered army posts at either end of Thorndale Avenue.

The avenue was bashed shabby, several houses boarded up.

'Ah, that's all right,' Jim the taxi driver said, as we pulled up outside the house. 'It's not one of the boarded ones.'

After a pause, while I looked at the down-at-heel but lived-in house, Jim said, 'Your grandmother must have had money, then.'

'She had lodgers,' I said.

'She could well have, these are three-storey houses.' Jim looked at me as if checking for distress or shock. 'This used to be a snob area, a real snob area.' From his tone, I knew he meant this to be commiserating.

'Doesn't look it now. Looks like it's been through the mill.'

'Oh, this area now . . .' he said, 'this area of Antrim Road, it's still where you'd find a fair bit of nastiness.'

'I remember it being really quiet, you know, we used to play in the street.'

Jim suddenly looked worried. 'What happened to your grandmother?'

'She went to live in Tipperary.'

'Oh, that's all right then.' He started the car. 'So you recognize it even so. Where else do you remember?'

'I don't know, we used to go to the zoo a lot, isn't that quite near?' ·

'A bit up the road. That would have been the old zoo, they closed it down because they were abusing the animals, but the new one's lovely.'

Abusing the animals? I didn't want to dwell on that – *abusing them*?

Jim asked me where I lived in England.

'I was in London for a few years,' he said. 'I did some work in a hotel. Kensington. But I missed Belfast.'

'You didn't like London?'

'It was OK,' he said dismissively. Then, as if he was worried I'd be offended, he added more brightly, 'It was OK, you know, but . . . Ach, you see how people are here, you know, they'd talk to you once in a while.'

To change the subject, Jim pointed to Cave Hill mountain ahead of us.

'You remember what they call that?'

'Napoleon's nose.'

'That's right! You'll soon get back to being a Belfast girl.'

Cave Hill, visible from all around Belfast, did look like a man's face. Why Napoleon, no one really knew. There were Neolithic caves up there but nothing French. Perhaps it was a revolutionary connection – at McArts fort on the summit the United Irishmen had plotted rebellion for two days and pledged themselves to fight for Irish independence.

We stopped in the car park of the new zoo. Excited children were bouncing up to the entrance, to what Jim said was supposed to be one of the most modern and humane zoos in Europe. As well it might be . . . Abused? I knew those animals, I'd wailed to be taken to see them every other day, they were my friends . . .

I had to know.

'What do you mean they abused the animals at the old zoo?'

'They got sick. No one was really in charge of it, it was too small and the animals were all diseased and neglected. They'd have been terrible-looking sick animals when you'd have been going.'

Obviously I'd loved them regardless. I did remember it had very small, smelly cages, with creatures pacing about crossly. I suppose if I'd really cared I would have called that 'abuse' but I'd had a far more disturbing interpretation of the word in my head. Luckily for any night's sleep I ever hoped to have in future, Jim had clarified the matter.

'Get out and take a look at the view,' he suggested. 'That'll cheer you up and you'll see why people don't like to leave Belfast.'

There was the ring of small mountains around the city, the Lough waters stretching away in front of me, the Lagan river valley below and the city spread out looking quietly dignified.

'Ten minutes from the centre, that view. Isn't it grand?' Jim said.

The view over the city was grand. But it was the sensitive, manic friendliness of complete strangers on the streets down there that would make London seem just 'OK' to someone from Belfast.

7. Witches, Bitches and Fishwives

Outside City Hall was a gathering of Belfast's teenage punk rockers, with bondage gear and big red Mohicans, the like of which had long since become extinct in London. There were some American tourists debating whether to go in for a tour of City Hall; then they decided they'd rather have breakfast. They took some photographs of the punks and went on their way, one of them saying, 'It doesn't seem how I thought it would be.'

Who knows what they thought Belfast would be like, but I'd guess no matter how much they'd been advised that Belfast was fairly safe now, they'd have expected it to be a lot more grim.

The whole fabric of the place felt exhausted, but in the shells of grand old edifices, shoppers picked over cheap goods in pile-em-high stores and discount supermarkets. Side-streets were full of tumble-down cafés and minicab offices, or had been paved over and filled with new branches of organic stores, cappuccino bars, designer clothes shops and book stores. Streets further from the centre, seemingly full of old, empty buildings, had sudden surprising art galleries and cafés – a sort of squatter bohemia. And there were so many night clubs I worried if I stood still too long someone would try and refurbish me for late drinking and dancing.

The population was notably young. Heading south, toward Botanic Avenue and the University district, the people were even younger, there were more cafés, more clubs, old bookshops, new bookshops, comedy clubs and arts centres. I was seeing different races – Africans, Indians . . . And students, students, students.

Queen's University was hard to get into these days, it had such a good reputation. The large numbers of Northern Irish school-leavers going to universities abroad wasn't all about escaping the Troubles. The high educational standard in the country meant there just weren't enough university places to meet demand, and at Queen's the competition for places was international.

My parents had met in the gothic halls of Queen's University, so I bought them mouse mats in the souvenir shop. They were constantly emailing me information about Northern Ireland, so they might be needing them.

'Check on the big goldfish in the Botanic Gardens,' my father's last message read. 'As a child I found them very exciting. Are they still there?'

Dutifully, I walked up from the university to see the condition of the fish. Hopefully I wouldn't have to investigate another report of abuse.

I was glad he'd sent me on this mission. Coming out of the Botanical Gardens on a sharp, frosty morning and into the flower-scented warmth of the glass palm house, startling with early daffodils of every possible shape and shade of yellow, surrounded by coils of strange greenery, I caught my breath and didn't want to leave.

Constructed in 1839, the palm house was an elaborately curvy palace of glass panels, framed in thin, white-painted cast-iron bands. On the hot interior, the bands of iron were rusting and glass panes were cracked and edged in mildew – this only added to the charm of the building. A couple of men were busy watering and feeding plants, humming songs, content in their work. There were labels to tell me what all the Garden of Eden madness of plants around me were called in Latin – but who cared what they were called, they were doing enough just by being there.

The original plan had been for edifying entertainments to be put on in the Botanical Gardens for the workers of Belfast on summer Sundays. In the nineteenth century, these entertainments were mostly Protestant preachers shouting for sobriety, thrift and avoidance of popery – occasionally provoking a riot. These days, there were big rock concerts in the summer months, but the Botanical Gardens really felt more like a park suited to a small string quartet. The sort of park where ladies in long pale gowns would stroll about with parasols, commenting on the wonderful curiosity of foreign plants in the palm house. And they might feel slightly overheated and decadent in the gardens' other building, the Tropical Ravine, a jungle housed in what looked like a plain brick shed.

The explanatory plaques on the balcony overlooking the artificial jungle bore no relation to where the plants were now – they'd grown and twisted to make a tangled, triffidy green wildness – branches and vines straining against girders, leaves flattened against glass roof panels, pushing to escape and overwhelm Belfast.

In the dark pools at the very bottom of the ravine, the over-large goldfish looked vaguely sinister but very much alive and unmolested. I didn't think they were as exciting as the general feeling of stumbling into a forgotten secret garden. I heard birdsong and realized there were dozens of blackbirds darting about the branches around me. I stood mesmerized by hot weird nature, until another person came in and I had to leave because they'd broken the spell.

The gardens felt familiar from way back. As did some slightly moth-eaten stuffed tigers in the Ulster Museum. I

distinctly remember being irritated by them as a child –
stuffed animals were not like zoo animals and smacked of
educational intent. The museum was asquawk with schoolchildren, chasing each other and trying to avoid educational
intent. Then some nightmarishly hearty bearded teacher gathered them in an exhibition annexe to sing songs along with
his guitar. These sounded like old folk songs, with flat-edged
tunes and lyrics mourning maidens spinning. Appropriate
enough, because there was an impressive display about the
linen industry in the museum. Huge lumps of brass machinery and live-action waterwheels. But for me the best part
of the linen industry exhibit was discovering the names for
various parts of the process: retting, hackling, beetling,
scutching – they all sounded like very satisfying things to be
doing. Of course they weren't. Linen was labour-intensive and
none of it was easy labour.

The pretty blue-flowered flax had provided clothing in
Ireland from at least the first millennium, building to a cottage
industry and export market by the sixteenth century. The
English government saw potential for this industry to
develop. They offered long leases and low rents to attract
people from Scotland and England to settle in Ulster and
take up flax production. Other new arrivals were the
Huguenots, French Protestants who had fled religious
persecution; they had considerable knowledge of the linen
industry. One of them, Louis Crommelin, set up innovative
manufacturing processes in Northern Ireland. Crumlin Road
in Belfast was named after this refugee entrepreneur – over
the years the local pronunciation of Crommelin became the
official name.

Spinning, weaving and bleaching techniques improved.
Linen became a boom industry, industrializing in the nineteenth century, with Irish linen becoming a mark of high

quality around the world. It provided work for a vast range of people from farmers to factory workers, from rich drapers to women who worked at home embroidering the cloth.

This home working was low-paid piece work. But better-paid jobs in the mills and factories had their disadvantages too. Scutching, the breaking up of the flax stalks for process-ing, created thick clouds of lung- and eye-damaging dust and, when mechanized, became even more dangerous. Clothing was easily caught in massive rollers and there were hideous incidents of workers getting their limbs mangled in scutch mills. The finest kind of dust, called 'pouce', caused severe respiratory illness. Scutchers were notorious for drink-ing whiskey as they worked, to clear their throats and chests – increasing the risk of other kinds of injury from impaired judgement.

When the flax had been scutched, it had to be sorted into types of fibres by 'roughers', separating it into heaps called 'stricks'. More dusty work. A more refined sorting called 'hackling' followed this. This was to separate the short, rough fibres, 'tow', from the finer 'line' fibres. Originally this was highly paid men's work but when machines came in, male children took over for a fraction of the wage.

The flax was then 'drawn', to make it into ribbon lengths called 'sliver'. Sliver was twisted into a loose thread called 'rove' and wound on to bobbins. Bobbins were taken by 'doffers' to the spinning room. Up to this point in the process it was dusty work, with side dangers of crushing, cutting and maiming. The spinning rooms were wet work. Linen fibres were kept flexible and fine by being held in a trough of hot water. Spinning in hot, humid conditions, then going home in the inevitably cold, damp Irish air, made spinners prone to bronchitis and pneumonia. The spinners would sit with their bare feet in the trough of water below them, developing skin irritations, swollen ankles, varicose veins and a particularly nasty inflammation of the big toe called *onychia*.

Weavers again had to work in humid conditions with hot jets of steam poured into factory weaving sheds. The condensation would drip on to the floors below them, necessitating work in bare feet – who had shoes to ruin in those days? – bringing more nasty foot and toe inflammations.

The cloth was then bleached and beetled – bashed smooth. Beetling machines were deafeningly noisy, hundreds of wooden hammers pounding the cloth, hundreds of fingers inadvertently pounded right off and workers too deaf to hear shouts of 'Watch out!'

Linen was extremely difficult to bleach. At first the cloth was boiled in an alkali solution of water, wood ashes and seaweed. Then it was steeped in buttermilk, then washed in soft water. The process had to be repeated several times, requiring an immense amount of water and power. Later, dilute sulphuric acid replaced the buttermilk, then a chlorine-based bleach. As an aside to the processes, coal yards and chemical works developed in Belfast. A railway network developed to bring coal to the mills – today tiny, seemingly inconsequential places have railway stations because they once had mills.

Bleachers were responsible for the quality of the cloth at the point of sale and became very powerful. They needed acres of land for drying the cloth, adding to their power and wealth in assets. Near the bleach mills, long lines of cloth would be laid along 'bleach greens', giving an impression in old photographs of stretches of ectoplasm trailed across the countryside.

The museum exhibit on the linen industry placed a woman I'd known when I was a child in a context for me. We'd always known she'd had a hard life, and that she'd worked in a linen mill, but now I had a better sense of the details.

Mary Eliza lived in an old white cottage beside Granny's farm. My brother and I once asked her how old she was, and she said, 'A few years over a hundred.'

This may not have been true, but it might have been how old she felt.

Mary Eliza would sit down in her armchair with a cup of tea, sigh and say, 'Well, thank God for nothing, because they can't take it from you.'

Generally, Mary Eliza was not of a cynical turn of mind and was a great favourite with children. She was small, bent, had a wart on her nose and permanently wore a black shawl around her shoulders. Any fears her witchy appearance generated were overcome by fascination with her and her possessions. Boy children liked her singing kettle. Girls were fascinated by her kitchen shelves, full of unmatched, brightly painted crockery that she called her 'fine china'. And she always had some kind of sweets to dispense generously from a fine china blue jar on the mantelpiece.

Mary Eliza was no relation, she'd just been incorporated into the family. I don't remember her displaying any alarming signs of foot rot but from the age of twelve she'd worked in the mill in the morning, barefoot in damp spinning rooms, and then she'd go to school in the afternoons. The schooling didn't take her far, she simply moved to full-time spinning at sixteen.

In old age, Mary Eliza pottered about, went on walks with Granny and took a long time choosing which cup and saucer to have her tea from. She'd cut pictures out of magazines for me to help with a project of mine, decorating Granny's hen house, in the belief that it would encourage them to lay more. I also sang hymns to them – I'd seen something on television about talking to plants and adapted it for hens.

Both Granny and Mary Eliza were very encouraging and would say to me, when I was hanging around their kitchens, 'You wouldn't believe how much more the hens are laying, would you ever pop out and give them a wee hymn. Maybe sing them a few.'

Mary Eliza was the first person I remember dying. I reacted with hysteria, just because I'd never heard of such a thing.

'But she was very old,' my mother told me, 'well over eighty.'

Age, it seemed to me, was no excuse for traumatizing me.

There was further trauma the next summer when my sister and I went to inspect Mary Eliza's empty cottage. All her furniture had gone and her fine china had been thrown out into the back yard, smashed and covered in hen droppings.

'Oh, the landlord's men are doing the place up for new tenants,' Granny said. 'And they just threw her things out because her brother didn't want them. They'd done it before I could stop them. I told them what I thought of them and that did nothing, so I told them it was worth money and they were fools not to sell it. That got them.'

Mary Eliza's brother was the local wild man, prone to drinking sprees, with no use for fine china. He was notorious for his peculiar turn of phrase when reporting a death on a nearby bridge: 'The poor woman was swept off the bridge in the storm and was found in the river, drowned and dead both.'

Mary Eliza had worked at Herdman's Mills. This company's main building had been a feature of the view from all around the area – constructed in pale yellow bricks, if it hadn't been for the tall chimney, it would have looked more like an Italian palazzo than a mill.

When, by the 1960s, other linen mills had long closed their doors, Herdman's had expanded, smartly moving into synthetic fibres when linen began to go out of fashion and flax became expensive.

As children, we used to be able to walk right by the extravagant mill building into the nearby village, Sion Mills. In 2004 I found the building hidden by ugly modern extensions, metal fencing and prefabricated sheds. Maybe I put a curse on it for making itself look less attractive, because two days after I'd been muttering about the spoilt view, there was news the mill was closing and the company moving to South Africa, where labour was cheaper.

My uncle Joe said people had thought well of Herdman's – they'd adapted to the times and kept their people in work. At their height Herdman's had employed over 1,500 people, at their closing they still employed 600. The closure was a shock and a disappointment.

The landscape of Northern Ireland was littered with closed-down mills, abandoned weaving sheds, rubbish-strewn mill races and stilled waterwheels. Occasionally museums, restaurants or stylish flats had been constructed in old mill premises, but there seemed too many to convert them all to something for the new millennium.

Apparently my grandfather could make long speeches about the villainy of the linen trade – he was very left of centre for an RUC man, even a Catholic one. The Herdmans were a religious family and had attempted to temper their villainy by providing a model village, Sion Mills, for their workers. They also provided schooling and created a successful local cricket team that made the news by beating a West Indian touring team in 1969.

The Herdmans made it a policy not to discriminate between religions, though they liked their workers to have a religion of some kind. And be sober. No public house was allowed in Sion Mills until 1869, when the Herdmans lost a court case. You'd still have to look a lot longer for a pub than a church in Sion Mills.

Most of Sion Mills was designed by a son-in-law to the Herdman family, William Unsworth, a student of Lutyens. He also designed the first Shakespeare Memorial Theatre in Stratford-on-Avon.

The village was a mix of half-timbered buildings and terraced cottages, with wide, grassy verges and chestnut trees in front of them. Behind a half-timbered gatehouse was the Elizabethan-style mansion, Sion House, where the Herdman family originally lived. Unsworth's Anglican church on the main street was based on a church in Tuscany. With tall campanili and vast semi-circular windows, it was a leap of luxury no one could have expected to appear in a small mill village.

Almost as exciting was the Catholic church, built in 1963, all strikingly severe lines, with a modernist representation of the Last Supper on the façade, by artist Oisin Kelly. This church was the one I remember going to, vying with cousins to be next to Granny, or picked out as the one who hadn't fidgeted once. With it being Saint Teresa's church, there was a recumbent statue of a dead Saint Teresa inside the front porch – at the time I appreciated her more than the bold modern architecture. I'd nearly choked with rage when one Sunday my forthright cousin Kay said to Granny, 'I'd like to be remembered like that when I'm dead.'

'I'm sure you will, aren't you just as beautiful,' Granny said to her.

My perfect cousin. I wasn't having it.

'I'd like to be a statue too,' I chipped in.

'Being a saint isn't about being a statue,' Kay crushed me and went off linking arms with Granny. I was so furious I hid out with the hens all afternoon, singing them hymns and urging them to lay such a spectacular number of eggs that everybody would see I was a saint without me even needing to die.

Being brought up a Catholic can do very peculiar things to a child.

We'd have more interesting crossings into Sion Mills than church-going – trips to the little shops that could involve an ice cream for the return journey. First we had to brave the Swinging Bridge, a suspension footbridge over a deep rocky gully and the fast-flowing River Mourne. The bridge didn't only swing as you crossed, it bounced, just enough to make you feel you could get tossed right over the edge and be drowned and dead both.

The bridge has been repaired since, but in our childhood, several planks were missing or broken, to keep the dangers below vivid in the mind.

'Don't look down the holes or you'll get dizzy,' Granny would say. I knew this meant that one glimpse down the holes and you'd be overcome and stagger crazily until you fell off the bridge. So it was a nightmare, trying not to even catch a glimpse of the holes while not treading in them, feeling the swinging and bouncing escalate as you neared the middle of the bridge, consoling yourself with the thought of ice cream as you came closer to the other side. But first . . . There was another bridge.

This was a concrete bridge over the mill race down to Herdman's waterwheel. Granny said the water in there was very deep and moved at thousands of miles an hour. Still, the bridge felt solid and was no trouble, until I'd asked her if there were fish in the mill race.

'I don't think so. Maybe some eels,' she said blithely. And because I thought eels were giant Sinbad's Adventures man-eating monsters, I'd have to run across the concrete bridge from then on, grabbing Granny and screaming, 'Eels eels eels!' until we were safely fifty yards on land.

She would occasionally lag behind, saying, 'You run on, dear, I'm too tired for eels today.'

So I'd be obliged to abandon her and watch anxiously until she caught up with me.

'You shouldn't worry,' she said one day, to reassure me or shut me up. 'They'd want a young one, not an old one.'

The little rectangular cottages of Sion Mills were unchanged and seemed entirely occupied by old ones. Walking around the neat streets on a damp afternoon, I smelt a familiar rubbery smell – turf burning. The elderly residents appeared to be taking the opportunity of a gap in the rain to have a front-stoop-sweeping contest. Furious swishing of brooms and little grey heads bent ferociously to the task.

Herdman's had sold these historically listed cottages to the occupants in the 1960s, at very low prices; their residents were ageing and the younger workforce preferred modern council estates, to the rear of Sion Mills, or in nearby towns.

On the main road, I tried to figure out which shops had been regular ports of call. The butcher's shop looked as though it had always been on the corner. As I went in, the man behind the counter struck up a friendly chat with some young boys buying meat pies, about whether the Strabane bus was going to be late and whether they had caught anything in their morning's fishing . . . He seemed as though he'd have time on his hands for nostalgic conversation. When the boys had gone, I explained my life history as quickly as I could and asked if this would have been the butcher's shop in the sixties.

'Well, no, the butcher's shop was round the corner then. This was a general store, that's what it was then. My brother had the old butcher shop, and when I took over, I expanded us.'

'Still, it's funny how familiar the village looks after all this time,' I said.

The butcher smiled. In a boomingly robust voice, he said, as if preaching from a pulpit, 'Sion never changes. Derry, Belfast, all over the North there have been changes, but not in Sion.'

He gave me a free meat pie for my journey, saying, 'Go on, it's the last of them, it'll only sit there looking at me.'

I remembered that in the general store days, this had been the shop where I'd be given free biscuits for showing off my English accent. Good to know I hadn't lost my charm.

A man locking up the gate at Herdman's scowled at me as I took a picture of the mill. He would be in no mood to be chatting and handing out free stuff. Although there was still steam coming from chimneys, it couldn't be long now until the gates were locked for good. Signs announcing that the banks of the mill race were now a nature trail called 'The Mourne Walk' didn't indicate there would be much replacement employment.

I took a meander along the walk, watching out for eels. The path wound upwards, overlooking the river – distracted by so many fears as a child, I'd never noticed how beautiful this area was. Two businessmen were walking the walk in the opposite direction – whispering, camel-coat-wearing men. Perhaps they were plotting some new venture to keep Sion Mills from fading to a lifeless future, conserved in heritage aspic – you could see it might go that way. Sion might never have changed, but without the mill it couldn't be the same.

By the nineteenth century, linen was only a part of Belfast's fortunes. Entrepreneurs were making money from shipping, tobacco, food processing and the gasworks, with the largest gasometer in the world. In 1888, Belfast was granted a city charter and the local businessmen wanted something to symbolize their new status. White Linen Hall, which originally stood in the centre of town, was a stylishly simple building, but it wouldn't do for the new city. The site was bought and Belfast City Hall was constructed – a domed and pillared shock of pomp, inside and out. For my taste it had just too much marble, carving, modelled plaster work, muralling and stained glassery, but the businessmen of Belfast had spent nearly a million pounds and wanted it to show.

On the green in front of the hall was a statue of Queen Victoria, supported by a muscular ship worker and a couple of waifs spinning linen. The live punk rockers were leaning on her in the rain, smoking in cupped hands and having an animated argument as I passed them – about whether *ER* was on television at nine o'clock or ten o'clock. So much for Anarchy in the UK.

Inside City Hall, our perky blonde guide coped well with a tour that had a rearguard of giggling French girls, who'd come in out of the rain, found the tour was free and tagged along without developing any active interest in the proceedings.

Not that it was always easy to be interested. Every stained glass window was explained to us and the origins of every type of marble . . . Upstairs, where the Great Hall and the Banqueting Hall were less overlarded with decoration, I began to settle into appreciating the grandeur of the building a little more. The Council Chamber, laid out like the House of Commons, had oak panelling everywhere and luscious-looking carpets.

'These are specially made carpets,' the guide cooed over them. 'Specially made from a silk and wool mix.'

I wanted to romp about on them barefoot, but though perky, the guide was quite strict in the way she kept us moving and might not have appreciated the delay while I indulged myself. We were allowed to sit in the councillors' benches. Most of us lazily settled into the benches nearest the entrance – these turned out to be the Unionist benches. Three of the French girls, in search of adventure, crossed the chamber and sat opposite us. The guide looked at them and laughed: 'That's funny because where you are is the Alliance party seats and there are only three of them.'

I wished I had danced on her carpets. I didn't think the anti-violence, anti-sectarian party should be so blithely ridiculed, however much they'd been excluded from the political mainstream. Mind you, she barely hid a look of distaste as she waved a hand to show where Sinn Fein members would sit, so she was unbiased in her bias.

On the way out, we passed a corridor lined with portraits of former mayors. There was a photograph of Rhonda Paisley, daughter of, in front of City Hall, where a banner was draped, reading: 'Belfast Says No'.

'Belfast says no to what?' I asked the guide.

'The Anglo-Irish Agreement,' she said, puckering her face into a disapproving grimace.

I thought about asking her how she'd have started the peace process but wimped out, irritated with her, City Hall and myself for not being brave and eloquent enough to publicly defend the Anglo-Irish agreement. Because of me, those French girls might never hear the other side of the story. Not only that, a few hours later, I got into such a severe disagreement with four women from Dublin, there was nearly an Anglo-Irish brawl in my hotel.

I was minding my own business, not looking particu-larly English or belligerent. The hotel restaurant was almost empty, but the four women decided they wanted the table right behind me. I'd glanced at them as they came in — hard-faced, hard-permed, middle-aged women, who twenty years ago you'd have seen selling fish out of a pram in Henry Street. Don't worry if you've never seen such a thing; believe me, these were the women the word fish-wife was made for.

They were all a larger kind of lady but they'd plenty of room to shift their table back the other way if they wanted the acres of space they seemed to demand from a restaurant. I shuffled my chair in and thought I'd left enough room. But next thing I knew I was being bashed and crushed from behind, as a lady tried to shift me with her ample rear end until I was face down in my Pavlova.

'Can she not move?' I heard another one say.

I tried to keep the peace and moved as much as I could of my own accord.

Still with the shoving.

'That's as far as I can move,' I said, pinioned to my table.

'English, Mary. Did you hear?' one of them said. And I was done with peaceful negotiation. I shoved myself backwards so I could breathe and waited for the wrath of Dublin to come down on me.

'Oh, I'll just ignore the silly bitch,' my pinioner said and shoved her chair back.

They started deciding what they would eat. I had to get out of there because if the woman behind me got one garden pea bigger I'd be suffocated.

To show that I had a Granny who'd been trained by Miss Bamford, I slid out of my seat, smiled and with icy polite-ness said, 'Excuse me.'

The echoing imitations of my 'excuse me' followed me up to the till. At a distance I felt braver and to hell with

Miss Bamford. I tutted and glared at them. They glared back. The cashier was taking a very long time to sort out my bill.

I was close enough to hear my assailant say, 'Is she still looking at us?'

'She is. What's she looking at?'

If I could still hear them they could lunge out of their seats and be on me before I got my change. Luckily, they had some whispered debate about what they were going to do to me, and I could make off up the stairs and lock my door.

In the morning I decided Miss Bamford would urge me in to breakfast to show dignity unbowed. They weren't there. I couldn't wait for them. I'd told Uncle Joe I'd be home that evening. He'd allocated the following day for an excursion with me and if I missed it, who knew when there'd be another gap in the 10,000 things to do he called retirement.

I wanted to take a big loop round to get to Portadown, so I could see some seasides, including Carrickfergus, where King Billy landed on his way to the Battle of the Boyne. And more intriguingly, where there'd been the last witch trial in Ireland in 1710.

I drove out of Belfast through stretches of heavy-looking Loyalist estates, the mountains beautiful in the background. It didn't take long to reach the edge of the city and have sparkling sea alongside the road instead of UDA-muralled buildings.

A few brave souls were heading out from Whiteabbey in yachts. Whiteabbey was where Anthony Trollope lived while working for the Post Office. He wrote to a friend: 'Though the North of Ireland is not the choicest permanent residence, it has some charms for the tourist.'

The view was charming. I pulled over to take in the seascape with less danger of crashing the car. The sun shone as if it had strayed up from a Spanish winter and a woman in a shop told me: 'Well, you know the old saying, if February's fair, every other month of the year is cursed.'

I said I hoped this wasn't an old saying that was true. She laughed and said, 'Well, when do you ever see this kind of weather in February? So they were just saying anything and had no proof of it.'

I agreed with her. I think.

I had to get on, I wanted to see the stocks in Carrickfergus where a witch had lost an eye from being hit with a vegetable stalk by angry anti-witchers.

After a ten-minute daze of sea-staring in Carrickfergus harbour, I remembered my quest and found the stocks. Some schoolgirls were playing in them, taking pictures. They asked me to take a group photo of them all piled on to the stocks.

'They put some witches in these,' one squealed. 'We're wee bitches not witches, but what's the difference?'

'Sorry about her,' another one said. 'We don't know who she is, she just appeared at midnight.'

Midnight apparitions did seem to be how the witch difficulties had begun. The witches came from the nearby peninsula of Islandmagee. The first victim of strange bumps in the night was at Knowehead House, home to John Hatteridge, the newly appointed minister. Mrs Hatteridge had stones thrown at her in her sleep and the covers were pulled off her bed by unseen forces. In the morning, some sort of beggar imp came into the kitchen, leapt about, ran off, then kept reappearing in the house, breaking things, stealing books and turkeys – and generally behaving badly. Next, he turned up in a surly mood, dug a grave in the garden and said it was for someone in the house. Soon afterwards, Mrs Hatteridge's mother, visiting the house, died in her sleep.

Sceptical?

Well what about poor Mary Dunbar, who came to visit and within two days developed pains in her legs? Leg pains a servant girl suspected had been caused by an unfamiliar apron found on the kitchen floor. The apron was burnt, but Mary Dunbar started to have fits, shaking and screaming, declaring strange young women were appearing to her and tormenting her. Considering she'd only been invited for a week, Mary had become a bit of a nuisance long-term guest, so the busy clergyman's wife employed young women of the village to look after her. Mary went wild every time a new one arrived, insisting they were part of the girl gang who were causing her terror and pain. Eventually, she accused eight girls who had the misfortune to be brought into her room to help her.

After a long day listening to Mary's yelping, the clergyman and his wife suggested she might like to return to her parents' house. The next morning Mary started to smell of sulphur, put on huge amounts of weight and couldn't be moved from the bed. A doctor interested in witchcraft came to see her and pray over her. While praying, he saw a petticoat flying around her room and a mouse ran out of her bed – this convinced him to have the eight girls arrested and imprisoned in Carrickfergus as witches.

At the trial, Mary had several fits, eventually vomiting up pins, wool and feathers to convince the court there was evil afoot. She said the eight tormentors were always appearing as apparitions, shoving these things down her throat – and here were the things as proof.

Mary Dunbar was an attractive girl and quite well to do. The eight girls she accused were all a bit plain, a bit poor and mostly illiterate. They lamely denied the charges but could do nothing as impressive as vomit wool and pins to make their point. They were pelted in the stocks and sent to jail.

Mary Dunbar continued to have fits long after she went to live elsewhere, claiming her witch tormentors were still at her with the feathers, the wool and the pins. She sort of disappears from history after a while – perhaps she died, perhaps she realized that she hadn't concocted the best method to win friends and influence people.

Carrickfergus town didn't seem witchy at all. It was touristy with little knick-knacky shops and cobbled side-streets. I couldn't find a bookshop, though there were several literary associations to the town. The Restoration dramatist Congreve lived at the castle as a child, his father was a soldier stationed there. Jonathan Swift's first job was at nearby Kilroot, where he wrote *Tale of a Tub*. The father of the poet Louis MacNeice was rector of Saint Nicholas, the seventeenth-century church in the centre of town.

Congreve's childhood residence, the dark, stark castle on the harbour, had once overlooked America's first naval victory in their Civil War. Paul Jones sailed by Carrickfergus and made off with the British fleet's HMS *Drake*.

Anglo-Norman John de Courcy built the castle to guard the approach to Belfast Lough and provide a stronghold in the region. Until the mid-seventeenth century, Carrickfergus was the only place in Northern Ireland where English was spoken. It was an important garrison and harbour while Belfast was still a village.

To make life more exciting for tourists, Carrickfergus castle held medieval banquets in the summer. Scattered round the courtyards and battlements were painted plaster effigies of soldiers loading cannon, shooting at things and looking disconcertingly colourful against the dark walls. There was a plaster representation of de Courcy himself, approaching the plaster statue of his wife, who was sitting at a window staring out towards her home, the Isle of Man. She looked as though she was pining and about to make a swim for it. Perhaps she started the trend for the east-coast Northern Irish to take their holidays in the Isle of Man. In the summer the island had once heaved with families from Belfast, but as soon as cheap packages to the Mediterranean came in, they dropped the poor island like a hot tailless cat.

On the way out, I overheard an American couple having a debate about whether it would be worth paying to see inside.

'You can say it's only an old castle, Ian, but what if we missed something great?'

'I'm just getting real cold.'

'A quick look, then, it's only three euros, oh no, pounds, is that more, or less? How much was it at Andrew Jackson's house? That was a steal.'

As well as having literary connections, Carrickfergus had been the home of this former American president.

Like many of the Irish of predominantly Catholic upbringing, I'd been led to believe that the Irish arrived to save America from not being Irish during the potato famine. But about thirteen American presidents were of Ulster Protestant origin; how many depended on who you were reading: sometimes the estimate was only eight, sometimes it soared as high as twenty-one.

As dramatically explained in *Gangs of New York*, the Presbyterians got to America long before the Catholics and were not happy to see their old neighbours turning up in boatloads, raggedy and escaping famine.

The Scots Irish, as the Northern Irish Presbyterians and non-conformists were called at the time, left because they had fought alongside the English, helped build up Belfast, the countryside farms and the mills but found they were discriminated against in legislation along with the Catholics. The established Church of England and Church of Ireland was the church to belong to if you wanted political or property rights. The eighteenth-century legislation was passed by Protestant King Billy, who wanted to destroy the Catholic elite and marginalize dissenters like Presbyterians, considering them too independent and too much associated with Cromwell. Betrayed, the dissenters got on boats and applied their diligence and sober determination to the new continent.

Many of the Presbyterian Scots had moved to Ireland in the hope of greater religious freedom and a society more dominated by their own beliefs. Further discrimination was a bitter disappointment. Those who remained in Ireland built up their power and influence by making money, until they were so wealthy they inevitably had power. By the late nineteenth century, the industrial wealth they serviced and largely controlled, was vital to Britain. By the early twentieth century, a Protestant was a Protestant and the denominations clung together, united by their determination to remain part of Britain. By the late twentieth century, Westminster's government needed the Protestant Unionist vote to maintain their majority. The churlishly treated Protestants had come a long way to get that kind of power. But then, further betrayal. They found themselves being told to sit at the same table as Sinn Fein and make peace. A pattern of loyalty ill rewarded by Westminster had repeated itself. Their 'No Surrender', 'never again' attitude today, that can seem so unfathomably stubborn, comes out of a hurtful history of being used and passed over.

It's estimated that by the year of independence, 1776, one in seven of the colonists of North America and Canada were of Scots-Irish origin. In the American War of Independence, generals and thousands of foot soldiers were Scots-Irish, fighting the English who'd been so ungrateful to them back in the old country.

Outshining all the Protestant Irish presidents, the Catholics did have Kennedy, his photo on many Catholic mantelpieces as if he were family. The Kennedys had played a romantic strain of their Irishness that struck a chord in a country full of immigrants – they'd come from starvation and poverty in the old world and now look . . . The Northern Protestants had always been interested in getting on, rather than recognizing the PR value of romantically looking back. When they did try romantic harking back, they didn't grasp that the victories of Cromwell and King Billy weren't quite of the same broad appeal as talk of famine and persecution.

Not that the famine had become a mere marketing ploy for Catholic Irish Americans. A meal was no meal without potatoes in my family. My aunt and my mother could discuss the quality and cooking of potatoes with the minute attention to detail of art experts looking for a tiny fleck on a canvas, exposing an old master as a forgery. They galloped at stereotype with some kind of racial sense memory and just couldn't leave a potato alone as a mere vegetable on the side of a plate.

'Soapy' was the worst thing a potato could be. Below this, and utterly unmentionable, were tinned potatoes. My mother had once pulled up short in a supermarket aisle and whispered, horrified, when she saw an English neighbour buying tinned potatoes: 'She's all airs and graces that woman and she's serving her family those wee bullets, those wee balls of lard-tasting stones. How hard is it to peel a potato? Look, she's bought a tin for every day of the week. God help them.'

Most potatoes had to be peeled, but a really good potato, a 'floury' potato, a Sistine chapel type of a potato that was very hard to get hold of in England, that treasure should be steamed in its jacket.

I realized my mother might still be able to hold her own in a potato debate, but she had succumbed to English ways and rarely served a steamed jacket potato. I'm sure she'll tell me it was not her fault, that she'd been worn down with trying to make a silk purse out of English potatoes – but she'd deprived me of the ability to eat a proper potato properly.

The potatoes would be served in a bowl, then you'd put yours on a side plate and deftly remove the skin with a knife. My aunt and uncle and even small under-cousins could do this almost in a single movement. I'd create a crumbled mash on my side plate, end up eating half the skin and generally reveal myself to have forgotten my heritage. People had died for potatoes and I couldn't even remember how to eat one with respect and orderliness. I deserved to have my throat stuffed with pins by witches.

8. Half Man, Half Bicycle

My aunt had abandoned us, off on a weekly spree as a bingo caller for the local pensioners. Uncle Joe and I had been thoroughly fed and given directions to various kinds of pies and cakes, should we have anything so shaming to her as room left for more food during her two-hour absence. So we were expecting to survive, but she had left us with a problem. She wanted to see Emma Thompson's film of *Sense and Sensibility* – our job was to tape it. This wasn't going to be beyond our pooled abilities, but the faulty video recorder could only record the programme being watched.

'So if you wanted to watch anything else you're sunk,' my uncle said, as he dutifully co-ordinated the technology. 'For myself I'm a great believer in all this kind of culture, as long as I don't have to partake of it.'

We spent the evening reading the papers, having the occasional flurry of conversation, with breeches and gowns flickering in a corner of the room. Then there was some moment of high drama in the film, some weeping into lace hankies over Hugh Grant, some fling of a dishevelled lady across a chaise longue that drew both our attention. The crisis seemed to pass. The ladies in bosom-pressing gowns were sipping tea, looking at apple blossom and talking with polite cheeriness of forthcoming picnics. My uncle watched for a while longer, slightly baffled to find himself involved. Then, to escape any accusation that he'd taken an interest, he coughed and picked up his paper saying, 'Well, it's all a far cry from paedophilia on the internet.'

My mother rang me later to check on my progress; I told her about her brother's reaction to Jane Austen.

'He's a wonderful strange kind of humour, he could always take me to the fair with the way he says things.'

When I spoke to my mother from Northern Ireland, she would take me to the fair, by throwing in some Irish expression I'd not heard her use in years. As if we were going back to the place together and she could let rip with a side of herself she'd put on hold, in case people had no idea what she was talking about.

I told her I'd bought some new clothes in Belfast, the city was full of bargains and I didn't seem to have a clean stitch left in my luggage.

'Oh, well now, you always think more about fashion than practicality. You want a few wee outfits to throw in a bag that wash like ribbons and never need to look at an iron.'

After this advice she needed detailed descriptions of the look and disposition of every cousin, under–cousin . . . I could clearly see the stars and moon over the fields outside my uncle's house and suspected I might still be on the phone for a clear view of the winter sunrise.

Conversations with my father didn't have so much active interest. He would ask what streets I'd walked down in Belfast, what monuments I'd seen and if peculiar memories, like large goldfish in the Botanical Gardens, were still unsullied. I could have just read to him from maps and guidebooks. Belfast was a fixed childhood landscape to him; he didn't want to hear anything had changed, been knocked down, blown up or turned into a car park.

I started to tell him about Thorndale Avenue, and he said, 'Just don't show me any photographs. Did you go into the new zoo? Apparently they've used the mountain landscape very effectively.'

He hadn't been back as often as my mother; he watched the news too much. He had no family of brothers, sisters-in-law, nephews, nieces, under-nephews . . . to keep a present-tense feeling of the country's ordinary goings-on in his mind.

Nevertheless, I had a notion that he'd like it if he went back, find more to recognize than he imagined. I did a hard sell on the present pleasantness of Belfast but only got him to a vague 'It sounds as if it's getting back to normal, but I wouldn't know it.'

Perhaps he was a real emigrant – looked back but didn't want to go back.

Uncle Joe had emigrated from County Tyrone to Armagh, so making a decision to visit his childhood home only involved the trauma of facing a day without golf. The journey back was an anniversary, almost. He'd made the journey with me on a summer day just over ten years before, when the countryside was prickly with checkpoints, soldiers and moments when you weren't quite sure if all hell was going to break loose.

Tired that day, having crossed through Tyrone and beyond, to walk the coastal path by Giant's Causeway, it seemed my uncle and I were stopped and questioned by soldiers every fifteen minutes. We'd headed home through what were then referred to in the press as 'The Killing Fields of East Tyrone' – an overstatement, but it was a district savaged by bombing and assassinations.

My uncle had just been telling me, as we drove a remote road – because he loved the closeness to the countryside you could only get on remote roads – that the trouble with such remote roads was you'd sometimes get checkpoints run by 'boyos' – paramilitary chancers wanting to hijack your car and beat the hell out of you if you objected. We turned a corner and the road was suddenly full of hefty men holding sticks. Ever cool, my uncle just gripped the steering wheel tighter and kept driving. Uncool, I was ready to shout, 'Give them the car, Uncle!'

But the men parted to let the car past and continued on their way to their hurley game, sticks hoisted over their shoulders.

That kind of edge was off the journey this time. We crossed the Sperrin mountains up towards Dungiven, where my mother and her brothers had their first family home, driving through thin drizzle and patchy mist.

'We'll not have much of a view, but then you're getting the privilege of weather typical of the region,' my uncle said.

The misty Sperrins had the same look as the mountains of Donegal: yellow gorse bushes, black turf bogs, infrequent sheep and a feeling of hard lives being eked out since very long ago, surrounded by bleak beauty.

The Sperrins were dotted with circles of standing stones and megalithic tombs. These built up the impression that the area drifted with otherworldly forces. Several houses in the mountains offered accommodation to visitors, advertising as a plus point one or two ghosts about the premises for an authentic Sperrin experience.

Aside from a vague frisson of spookiness, walking and fishing were the main visitor attractions. The recently opened Sperrins Heritage Centre offered a chance to pan for gold in the rivers. The tales of how much gold was in the hills varied, but there was enough to create speculation of possible fortunes yet to be made. A couple of Northern Irish jewellers made expensive one-off designs in Sperrins Gold. A medallion of the gold was given to Barry McGuigan to celebrate his world title. But anyone planning on digging up the

mountains on the off-chance there'd be a huge mother lode
. . . They'd have to get past my uncle first.

'Your aunt teases me that I love it up here so much, I'd
be happy all alone in a hut, with visitors on Sundays to bring
me pipe tobacco and the papers. She might be right.'

'When you'd read all the papers, what would you do?'

'Walk about, take it all in, I'd be fine.'

My uncle often muttered about Edens of solitude but
rather undersold himself as a hermit to me by being
gloriously gregarious.

The part of his vision of himself as some other self that
rang true was the need for pipe tobacco. Having been warned
off cigarettes by doctors, he chain-smoked a pipe, getting
up a nice fog in the car as we kept the windows closed
against freezing fog descending outside.

'On a clear day, and there are some, you can see right
across to Donegal,' he said as we came over the top of the
mountains and down towards Granny's farm.

As we'd made our reconnaissance of the territory ten years
previously, I knew there was no more Granny's farm. The old
grey square house, with Bimpa's vegetable patch beside it, had
been flattened and replaced by a huge ranch-house-style
bungalow that we all referred to as 'The Hacienda'. The
owners of the Hacienda cut down ancient trees and bulldozed
dry stone walls out of the way, to be sure their show-off
ridiculousness of a house could be seen clearly from the road.

The farmyard and pig sheds were still there, as was the
tin-roofed barn where an electric generator had whirred and
groaned noisily. Sometimes, we'd have to cheer Bimpa on
as he restarted it after some cantankerousness had plunged
it into surly silence. Sometimes the whole thing had to be
dismantled and beaten with hammers before it would get
back to work.

If we were on our own, the barn was out of bounds. But we felt more confident than adults that we wouldn't have an urge to stick our heads in the generator, so we ignored this rule because we absolutely had to go in the barn to fetch straw to make dens or, one summer, to look for kittens. Evil old farm cats had somehow produced these loveable creatures. They were probably fathered by the scarred and ferocious Mick MacManus, chief of cats, named after the wrestler Granny adored.

Gradually, the kittens were given away, except one little crookedy blind one. It staggered around the barn for a week or so, then disappeared.

'It was drowned,' Granny said when I inquired after it.

'How could it be?' I couldn't imagine how the little sight-less thing, with a dragging leg, could have made it down to the river and fallen off the Swinging Bridge, drowned and dead both.

'One of the farm men put it in a sack and drowned it in the rain barrel,' Granny said breezily.

I started to wail.

'Look, Mick MacManus and those other cats would only have tortured it to death.' Granny softened, recalling that I was not really a farm child accustomed to pet euthanasia. 'It was the kindest thing. It was in pain.'

I made a point not to tell Granny of any aches or pains for a while after that, in case she took such a brisk attitude to me.

But the next pain I had was so drastic I couldn't keep it from anyone – a spectacular accident, with blood every-where and the top of my left index finger nearly separated from me. Fortunately, it was horrific enough to mean I avoided retribution for the accident being my own fault.

Rain was falling, the kittens were adopted or assassinated,

the hens had heard a full repertoire of songs from my brother and me, and we were getting bored. We decided to inspect Granny's latest entrepreneurial project, baby turkeys we'd been forbidden to visit unsupervised in case we annoyed them.

Granny had them in a child's cot lined with straw, they were the ugliest beasts making ugly, strangled sounds.

'Let's touch them,' I urged my brother.

We poked our hands in – the feel of them was so repulsive, I leapt back squealing and smashed my foot down on a light bulb on the ground behind me. The shattering of it with a firm stomp of a wellington boot had been quite satisfying, so what a gift to find there was a pile of used light bulbs in the corner of the shed.

Who knows what Granny was collecting them for? Maybe they could be sold to someone for recycling when she had amassed enough; maybe she was trying her hand at conceptual art. Money-making schemes went on in Granny's head so feverishly it was strange she never got to see the day she was always talking about – 'the day my ship comes in'.

I didn't see money or ships arriving with the light bulbs – I saw a way my brother and I could have some fun. I think he may have questioned my whisper of, 'Hey, let's smash these.' But he knew better than to seriously question my authority when some red mist of destructiveness had risen in my head. We stomped and smashed, stomped and smashed until there wasn't a complete light bulb left. Then we had to smash the pieces of broken glass as small as possible, not for any reason, just to keep smashing.

'None left,' my brother said disappointedly, after a frenzied stomp around. He'd got the red mist now. To help him feel he'd had a fair go at all the glass, I spotted a large piece and generously put it down at his feet. I didn't move my hand away fast enough, my brother stomped, I screamed, blood poured out of my finger, he screamed, ran out of the shed and brought back Granny, my mother and a younger uncle, Martin. My mother screamed, my brother had stopped screaming but started again, Granny pulled off her apron and wrapped it round my gushing hand, Martin threw me in his car and rushed me to the doctors in Strabane.

I fainted twice in the car but surprisingly remained conscious while a wheezing old doctor cleaned my wound with shaking hands and stitched my finger together, with the steadiness of someone having witch-tormented fits. My uncle loaded me up with sweets on the way home and told my mother, 'The usual doc's on holiday, they had some old boy in there they said was a locum, but he seemed as skilled as a trained calf.'

I can't bend the top of my finger to this day, but it's an ill wind. The horror of the calf-handed old doctor, on top of all the blood, meant I was the princess of bravery for a week and never had to stand trial for the massacre of the light bulbs. Everyone knew my brother was never to blame for anything, that it would have been my idea, so he escaped persecution as well, although he now claims I got all the sweets and accolades for bravery, while his post-traumatic stress syndrome and survivor guilt were completely ignored.

Mary Eliza's cottage was fresh painted and in use; the farm opposite looked the same, extended somewhat, but it had old white outbuildings, with red corrugated iron roofing, that seemed familiar – only the Hacienda had landed crassly in the middle of our memories.

Uncle Joe decided he'd seen the Hacienda quite often enough, parked a disapproving distance up the road from it and skulked in the car with his pipe, while I went out into the drizzle to wander around and maybe have yet another bounce across the Swinging Bridge.

A middle-aged man was scraping mud off the path to an old house on the way to the Hacienda. He looked at me, as if he knew me from somewhere but couldn't quite place me. I smiled and was going to go on with my bridge-bouncing mission when he asked, 'How are you?' in a way that implied he'd like to know who I was and what I wanted, more than how I was.

'I was just taking a look round. My grandmother used to live up there, in the old house.'

He looked at me for a moment, hesitant but had to know.

'Who was your grandmother?'

I said her name and he grinned.

'Married to the police sergeant. I used to be friends with those boys.'

I was about to tell him that one of those boys was in the car up the road, when he named my youngest uncle.

'Eamon, that played football, I was at school with him . . .' Then a spark came in his eyes, his heart seemed to leap. 'Are you his sister?'

After a moment to register what age he'd accused me of being, I said, 'No, I'm her daughter.'

The hopeful spark flickered and died away.

'Ah right, so she's married now,' he muttered.

Disappointment shadowed into his eyes, as if he'd been there lurking outside the house in hopes for a matter of months, not decades. And then, as if to serve my mother right, he said, 'Well, I'm married myself now.'

My mother says I'm imagining a pining suitor at the end of the path, she doesn't remember the man at all.

Still, if she was being admired from afar, she might never have known.

The man didn't remember Uncle Joe: 'He'd have been older, gone away to school. But I knew the young one. And the policeman. We'd go in the car with him to Strabane sometimes.'

He remembered Mary Eliza and was pleased to be given the name 'Hacienda' to call the new house.

'It's that all right.'

I thought it was time I went back to the car to tell my uncle why I was talking to a strange man.

The man said goodbye, then added, shyly, 'Tell Eamon you met Kieron Smith at the head of the Duck Walk.'

He grinned to himself as I left and sauntered back toward his house.

The Duck Walk was the slope that led down to the Swinging Bridge. Maybe ducks did walk down there to the river, but I think it really had the name because it was steep enough to make you waddle coming back up it from Sion Mills with shopping, or a few whiskeys inside you.

Uncle Eamon knew who I was talking about. 'He wasn't a friend of ours really, but we sort of tagged him on to us. How funny he thought you were sis. But you probably look like she did the time he'd last seen her.'

Seen her whilst pining from the end of the path I'm sure. Still, he'd had a go in Bimpa's car, which was such a rare excitement it was also worth pining for. Bimpa hated to drive and went so slowly everyone might as well have walked. Pre-Hacienda days, the track out of Granny's house had high walls on either side, quite difficult to see out of, but leading on to a tiny country road, not the M1. Nevertheless, Granny had to stand in the road and wave Bimpa out, after checking and double checking that nothing was coming for miles.

'If your Granny could have walked in front of the car with

a flag all the way he'd have been happier,' Uncle Joe told me, 'but people weren't doing that so much in the sixties.'

This strange nervousness didn't go with the rest of Bimpa. He'd been a crack shot, an RUC champion boxer, a badminton enthusiast and had cycled a long mountain beat alone in Catholic territory for years.

As we retraced some of his beat, I asked Uncle Joe if Bimpa had been in danger.

'It was quieter then. And these hills were quite mixed – the lower slopes with the good land were Protestant, it's only higher up it's Catholic. There were outbursts of spitefulness, but I don't remember any directed at him. People knew he'd converted so he was almost all right with both. Later, that sort of subtle distinction ceased to apply. There was a police-man shot up here a few years ago. There'd be no going around on a bicycle now.'

Impressive though, long gradients on forty Senior Service a day. Possibly the sportiness acted as an antidote to cigarettes, because Bimpa lived till the mid-1990s. He was a long time without Granny, who'd died in the seventies. From the generation of men who couldn't even bring themselves to glance at a cooker, he moved down to the Portadown district to be near family who'd feed him. And to avoid possible spitefulness in Tyrone.

In Portadown he had a modern terraced house where he was regularly visited by grandchildren. He bought a very large colour television that delighted him, all the sport as like as life. And he claimed he had the children's programmes on in the day to amuse any grandchildren who might drop round, but my uncle Eamon suspected he enjoyed them himself. 'All those strange wee creatures in bright colours, I think he's fascinated. He's fixed in front of that television from the moment the children's programmes come on.'

When I'd gone over to visit Bimpa and his television, Eamon said, 'Don't worry if he doesn't have much to say. He doesn't have much to say.'

The first shock for my uncle was that, as I sat down, Bimpa turned down the sound on the television.

'He never does that for any of us,' Eamon confided later.

Bimpa asked about my parents, my work, but soon the conversation ran dry. I had no clue what to ask him but wish now I'd asked a million questions. Not that he'd neces-sarily have answered; he'd been a closed book for a very long time. He did give me a talk on his favourite topic, the trouble Ian Paisley was to the country . . . Then we hit another lull. He picked up his Senior Service and asked me if I smoked.

I wondered if it was a test, to see how nicely I'd turned out, but then was grateful for the real wonder of smoking, the bonding in it and the chance of a long conversation about smoking. He agreed it wasn't good for you – but look at the number of people killed on the roads . . . He could quote car-crash statistics as if he'd witnessed every accident in Europe himself.

Uncles and cousins told me the cigarette was a sign I'd been a hit with him. I'd have had no other way of knowing.

When Bimpa died, a few years later, my brother conducted the funeral mass. My brother had managed to recover from the post-traumatic stress I'd caused him in the turkey sheds and gone through the tough years of training required to become a Catholic priest; or he became one because of the turkey shed, to minimize female presence in his life. In all the vast number of cousins it had been one of us English ones who'd taken up the old faith with determination. I'd completely failed to understand why he'd have done such a thing. But at Bimpa's funeral, my little brother, up there in front of a large congregation of people at a sensitive moment, delivered the perfect blend of personal and authoritative in his eulogy.

My brother had been at a seminary in Dublin and had spent a lot of his holiday time over in the North with the relatives; he knew them better than I did. They'd been far more caring and supportive through his long haul to ordination than a punk rocker, heathen sister back in London. I still didn't understand, but I was proud of him. More so when we were all leaving the church after the funeral and I spotted him, snuck out a side door, thinking no one would see, weeping like his heart was going to break. I had a big sisterly urge to rush up to him – but realized he didn't want anyone to know this had happened to him.

Five minutes later, he joined everyone on the walk to the cemetery, calm, coaxing and comforting people twice his age. There was something about him.

There was something about Bimpa too. For all his taciturn distance, he'd set up something in our family that prevailed. A belief that you walk down the middle and follow your heart, because sectarianism is nothing to do with real life. And by being whoever he mysteriously was, he created one of those moments that can be held up as an example of Northern Ireland not being the place people think it is.

At his funeral, senior RUC men, who'd started in the force under his training, attended respectfully – they said he'd been an inspirational teacher. The Portadown RUC lined the route to the Catholic cemetery saluting him and his Catholic family. People from houses along the road came out and asked whose funeral it was. They'd remember what they were told. It wasn't just a funeral, it was a pause, where someone was given his due, regardless.

He was buried beside Granny. From what I've heard not

so much resting in peace as in long, cross silences and irritated bickering. But they had far more to them than that. Somehow they catapulted four sons and a daughter way off the farm and knew that education was the way to do that. A route through higher education into a good future was found for all of them, whether they'd liked it or not.

Perhaps Uncle Joe had become a great educator because he had hated his own schooling so much. His boarding-school days in Derry had been so torturous, he'd still scowl at a mention of the city. Another pupil at this grim boys' school had been the playwright Brian Friel: 'We weren't in the same year but he did something that marked him out to me as someone interesting. There was a headmaster who was a bit of a wag, or rather fancied himself as a bit of a wag. One morning, he was giving a school talk that he sprinkled with jokes, and pupils sniggered dutifully as appropriate. Suddenly at one of his jokes, Brian Friel started laughing really loudly, holding his stomach, choking . . . Then he fell off his chair, rolling about the floor, still convulsed with laughter. A master hauled him to his feet. The headmaster asked him what was wrong. He said, "I am sorry, sir, it was just so funny." And he appeared to make a great effort to pull himself together. His excuse was made so convincingly it had to be accepted – but you could see the headmaster had a tiny doubt about whether Friel was taking a rise or not, as did the boys. And Brian Friel never said anything about it afterwards, never bragged about it, just kept it to himself – something he may or may not have done to amuse himself.'

Stories, stories. We were up in the hills of Bimpa's beat now, passing the old police barracks house where the family had lived for years. Uncle Joe pointed out the house of a neighbour who played the piccolo. He'd worked in the steel mills of Middlesbrough and taken up the piccolo in the works band. Over there was a hotel where Bimpa would have to rest himself in the bar after his long cycle tours.

The bar had been run by a woman who'd stayed single and prosperous for years. Late in life, she'd taken up with a younger man from Strabane, a bit of a layabout. Everybody feared he was a gold–digger and waited for the worst. But the hotel and the older woman were the making of him, he made it even more profitable and expanded the business, so then all the doom–sayers were the ones saying, 'People always predicted the worst but I knew she was too shrewd to marry a gold–digger.'

This hotel was in a district where everyone had strange long names. Allison Kate Mary Brian Lockrie; Paddy Kate Brian John Lockrie. Because so many people had the same surname, the names of parents and grandparents were thrown in to differentiate.

Another common surname was O'Kane. Granny's surname. Originally they were the OCahans, a very old clan name. The OCahans were from the hills round Dungiven and they spread out all over the area, right down to Strabane.

Near Dungiven town, in the remains of the Augustinian priory, was the tomb of Cooney na Gall OCahan, who died in 1385. A sculpted figure wearing armour lay in the chancel. In niches below were carved warriors in kilts, representing his Scottish mercenary troops, hence his nickname, 'na Gall', meaning foreigners.

Whatever ancient Irish clout we'd had then had diminished somewhat by the time of Granny's parents, although Uncle Joe was sure her mother was a native Gaelic speaker – a fairly ancient Irish kind of thing. And in what would have been OCahan hill territory, Granny's brothers farmed, living side by side in low grey houses. As children we'd take a long, long trudge up from Sion Mills with Granny to see them. Worth it, because one of the houses was full of ornamental china dogs and in the other was a great-aunt-in-law who made bright pink marshmallow cakes.

In the early nineties, Uncle Joe and I had found the houses empty but standing as if ready for new occupants. This time we nearly missed them, they'd become so overgrown – weeds twining through empty window frames, roofs caved in, saplings straining through the gashes in the walls, a tree fallen across a door . . . I don't know how old it made my septuagenarian uncle feel, but I felt ancient to see trees growing through rooms where I'd once coveted china dogs and gorged on marshmallow cakes.

'There was a family down there.' Uncle Joe pointed out a cottage still in use. 'They were all what you'd call a bit slow. You know, the types whose IQ is written on their forehead. One time me and my brother James had the mumps and seemed to get better very quickly. So the father from the slow family came over and said to my uncle that his boys had the mumps and he wanted them to have the ancient OCahan cure that we'd had. My uncle didn't believe all the old pagan country nonsense but felt it would have caused neighbourly ill feeling to refuse. He took the two boys with mumps to a barn and put them inside a big plough horse collar. He gave them a bridle to hold, turned them round three times, then led them to the spring down the road. He told them to drink three times from it and led them back up the hill to their sickbeds. In a few days they were up and about. So . . .' my uncle puffed on his pipe smiling, 'now us clever modern ones might talk about the power of suggestion but my uncle said the idea of what to do with them came into his mind as he went along, so he couldn't be sure if he was making it up as he went along, or if he was being inspired by myste-rious forces.'

The two slow brothers had lived till a very old age: 'They'd never have made it in the city but out here they'd pleasant enough lives. They'd farm in the daytime, have a meal about five o'clock, and rest until it was time to go out socializing. They were great socializers.'

They may have been the boulevardiers of the backwoods but where would they go? The hotel was miles away, the pub was miles away . . .

'They'd visit people in the houses around, talk and play cards. Of course, all this went on from about ten at night till one in the morning. It wouldn't do for ones reared in England who can't sit up at night.'

'I don't usually tire out so easily. I think it's the fresh air, too much ozone.'

'Maybe that's what it is.'

I certainly couldn't get into the rhythm of life at my uncle's. I'd be thinking I might go to bed just as they'd be heading out to play cards. People would arrive for visits at times of night I'd take to mean an emergency – but it was just the hours people kept.

Card-playing had been a major recreation with the adults on our Buncrana holidays. Uncle Joe and Aunt Helen still played two or three nights a week, although their card school was not what it was.

'It's more in the nature of something you'd see on a comedy programme than anything like the Cincinnati Kids we used to fancy ourselves as when young. Two of the players are nearly blind and one is nearly deaf. There's another one who's very blind but won't admit it. So there's chaos, with me the only one with any faculties left trying to keep patience. Helping people see the cards who won't admit they can't see them and shouting the bids for the deaf one. And then there's a lot of time spent discussing our ailments; the ailments or passing away of others known to us, or unknown to us but in the newspaper . . . So the actual card-playing time is very restricted. Some ruthless card sharp could join us one night and make a fortune. If they were a ruthless card sharp with a limited idea of a fortune. Your aunt cleaned up on Sunday night and made twelve pounds, so it's all high-rolling stuff.'

He said card-playing was regarded by some of Bimpa's Protestant kin as a vice, but it was the pastime of country people who didn't want to go to pubs. It gave shy people something to do if they couldn't make conversation; it gave scattered communities a harmless focus and enabled older people to keep tabs on each other. I asked if he thought it kept people's brains sharp.

'If they have the blind and the deaf and the lame to co-ordinate diplomatically like I have, then it certainly would.'

Our anniversary journey through County Tyrone didn't take in a diversion to walk the Giant's Causeway coastal path.

'That's one I'll have to admit old age has cancelled out for me,' my uncle said. 'Although when we did it before, you in your innocence didn't realize you were walking miles with a man who'd just had a heart operation.'

'I did know. I just thought as you'd said you wanted to do the walk, that walking must be good for you.'

He laughed. 'At that stage in my life, telling a young niece a stroll on a coastal path was beyond my abilities wasn't part of a habit of life I'd got used to. I still liked to see myself as a fellow just past middle age and of heroic disposition.'

'It was pretty heroic, I was exhausted.'

'It stands out as a heroic piece of walking in my memory.'

We'd walked the steep path slowly and made stops to look at seabird nests, or ships on the horizon – really rest stops for both of us. Reaching the end, it seemed we'd have to turn round and walk all the way back – but I spotted what I thought might be a short cut across the fields to the car park.

'What if it wasn't?' my uncle had said. 'What if it was some way that actually turned out to take longer, wouldn't you just die?'

I don't know if we'd have died, but we might have had to sit down in the fields and weep until rescued.

There wasn't just my uncle's better adjustment to the constraints of age making him less enthusiastic about another trip to Giant's Causeway. According to him, Giant's Causeway and the Antrim coast were sights all visitors to Northern Ireland should see once, but they became a bit less exciting every time. Unlike the Sperrins – an enduring joy, because the Sperrins were changeable: gaunt and full of secrets in winter shadows; exquisitely pretty in the sunlight. They had no well-trodden paths or gift shops. They had the sort of unoccupied ancientness people expected of the Irish land-scape but found less and less.

Not that the bizarre basalt columns of Giant's Causeway were a bad thing, they just got all the attention.

The honeycomb rock pavement was created by volcanic rock shrinking and splitting as it cooled, forming a platform of 40,000 stepping stones that disappeared into the sea. The basalt columns were a natural feature that looked too geomet-rical to have just happened, but apparently they did. There were many legends to explain them away, the most well known concerning local warrior and giant, Finn McCool. Finn McCool was supposed to have constructed the cause-way to bring over a lady giant from Scotland to be his bride.

There were similar rock formations on the facing Scottish coast, so if we clever modern types didn't know about volcanic rocks . . .

Our previous journey had taken us to a very different Strabane. From the sleepy market town of my childhood, it had become a heavily shuttered shell of a place by the early nineties. There were massive steel-protected army and police bases, armoured cars had rolled through the streets at all hours. It was strange to try and imagine that in the eighteenth century, publishing and printing had been the town's genteel industry. Strabane hadn't returned to genteel with the removal of all the armoury. There were new shops, one selling racks of white satin holy communion dresses at a massive discount. There were new cheap food marts, refurbished pubs serving Italian coffee, a few tubs of plants stuck around the central car park, but unhappiness seemed to have welled up in Strabane and couldn't really be disguised with mock Victorian street furniture, new shops and a lick of paint.

Strabane had been poor for a long time – emigrants flooded out of the area long before the famine – publishing, linen, whatever business was thriving in the area excluded vast numbers of the Catholic population. This exclusion had festered to make Strabane one of the worst places in the Troubles. Levels of unemployment, crime and vandalism were still very high.

Exemplifying the perversity of human nature, one of Ireland's funniest writers came from poor old Strabane – Brian O'Nolan, aka Flann O'Brien/Myles na gCopaleen. People assume he was a Dubliner, the archetypal Dubliner, but there was an easily missed blue plaque by a car park, marking the Strabane house where O'Nolan/O'Brien etc. had been born into an insistently Irish-speaking family. He went on to a brilliant academic career at University College, wrote mind-bending comic novels and a column in the *Irish Times*, called *Cruiskeen Lawn*, in which he championed the Irish language and mocked any stupidity and pomposity that he came across in his Dublin life.

If the writer's family house had been in Dublin it would probably have been a museum by now, full of O'Nolan/ O'Brien/Myles na gCopaleen mugs, pencils and mouse mats. But Strabane had barely caught up with itself, let alone had a chance to cash in on its overlooked treasures and chase after the lucrative literary teatowellery that thrived in Dublin.

There was a small National Trust museum in Gray's Printing Shop on the main street. In an upstairs room were glass cases of war memorabilia belonging to men from Strabane who fought for Britain in both world wars, alongside a display of pottery by local children. Downstairs, an exhibition named Strabane as the birthplace of John Dunlap, printer and distributor of the American Declaration of Independence. Another Strabane printer who emigrated to America was James Wilson, grandfather of President Woodrow Wilson.

'Somewhere round Strabane the French people related to your Granny lived. This would have been on her father's side, her grandmother was French. There were many theories, but it was likely her family had come over from Brittany to work in the linen industry.'

'So we're a bit French?' I said as we drove home, the card table calling to my uncle.

'Not enough for them to give you a passport,' Uncle Joe said, 'and probably not enough to brag about.'

I'd been planning to brag when I got back to London, but maybe he was right. I had enough different bits and pieces in me anyway. Real North Western OCahan Gaelic, Presbyterian mix on my mother's side; Belfast Grandma was really from Tipperary, and her husband had been Church of Ireland, of English ancestry. Wanting to be French as well was just greedy.

On mountain roads again, I thought about Flann O'Brien's novels and of Bimpa on his bicycle. According to the 'atomic theory' in O'Brien's *The Third Policeman*, the particles everyone and everything was composed of began to interchange when they came into contact too often.

'The gross and net result of this is that people who spent most of their natural lives riding iron bicycles over the rocky roadsteads of this parish get their personalities mixed up with the personalities of their bicycle as a result of the interchanging of the atoms of each of them and you would be surprised at the number of people in these parts who nearly are half people and half bicycles.'

No wonder Bimpa had to have rest stops at the hotel bar; he was trying to save his atoms from bicycleness. Perhaps being part bicycle was why he didn't like to be in cars.

The Third Policeman had been written in the 1940s; it was possible that Bimpa on his bicycle could have been an inspiration for Flann O'Brien's strange cycling mountain policeman. Who could say? Like being a bit French, it was probably a dubious boast I'd better keep to myself. But I would, and hug it to myself.

We skirted back past Gortin Park, miles of forest that had been planted for timber, now preserved for their beauty. In World War Two, American soldiers had camped there; locals had been curious to see black American soldiers, living in a separate camp to the white soldiers. They'd been puzzled to hear the local police had to go and help the American military police break up fights between the black soldiers and the white soldiers — and to hear reports that the black soldiers' camp had far fewer amenities than the white soldiers' camp.

The forest had no shouts in the night now. It did have a night walk advertised that I was sorry I'd miss: 'World of Owls' night'.

'Is Gortin notorious for its owls?'

Uncle Joe pondered this a moment. 'I expect they wouldn't be so impudent as to claim a world of owls if they didn't have *some* owls.'

Outside Omagh, we passed signs for the Ulster American Folk Park. Uncle Joe waved his pipe at them.

'I've not been there, but going by reports I've had from my grandchildren, even a very poor quality display of owls would be more entertaining.'

Unimpressive for local children, the park was however a smart move for attracting American and Canadian tourists who were tracing their ancestors. It had data banks on Irish emigration, replica American log cabins and farmsteads and the boyhood home of Tyrone emigrant John Joseph Hughes, who later became Archbishop of New York. This farmhouse was moved from a few miles away, stone by stone, and rebuilt in the park, as was the eighteenth-century home of Rocky Mountain pioneer Robert Campbell. Opened in 1976, the folk park developed around the farmhouse where Hugh John Mellon was born in 1813. His son built the steel town of Pittsburgh; the growing Mellon fortune helped build the Waldorf Astoria, the gates of the Panama Canal and San Francisco's Golden Gate Bridge. Other notable locals included the grandfather of *Apollo 15* astronaut James B. Irwin; James Shields, one of Lincoln's most successful generals; and Davy Crockett's grandparents.

We passed through Omagh. Apparently my uncle Martin

had been in the street where the bomb went off, and left just twenty minutes before.

'That's the story with a lot of people round bombs in Northern Ireland. Most of us have just missed one.' Uncle Joe lit his pipe and thought for a minute, looking for a way to defeat the dark topic. 'But, as your grandfather would say, how many people just miss getting hit by a car every day?'

9. Sodomy and Sailing

I'd rung my aunt Helen the previous summer, at the start of July, and gabbled on about how I was going to write a book about Northern Ireland, and was coming over because I'd never seen the Orange marches.

'But we're just leaving, dear. We'll be in Buncrana tonight. None of us stay in Portadown at this time of year. Wouldn't you think of coming another time?'

'But it kind of has to be now, really.'

'Well you're very welcome to see us in Donegal but we'll be away all summer.'

I worried my aunt had gone off me, but she had been very ill, she was trying to pack . . . And she just hadn't the time, or the heart, to explain to me why I was asking the impossible. I was so out of touch I hadn't registered they lived where Loyalist gangs had been on sprees of killing Catholics in the eighties; where Catholic churches were petrol-bombed; where Drumcree was a couple of miles down the road; where the Orange marches just weren't something to be idly curious about.

There was no evidence she'd gone off me when I came back at a less fraught time of year. We were on one of our many trips out to teashops when we started talking about books we'd read on the subject of Northern Ireland. We both agreed our favourite was Dervla Murphy's *A Place Apart*.

'It's a while ago since I read it, but there is one bit that really sticks in my mind . . .' I began to say.

My aunt nearly leapt across the tea table. 'Where she goes to Ian Paisley's church?'

'Exactly. That's exactly what I was going to say. She's been really easy-going and suddenly she just gets this chill, this feeling of real hatred rising up in the place.'

'That bit stayed with me!' Aunt Helen was exuberant and definitely did like me, for sharing this remembered piece of reading with her. 'I can still feel what it was I recognized when I read that. I was so grateful to her for describing it. Because that man . . .' She looked tense, she was going to have to do something she didn't like to do, speak ill of someone. But this was an exceptional case. 'I remember when I had my first baby we lived in a flat in Armagh. Your uncle was away for a couple of days on a training course and I was alone in the flat, listening to the radio, and on the news Paisley was speaking. The things he was saying about Catholics . . . I locked the door and drew the curtains and prayed for your uncle to come home early.' She shook off the memory and shrugged. 'I was young, you know, a bit more timid than I am now, but the chill Dervla Murphy described feeling in his church, that's what I felt when I first heard him.'

Many of the things Paisley said were more peculiar than chilling. He accused Catholic ceremonies of being an 'amazing exhibition of carnal tomfoolery'. Which showed very little understanding of any Catholic church I knew; carnal tomfoolery was the one thing Catholics, especially girls, were taught to live in fear of.

When the Queen Mother and Princess Margaret visited the Pope in 1959, Paisley was apoplectic, foretelling that 'God's curse will fall on England.'

Born in Armagh, in a predominantly Catholic area, Paisley had a fire and brimstone preaching father, and mother. When his father fell out with his superiors and set up his own Protestant sect, the Paisleys suffered ridicule, isolation and extreme poverty – depending for food on donations from his father's few followers.

When Paisley was growing up, there were Catholic preachers who spoke against Protestantism as 'heresy'; they'd tell their congregations not to associate with Protestants, and certainly not to marry them or go to their schools. Being outlawed and persecuted for so long, some of the Catholic clergy in Ireland had become very hardened, fearing any chink in their armour. There was a mood of angry separatism and conservatism in much of the Irish Catholic Church that my father remembers as 'narrow, obsessively anti-English and draconian'.

Paisley hadn't single-handedly introduced bigotry to Northern Irish society, of course, but his name was almost synonymous with it in our family. I read a lot about him, fearing he might have kicked Bimpa in the playground and we'd all inherited a prejudice. But for one thing, Bimpa would have just kicked him back.

For another thing, Paisley created situations, and then covered his tracks claiming to be elsewhere at the time, praying at the time . . . There wasn't much leeway to give him the benefit of the doubt or suspect we'd misunderstood.

In June 1959, Paisley had spoken at a rally in the lower Shankill Road, organized by Ulster Protestant Action. Addressing a mainly young crowd he said, 'You people of the Shankill Road, what's wrong with you? Number 425 Shankill Road – do you know who lives there? Pope's men, that's who! Forte's ice-cream shop, Italian papists on the Shankill Road! How about 56 Aden Street? For ninety-seven years a Protestant lived in that house, and now there's a Papisher in it. Crimea Street, number 38! Twenty-five years that house has been up, twenty-four years a Protestant lived there, but there's a Papisher there now.'

The crowd marched up the Shankill Road and headed straight for the Catholic homes, throwing stones, breaking windows and painting 'Taigs Out' on the doors. Shops thought to be Catholic-owned were attacked and one, with a display of crucifixes in the window, was looted.

It wasn't only Papishers he didn't like.

Homosexuality was decriminalized in Britain in 1967 – but not in Northern Ireland. In the late 1970s, gay campaigners in Northern Ireland began to pressure Westminster to bring the province up to date and decriminalize homosexuality. Paisley began a campaign called 'Save Ulster from Sodomy' and caused such uproar Westminster didn't change the archaic law. In 1982, the European Court of Human Rights finally forced through the legalization of homosexuality in Northern Ireland.

Homosexuality wasn't legalized in the South of Ireland until 1994. The Pope was still calling it 'evil' in 2004; but the grip of the Catholic clergy on Southern Irish politics was slipping. Paisley pointed to this as a proof of the religion's feebleness, rather than as a sign of a more secular and liberal society developing over the border. And he continued his loud battle to prevent a secular and liberal Northern Irish society.

Who followed him? He had a rank-and-file Protestant congregation that the other Protestant churches and the Orange Order couldn't get away from him. Protestants fearing the declining number of jobs would be taken out of their hands; fearing union with the South would mean Catholic domination; fearing Sinn Fein would come to power and take terrible revenge . . . Then there were the fundamentalist Protestants who agreed with him that evolution shouldn't be taught in schools. And Paisley appealed to something darker, a revulsion that Protestants from a mixed range of backgrounds felt for Catholics – as powerful and irrational as racism.

Aunt Helen lived surrounded by Protestants and she had no difficulty with them, if they weren't the kind who wanted to drive her out of her home, or petrol-bomb her church. She fretted over her young Protestant cleaner as if she was an extra daughter, worried for hours when she thought the cleaner was headed for a big domestic row with a volatile husband over a phone bill. She ran in and interrupted Uncle Joe's golf-watching, she was so relieved to get the news that the cleaner's husband had been managed and there'd been no hideous scene. She was proud that the cleaner had once said, 'All my best customers are Catholics. They treat you well and have a bit of consideration.'

My aunt even felt sorry for one of her pensioners group whose grandson was in a Loyalist gang and had been arrested for involvement in a back-street stabbing. But she did prefer to be in Donegal during what she and a lot of Catholics around Portadown didn't refer to as July, or the holidays, or even the marching season; it was 'Drumcree time of year'.

So I'd snuck into Belfast in July, to see the other side of life. I was early for the marching and I had other business down the coast. I could pass the time, even if I had to pass it alone.

When my parents were first married, my father had a teaching job in Downpatrick, we'd lived near lakes, then moved to the seaside at Newcastle. My memory of Downpatrick was hazy. As Flann O'Brien said, 'I was very young at the time I was born.'

I know my parents had fun in Downpatrick. Apart from a gorgeous first child, they had a share of a racing dinghy on Strangford Lough and in the evenings they sang in pubs with their fellow amateur sailors. Northern Ireland was like that, you could live a fine life on a schoolteacher's salary. To revisit this unremembered joy, I took the bus from Belfast; buses were better for seeing the countryside and eavesdropping than driving.

Through disappointingly smeary bus windows I managed a squinted view of pretty villages festooned with Union Jacks and the Red Hand of Ulster flags. Sometimes there were black flags with crests on them – this represented a section of the Orange Order, the Royal Black Preceptories, who were more ritualistic and religious than the rest of the order. So many flags flying defiantly in immaculately tended front gardens.

The Red Hand of Ulster flags were the cross of Saint George with the hand emblem at the centre of the cross. If it hadn't been for the emblem, you might think the flags were out to support England in international football. But these flags hadn't had their meaning simplified by fashion.

The meaning of the red hand was often disputed. A right hand was a common European heraldic device, representing the right hand of God. It was on the Ulster flag because it was the kind of thing that got put on flags. The legend that Heremon O'Niel, racing a rival chieftain for possession of Ireland, cut off his hand and hurled it ashore may not be true, and is a common Norse legend, not unique to Ulster.

The Star of David is also on the Ulster Flag because the star was another shape commonly used in heraldry. It probably doesn't mean that Ulstermen are the lost tribe of Israel – although there are websites forcefully arguing the case for this.

But then, if everything on websites was fact, the world would be a very peculiar place.

★

Downpatrick was a predominately Catholic town with a Protestant hinterland. The bus station was rustically old-fashioned, but opposite was a giant modern food mart, a giant pizza joint, a giant cheap clothing store . . . Somewhere under these was the house I'd first lived in.

I'd booked myself into a guest house an American friend had recommended – why had I listened? It might be charming but it was a mile out of town. I went into a minicab office by the big stores. It was full of drunk men and cross women with bags of shopping. The stressed cab controller knew where I wanted to go but warned me, 'The main road up that way is closed. He'll have to take you round the hills, so it'll cost a couple of pounds extra. A fiver?'

I immediately assumed the road was closed for reasons to do with the marching season.

The reason I'd jumped the queue wasn't because I was sober and English. The people hanging around were waiting to have a full group to share cabs to their estates.

The driver again apologized that my route would be more expensive than usual. 'They're doing tarmacing on the direct road.'

Strike one to me, there was nothing going on that was to do with the Troubles.

The severely tattooed cab-driver had worked in North London and asked me if I knew a Colindale pub he'd frequented.

'It was a good pub. They had lock-ins for all comers, you know. There were pubs in London in the seventies when it was difficult to have a Northern Irish accent and get served.'

'Did you go to Kilburn?'

My cousin Paul had been taken to Kilburn by a helpful workmate when he'd first arrived in London. He'd been horrified. 'All those people from the South glared if I spoke, so I kept my mouth shut. My English mate fitted in better than me, we're just not like those Kilburn Irish and they don't like us. Maybe they think the Northern Irish have given them a bad name, I just couldn't figure it out.'

The Downpatrick cab-driver had a similar view.

'Kilburn? I was better off in an English pub. That's what I didn't like about being in London, it was our own were the worst to us.'

He didn't go into a tirade cousin Paul liked to indulge himself in, after a few beers, about how those Southerners had sold us Northern Catholics down the river at the time of the partition and never looked back.

We were driving up into idyllic countryside, old mills by meandering rivers, grand houses, gnarled trees and deer standing staring across green hills – big-antlered proper stags at bay.

'It's beautiful up here,' I said.

The driver didn't comment. He swung into the drive of my guest house, after narrowly missing a pheasant on the road.

'Well, good luck to you in there,' he said to me in a slightly ominous way.

The guest house was very fancy. There were no Red Hands flying, but I think he felt it was no place for a Catholic girl – he'd craftily established my tribe with questions about where in the town my parents had lived, where my grand-parents lived . . . People just had to know.

The garden would have won awards in the home counties for its triumph of roses, dahlias and absolutely perfect borders. I was in no mood to see the pleasantness. I was thirsty, hot, tired, so to me the place seemed irritatingly fussy and chintzy.

I saw from a notice in the window they had their own rare breeds farm that supplied their organic meat. I could see pigs the size and colour of Jersey cows in a field behind that looked rare enough. There was an organic shop on the premises, they cured their own bacon, made their own bread, laid their own eggs . . . I really regretted booking into the place, I'd be bound to stain something, break something – and I certainly wouldn't be allowed to smoke. More worryingly, they'd got my deposit in advance but no one was answering the door. I rang, I knocked, I peered in windows . . . A lot of polish, pastels and water-colours, but no people.

Some men were trimming a hedge up on the main road, watching my plight with interest. I decided if night fell and I was still on the doorstep, they'd have to take me to town on their tractor.

I thought I was saved when an old couple drove up, but they were looking to buy some special loin of rare pork. They joined me in a tour of the exterior looking for clues. A perfect Siamese crossed our path.

'No,' said the old man. 'Nobody here but the cyat.'

I'd forgotten that cat and car are words with a 'y' in them in parts of Northern Ireland. In other areas they're definitely a kat and a kar, a 'c' sound so hard it had to be written 'k'.

'There's a disappointment,' the man said as they returned to their cyar. 'I was looking forward to the pork. Well, good luck to you, dear, I expect they'll appear eventually.'

I was alone again, with no one to help me but the cyat. Just as I was about to go and ask the tractor men for rescue, another, as I would call it, car, drew up.

'Oh dear, I am sorry. My daughter told me you'd be arriving and I completely forgot. Have you been waiting long? She will be annoyed with me. I am sorry.'

She was so worried, and such a cuddly, fluffy, grey-permed, grannyish old lady, all my annoyance evaporated. She showed me to a room, with French windows on to my private section of the rear garden. The room itself looked as though it had been decorated by Dale Winton's maiden aunt. It didn't have a surface that wasn't covered with a delicate crochet mat, a piece of furniture that wasn't trimmed with extra helpings of fabric and braid. I had three types of shampoo, a towelling bathrobe, every size of towel, sachets of luxury bubble bath, organic soaps, sweets in jars, assorted rare teas, a silver coffee pot and ground organic coffee.

After showing me my room, the lady gave me a full tour – dining room, sun parlour, sitting room and cabins they were building at the back. 'For families, when it gets busy. My daughter never stops . . .'

She looked at me with sudden concern. 'You must be tired, dear, imagine coming all the way from Belfast on the bus. I'll make you a cup of tea. Let's sit here in the sun parlour where there's a lovely view. You can only see the pigs in the field from the sitting room. Some people find that interesting because they're a rare breed, but I don't think we're interested, are we?'

She was English, from Kent, she told me over strong, sweet tea. Her daughter had married a Northern Irish man she'd met at university.

'When my husband retired, my daughter kept saying we should move over here. I wasn't sure, but she is our only child. So we live in the next village. A lovely village. And we get to be near our grandchildren. My daughter and son-in-law are so busy with all their projects, they've just opened a second organic shop. My husband loves it here, he has golf galore and gardening.' She paused, knowing that she was here now and there was no going back to Kent whatever she felt and there was no point telling a perfect stranger how she felt, so she might as well make the best of it . . . She pointed to the hill dotted with deer and edged with spreading trees. 'Round here is what I call "rural". I love to see trees like that, trees that have been left to grow in their own natural shape.'

I said I was amazed to see the deer.

'They do look good up there, don't they? They're farmed. There's a restaurant in Killileagh, our village, where they serve the venison from here. And pheasant, there's a lot of pheasant. It's all very rural. In the spring near our house there's a dell of bluebells . . .'

In every sentence, she was making the best of it. Not that she wasn't proud of her daughter's enterprises.

'They started with a little bit of land and a small house and they're making such a go of it all. But she's her father's daughter. She'll just struggle on. I remember when she was doing her finals, I said, "Do you have to work so hard?" And she said, "Yes, Mum, this is how it has to be."'

We talked a great deal about London and a little more about the lovely ruralness of County Down – then very sweetly she said in lowered tones, 'Now, dear, have you ever been here around this time in July?'

I said I hadn't, but I knew it was a tricky time.

'Oh,' she said. 'We just don't leave the house, because it can be very dangerous, they can pull you out of your car and all sorts.'

My heart went out to her, thinking she should warn me in case I was as lost as she was. She was relieved when I told her I had relatives in the North – I lied that I'd be moving on to see them in a few days, just so she wouldn't have to think about me roaming alone in all the danger.

'Now, you know,' she said, 'I'm worried about what you're going to eat this evening. I could give you a lift to a restaurant, but I have to go and cook for my husband, so you might have to get a taxi back.'

I assured her I had been eating all day, had fruit in my bag for emergencies and I'd be happy with an early night, rather than venturing out to restaurants.

She looked as though she might accept this but gave me a packet of biscuits, just in case.

'My daughter should be back in a couple of hours. Don't hesitate to ask if you need anything.' She stood to go, reluctantly. 'I better leave you to get settled. Goodness, you'll say that landlady's mother is a real jawer.'

I said, 'No, it was lovely talking to you.'

She said, with a great well of feeling, 'Yes, yes, I loved it too.'

And off she went, back to her life in a country she didn't really like, despite the trees and bluebell dells.

After I'd used the alarmingly luxurious bathroom and managed not to break anything, I fell asleep on my hand-embroidered pillows. A storm had got up when I woke, wind crashing about in the rural trees and the rare pigs were making an Armageddon type of noise somewhere in the darkness. I sat, huddled in my coat, on the steps outside my French windows, smoking and feeling vaguely tearful. It was sad, I thought, to come back to the place I'd been born and have no one to talk to but a sweet old lady from Kent, who thought I didn't know the place.

It had been an odd day anyway. I'd had a four-hour wait at Belfast bus station to get to Downpatrick, after an early-morning flight. I'd eaten burgers and chocolate to comfort my tiredness and made myself feel slightly sick.

My plan was to buy my ticket then doze off the burgers, chocolate and creeping nausea. There was only one ticket window and a long queue of people, who all seemed to be irritated. In front of me was a tatty woman with a black eye and a whimpering little boy in a T-shirt that read 'I'm British'

over a Red Hand of Ulster. She kept telling the child if he
didn't shut up . . . 'If you don't shut up . . . If you don't
shut up . . .' I nearly swung her round and said, 'What? For
God's sake at least be specific or I'll black your other eye.'
But finally she stopped, the child stopped whimpering and
I simmered down from homicidal to merely grumpy.

I managed to find a space on a bench, was getting settled
for a long rest, when an excessively bearded tramp came up
to me, empty-handed, and asked if I wanted to buy a newspaper. I looked confused and he said, 'Come on, you bitch,
give me fifty pence and I'll get you a newspaper.'

I ignored him and he went off to call someone else a
bitch.

I decided to close my eyes so I'd look asleep if anyone
else wanted to engage me in such charming banter.

My aunt wasn't the only one making an exodus. Two
young men behind me were talking about leaving 'until after
the 12th'. From early in my eavesdropping I gathered one
was twenty-two and had a shared house, the other was
twenty-three and had just joined as a sharer.

Twenty-two was from Fermanagh and a Catholic;
Twenty-three was from Roscommon, a Southern Catholic.
They were talking about their house being mixed, with two
Protestant house-mates. Twenty-two said they'd discussed
putting in the advertisement for a house-mate that theirs
was a mixed house, but then thought they could be asking
for trouble. They decided to say nothing and if someone
turned up wearing a Glasgow Rangers shirt, they'd think,
maybe not.

The Protestant house-mates, Julie and Hazel, had been
teasing Twenty-two that they'd joined in Saint Patrick's day
celebrations with him, so maybe the Catholics in the house
should put on sashes and march up and down the living

room for the 12th. Interestingly, he thought it showed good spirit on the girls' part to join in Saint Patrick's day, but for him, 12th of July celebrations were out of the question.

Twenty-three was pleased he'd found a place in such a friendly house. He had some intriguing stories about his search for a home in Belfast. A girl he worked with had offered him a cheap place, but it was right in the middle of Loyalist Sandy Row. 'I just didn't want to run the risk.'

Before that, he'd lived in the area up near Paisley's church, quite a pleasant middle-class area – but near Paisley's church.

Twenty-three would go into the library to use the computers and one day he was in there, emailing, and a little boy came in, 'All shaved head and Chelsea shirt, you know, a real wee bastard. And he stood in the door of the library and shouted, "I hear you're a Taig!" I froze. I thought, Jesus, I'm spotted, I'm branded and I have to live round here. But he was shouting at another kid, a wee girl with a speech impediment, so she couldn't rightly say what she was. So anyway, I was pleased I'd had a narrow escape. Then a few weeks later I went back to the library and I wanted to check if there was any mail on my Eircom box. The computer kept saying it couldn't access the site. I went to the desk to complain and the woman made a real stuck-up face and said, "No, we can't help you with that." I was so irritated with her, I asked if I could talk to her supervisor, and she said, "She's gone on her tea break but she'd tell you the same thing." I asked how she knew she'd say the same thing. She looked at me cheekily and said, "She just will." I couldn't believe it and I was trying to think what kind of a scene I could make, but people were standing around listening in, I started to get nervous. I sarcastically said, "Thank you for your help." And I was fuming for days, so I wrote a letter of complaint to Belfast Libraries, a real fuming letter. But that was no satisfaction, of course, because I decided I'd better not sign it, or give my name and address, because you just never know.'

Twenty-two understood. 'No. I know. Whenever anyone in Belfast asks where I'm from in Fermanagh, I never say the south, I always say, Enniskillen, a big mixed place, because you never know. It just takes one lunatic. I had a mate beaten senseless by three thugs with a baseball bat because he'd been walking home carrying hurley gear. It's weird, you could decide to walk home a different way, or turn off a main road and you're in the middle of hell.'

As my mother told me, no good comes of eavesdropping. I didn't want to hear this conversation. I blamed Twenty-two and Twenty-three for putting me on a doorstep at midnight, listening to howling wind and squealing pigs, chain-smoking and feeling weepy. I didn't want to hear base-ball bats, or that Belfast Libraries would be downright rude to anyone who wanted connecting to a Southern Irish inter-net service. I wanted seasides and lakes; I'd built myself up to expect them. I felt stupid, lonely and very naive.

In the morning of course, things weren't so bad. Sun shining, lavender and roses outside the French windows all refreshed from the storm, and scented summery. I had some of my real organic personal coffee and realized it was ridiculous to panic that I was wrong about Northern Ireland because of overheard war stories from a couple of lads in a bus station when I was hot, tired, full of junk food and set upon by tramps.

The dining-room tables had frilled cloths and hand-made pottery containers for home-made everything. I was given an Ulster fry that didn't seem to have been fried but prepared by little gourmet elves, using secret processes to make the national dish without the usual side effect of craving a triple heart bypass immediately after breakfast.

The determined daughter, Jennifer, was bouncing her good health around the dining room. I could tell by her glances that she was a little curious about me, as I didn't seem to fit with her guests at all. There was a big, amber-beaded, Margaret Rutherford type English lady and two sets of elderly Americans.

As well as new tourist attractions going up with heavy emphasis on the Protestant emigration to America, there were efforts being made to sell the 12th of July to Americans of Protestant descent as something that was theirs to enjoy, if they'd never felt comfortable in all the frolicking green-ery of Saint Patrick's day parades.

My father had always complained that Northern Ireland would be a better place if the Americans would leave it alone; he argued that both sides were funded through the Troubles by donations from American sympathizers of similar religion. My mother would snap his head off and say, 'It's the English, it's nothing to do with America.' She also vehemently blamed the South for abandoning the North, then profiteering from gun-running. On the plane over from Belfast I'd got talking to an old man from Lisburn who blamed the Troubles on inbreeding in rural areas: 'What we need is immigrants, blacks and Bosnians, the more the merrier, so there'll be less of this inbreeding making people daft.'

I had a feeling I could go round for months with a clip-board asking people to list the causes of the Troubles and I'd never get the same answer twice. But it was possible there were more interesting things to do with my life.

I walked into Downpatrick deciding to risk the direct route, as a mile walk would be good for me, but three miles, well, there was no telling what kind of malfunction that might cause in me or my ageing trainers.

The road surfacing seemed to be done with, but cars were

still being kept out, so I had perfect peace to feel nature-hugging about the scenery. This was very old countryside, used for hunting and livestock-rearing back through the centuries. Elegant houses sat proud in the dips and dales – you could have filmed a Jane Austen film and only had to move a couple of television aerials for an authentic, quaint country feel.

I saw a familiar tractor, and sitting at the roadside drinking tea were the two men who'd watched my long lock-out from the guest house. They did the strange, wary thing Northern Irish people can do, hesitating to be the first to acknowledge they knew me, but poised, ready to be friendly if they were given an opening.

I smiled and said hello. They immediately relaxed, broke out their smiles.

'So you got into your B and B eventually?' the older one asked.

'Eventually.'

'They have that place very nice.'

'Once you can get in it,' I said.

They both laughed. I noticed the young one was disturbed by my scruffy trainers.

'Are you walking into town?' he asked, shifting his gaze from my disgraceful feet.

I said I was, because it was a nice day.

'Aye it is,' said the older one. 'But don't wear yourself out. If you're walking back, remember it'll be uphill.'

While I was still unworn out, I walked uphill to the cathedral where Saint Patrick was supposed to be buried under a massive stone slab, along with Saint Brigid and Saint Colomba. Some Americans were standing looking at the slab, one of them asking what I was thinking: 'How do they know it's really them in there?'

Not that it mattered. As anywhere else with a Saint Patrick association, Downpatrick had built on the legends and counted the money to be made.

The Down County Museum, along the road from the cathedral, had a section devoted to Saint Patrick – I skipped it and moved on to look at the main exhibit. This began with lists of people hanged in Downpatrick through the ages and what they'd done to deserve it. The museum was housed in the old gaol, built in 1798, whitewashed clean now, but with plenty of descriptions on the walls of how crowded and smelly it had been. There were plaques telling stories of the minor crimes of poverty that had ended people up at this bad end.

A popular County Down ballad, 'The Man From God Knows Where', was written in 1946 about the United Irishman Thomas Russell, who was hanged at the gates of the old gaol. It was a popular song on the American folk and country circuit, and had recently been revived by an American folk singer calling himself Tom Russell. The original Thomas Russell wasn't actually from God knows where but from Cork – in the song he's just a mysterious stranger in Downpatrick, no slight on Cork intended.

Convicts from Down gaol were often transported to Australia. Downpatrick had a growing number of ancestor-seeking Australian visitors – apparently convict ancestry, particularly Irish, was now no longer a stigma but something to show off about. A small exhibition displayed photos and happy letters from one Australian who had traced a female ancestor back to County Down gaol.

The more recent past of County Down was displayed in an exhibition of black and white photographs. They were all of the late 1950s and early 1960s and, like my parents' photos of the area at the time, they looked older. Something about the countryside, the cottage industries, small shops and hand-made clothes seemed to come from ten or twenty years before. The photographs resembled the streets, lakes and countryside that I remembered – but I remembered similar photographs.

County Down Loyalists had a moderate reputation, compared to those of County Armagh, but I still felt taken aback to walk off the main road from the cathedral and find a Red Hand of Ulster flag in every garden. I was looking for the high school where my father had taught. A building that looked like an army barracks turned out to be the school. It had always had a big stone arch in front of it because after the museum gaol had been deemed too small, there had been a gaol on this site. The arch was a piece of history, but the new fortifications round the school were a modern necessity.

The Catholic population of Downpatrick had grown through the last three decades and Unionist politician John Taylor had recently criticized the school for taking in too many Catholics, keeping places from Protestants. The school had been outraged: they insisted that they had a policy of taking people who were smart enough, whoever they were, and that was that.

High fencing and tough security in schools, including primary schools, had become common. Schools were attacked for taking in the wrong kind of pupils, for being the wrong denomination . . . But integrated schooling was on the increase, slowly.

Started in 1981 by a group of parents in Belfast, the integrated schools movement gathered enough funding and support to start East Belfast's Lagan College with twenty-eight pupils. Mixed schooling did exist, where schools took pupils on a merit, or scholarship, basis, but this was the first determined drive to stop separation of cultures at an early age. In 1989, the British government agreed that if a school could ensure enrolments for three years and if 60 per cent of the pupils came from the existing majority in the area, the Department of Education would fund integrated schools.

By 1999, Lagan College had 900 students and there were forty-five integrated schools in Northern Ireland. This represented a small percentage of the population, and the movement still faced opposition from both sides. Catholic opposition came from religious leaders who feared the secularization of schools; some groups of Catholic schoolteachers feared the future closure of Catholic schools would leave them high and dry, with jobs being taken by teachers from the Protestant majority. Protestant religious leaders feared the secularization of schools and some Protestant teachers felt their jobs would go to Catholics, to maintain a mixed staff in areas that were once strictly Protestant . . . Then there were the extremes on both sides who just didn't want any mixing and tainting.

In spite of all this, the demand for places in integrated schools was very high. The movement had acquired the backing of celebrity campaigners including Kenneth Branagh, Joanna Lumley, Stephen McGann, Brian Friel, Barry McGuigan, Ardal O'Hanlon, Daniel O'Donnell and David Montgomery. Their involvement might bring the moderate success of this quiet, commonsense movement a scrap of the attention given to high-drama bad news.

I wandered into Downpatrick's dilapidated high street. The street seemed to be full of people with nothing to do. Two of them were PSNI men, standing opposite the dourly secure police station. I was going to ask them the way to the Tourist Information Office, which no longer seemed to be where it was marked on the map. They were chatting to each other, looking quite affable, but went stony-faced when they noticed me.

'Did you want something?' one of them asked. The other just stared at me.

I asked them for the Tourist Information Centre, and they looked annoyed.

One reluctantly said, without looking at me, 'I think there's something like that in the arts centre.'

The other one looked dubious. 'No. The Saint Patrick's Centre down there, try there.'

They were barely managing to mutter these answers. Then they turned away to look at their police station, perhaps checking I was being caught on camera.

I suppose the former RUC might be insulted to be considered mere soft bobbies with nothing better to do than tell you the time, or give you directions. Perhaps recent history had taught them that in the Catholic town centre of Downpatrick, someone approaching them might not be a harmless idiot.

In the shiny-glass, enormous and unmissable Tourist Information Centre I met with an eager gaggle of staff, pressing their helpfulness on me, and an elderly Dutch couple. The couple might have been Dutch just because they were, but I wondered about the connection to Dutchman King Billy. Was there a Dutch tourist trail to the Orange parades opening up?

I kept picking up guidebooks and asking the girls the price.

'That's free of charge so it is,' they'd say cheerily. 'Yes, that one's free too.'

I staggered out of the place laden with free books, maps, brochures, booklets, leaflets, postcards . . .

The tourist complex also had a garden restaurant, an art gallery, a classy souvenir shop, conference facilities and a very exciting-sounding 180-degree audio-visual flight around Ireland. I was clamouring to get in to that, but it had a technical hitch and was closed.

The helpful staff didn't want me disappointed. 'Look, we are sorry about this, what about if we give you half-price admission to our Saint Patrick exhibition?'

'No, really, I . . .'

'Here, half price, in you go, no bother.'

I trudged dutifully into a high-tech exhibition explaining how Saint Patrick brought Christianity to Ireland – the whirl of audio, video and projected Celtic artworks didn't really distract me from the pain.

The whole tourist complex cost £6.3 million, looked stunning but overlooked a car park, Argos, a gigantic cheap supermarket and a depressing, smoke-filled coffee shop. All these places were milling with people who looked miserable and pasty, with accompanying unhealthy-looking children. The split personality of the town started to feel peculiar.

I decided I had to get out of town, escape to Portaferry. The same harassed controller was in the cab office, telling drunks and women with shopping to 'Wait a minute, Jesus, what did I say? It'll be ten minutes.'

To me he said, 'There's a bus, you know,' then told me to get in the red car outside.

'Portaferry and Strangford?' The driver whistled. 'OK, but it'll be a tenner.'

I said I'd manage that, realizing sadly that Downpatrick must be full of people who couldn't.

The driver asked me what brought me to Downpatrick. I started thinking what would be the best thing to say to the driver to make him feel I was on the right side, got fed up with the whole Protestant/Catholic tightrope walk and just told him the truth, most of my life story back to boating babyhood.

'Those were the days, eh?' said the driver, who was probably my parents' age. 'It's got more upmarket, the sailing, but used to be anyone had a boat. What we'll do is we'll cross over on the car ferry if you like, I mean if you're just touring. The view of Portaferry from the Lough would take your breath, it really would.'

It really did. Low terraces of brightly coloured houses and shops in the sun by blue-green water. We crossed on the little car ferry, getting out to look back at Portaferry and up the Lough. A rowing boat made slow, steady progress among skittering dinghies.

The ferry crossed 'The Narrows', where the Lough met the Irish Sea; a sharp breeze took away all the drowsy feeling I'd been getting from too much walking around on a hot day.

'I'll make you a confession,' said the driver. 'When I'm in a bad mood, I cross on the ferry just to calm down.'

I saw how that would work, although the ferry ride to Strangford took less than ten minutes, so he must have had an easily calmed nature.

Strangford had a post-sailing singing pub my parents frequented. The driver said he wasn't a man for pubs, so he couldn't tell me if there was still that kind of jollity.

'But if people are in a pub, don't some of them start singing eventually, even if it's just to themselves? There's a big sort of carnival round here at the end of July. Plenty of music there and clowns for the children, that kind of thing. And that's the time to see boats! There's all kinds gather on the Lough. Fine old boats. And there's always a big gathering of Galway Hookers.'

He paused to look at me in the mirror, having his little joke.

'In case you're wondering, that's an old type of boat from the west of Ireland.'

I laughed obligingly. He started to tell me that if I really wanted to see beautiful scenery I should go to the west of Ireland.

'We've nothing to compare to it.'

I disagreed, it did compare. I always found the west of Ireland, especially round Galway, oversold and overpriced. Maybe Strangford Lough turned a bit touristy when the Galway Hookers came in, but we'd hardly seen a soul all day – just water, boats, birds and the castle towers of old plantation houses in the hills.

'It's not crowded, I'll give you that. But I still think of Galway when I think about retiring.' He laughed. 'Bear in mind the expense I'll be facing, if you were thinking of tipping me.'

When we arrived back at the cab office, he glared at a pair of drunks leaning against the outside wall.

'I expect I'll have them now. A two-pound trip they could walk if they weren't so senseless.'

I walked away from the cab office as fast as I could. It was all very well being told that in my parents' day any old person could own a bit of boat, but I still felt like some privileged brat who'd no idea what really went on for people in Downpatrick.

Back in the crochetery of my guest house I fell into conversation with Jennifer, the landlady herself, as she stocked her shop fridge with locally made rare cow and raspberry organic-untouched-by-anyone-who'd-ever-smoked-or-eaten-lard type of ice cream. It was as if she'd been waiting for me, wanting to double check information her mother had passed on.

'I hear you were born here?'

'We moved down to Newcastle when I was two. So I don't know what I remember, or what I've seen in photos, but it doesn't seem very familiar. My parents' photos were of a little quiet market town, very old-fashioned. I suppose it was a long time ago.'

She put down the last of the ice cream and sighed.

'Oh, Downpatrick's changed. It's got very down at heel. It used to be exactly as you say, a quiet market town, surrounded by agricultural land. It had a properly integrated community. But then . . .' she looked at me as if deciding whether I could be trusted, 'then in the late seventies and eighties, they started to move people out of the slums of Belfast and built all these cheap, bad housing estates. And Downpatrick was suddenly swamped with people. There was no work for them and the transport system's not good enough for them to go to Belfast and work. So they're all here, with no work and they drink in the pubs and cause trouble, so no one else goes in the pubs. And there's no nice shops any more − just these big stores for people without much money and loads of kids, you know, stores with cheap food, cheap clothes, cheap children's clothes . . . They're a giro culture; it's not their fault, all dumped on these terrible estates with no industry for them, no future.'

So I hadn't been imagining that Downpatrick felt dislocated and dilapidated. The atmosphere wasn't some natural side effect of ill-thought-out modernization. Downpatrick was artificially overgrown and full of people who didn't know what to do with themselves.

Those who did know what to do were obviously working to build up the tourist industry, but they had all these poor people around . . .

The poor people hadn't exactly been dumped. Most of them had fled Belfast when Protestant gangs started burning Catholics out of their homes. There'd been an evacuation to quiet Catholic towns like Downpatrick. It had been hoped this was temporary, but there was no going back.

I was glad to be leaving in the morning. I didn't feel comfortable up among the flowers and crochet, where poor Catholics were regarded as spoiling the view, the town prospects and without an ounce of enterprise to make a future for themselves. And who did Jennifer think was driving the cabs? Who did she think was working in all the cheap shops for the people to buy the cheap things, creating a working-class, admittedly unattractive economy? I preferred her mother, who'd just known something didn't feel right and she'd rather be back in Kent.

From feeling uncomfortable with the social injustices of life in Downpatrick, I got off the bus in Belfast and realized I was suffering from a discomfort I could do something about. The disgraceful trainers were tearing holes in my feet where they were still connected to me and were all holes where they weren't.

I found a shop selling cheap shoes suitable for the likes of me and my eye was drawn to some bright pink trainers. They were not only pink, they had all manner of strange cross hatchings and side effects and Velcro flaps. They were reduced to ten pounds, fitted like lovely decorative feet cushions and I just had to have them. The polite shop assistant started the usual shoeshop sales talk as I pranced up and down in front of the mirror: 'They're great, aren't they? And they'd look good with jeans, or they'd be fine with a skirt and . . .' Suddenly her real thoughts burst out of her, she looked at me with concern for the terrible mistake I was making and asked gently, 'Do you really like pink shoes?'

I assured her I did and I'd wear them out of the shop. She took my money, looking ashamed that she hadn't been more firm with me.

I bounded to the city-centre bus stop I needed, I had pink shoes, nothing bad had happened to me yet and I was off to the parade.

10. Lions and Headhunters

I told myself to forget anything I'd ever read, heard or absorbed genetically about Orange marches. I would spend a few days in Protestant East Belfast, trying to imagine I was from some remote place, never reached by news from Ireland. I wouldn't be looking for signals and subtexts, I'd just take the marching season as I found it.

It became hard not to see signals and subtexts the minute I boarded the bus to go up the Newtownards Road. I asked the driver to drop me off at the crossroads the landlady had told me to ask for, and he looked troubled. He said he didn't know it, was it near such and such? I said I'd never been there. He looked more troubled.

An elderly lady sitting opposite the driver had been listening. Something about my request was bothering her too.

'I know the place, I'll let you know,' she said, almost in a whisper.

Neutrality and empty-mindedness were too difficult to maintain as the bus progressed along a road slapped with flags and militaristic Protestant murals.

I passed wall after wall painted with the badges of various divisions of things beginning with 'U'. There was a mural of men shaking hands, with the words: 'Surrender of all our Dead Comrades'. A reference to peace talks. Down side-roads I could see muralled estates with more Union Jacks than you'd ever think had been made. We passed a big black building with heavy security; shortly afterwards the bus-driver said, 'I think it's around here you want.'

I saw the guest-house signboard. 'Yes, that's the place.'

He wasn't at a stop but he pulled up, glanced at the guest house, then at me. 'Are you staying there?'

He seemed surprised and regretful. The old woman looked really distressed. As I got off the bus she was still looking at me as if she wanted to tell me something, or just shout, 'Don't!'

The guest house didn't look as attractive as it did in the guidebook photograph, but there was nothing obviously alarming about it.

When the bus moved away, I saw the house opposite was burnt out.

The big black building down the road was the UDA head-quarters. A woman in the shop near by told me, as if I was extremely stupid or pulling her leg. At least I wasn't going to be somewhere ambivalent.

I'd gone down to the shop to pass the time because, yet again, I'd arrived early and found no one to let me into the inn. The shop didn't have much in it – soft drinks, cigarettes and lots of small newspapers belonging to organizations beginning with 'U'.

I sat on the guest-house doorstep drinking lemonade and enjoying the sun, contemplating pointing out to the Tourist Board that the trees photographed in front of the guest house no longer existed and unwitting foreign tourists might not be seeing the best of Belfast looking at the burnt-out build-ing opposite for a view.

I wondered again about the people on the bus: did they notice I had some kind of Catholic aura? Well, that could certainly prove a nuisance if I was trying to mingle a few doors down from the UDA.

The landlady swung her car into the tarmac in front of the double-fronted Victorian house.

'Annie Caulfield?' she asked as she slammed her car door shut. 'You're early.'

She would probably think of her manner as brisk; I thought she was rude. Again with the paranoia, but Caulfield was a name that could go either way. Maybe it was the Annie that was a bit Catholic . . . Maybe she just didn't like the look of me in general.

I didn't like the look of her guest house. It had a feel of cheap London bedsits, everything stained and worn. Every flower was plastic and every curtain was faded dralon. Still, at least I could smoke. If the rest of the street was anything to go by, I could torch the place and no one would mind.

My room was just about clean, but as I flopped down on my duvet for a rest, I smelt old sweat. Not mine. I hurled the smelly duvet on the floor and hoped the hot weather would continue into the night and I wouldn't need it. I might have enjoyed complaining to the rude landlady, but I was trying to take a positive attitude . . .

I went out for a walk, wandering side-streets – not streets, avenues, much Union Jacked and Red Handed. Again there were a couple of burnt-out houses, on fine Victorian terraces with trees in front of them. Houses that weren't burnt, or boarded up, were well cared for. This should have been a nice part of town to live in.

I turned into another avenue and on the corner was a group of what I'd learnt to recognize as 'real wee bastards' – kids with shaved heads and Chelsea shirts. I told myself they might look unpleasant and it was four against one – but they were only about twelve years old. They were watching me, talking about me. They looked like they might throw a stone at me for something to do.

I'd seen a lot of Chelsea FC shirts. Protestant support for Rangers and Catholic for Celtic was a division all over

Scotland, as well as Northern Ireland, but Chelsea was a strange one. Little logic to it, considering that Liverpool was the soccer team founded by an Orangeman.

There was a group called the Chelsea Loyalists, with a website full of talk of 'Republican scum', displaying photographs of East Belfast murals. They were part of the British Ulster Alliance, formed in 1999: 'Supporting Loyalists and highlighting issues on the mainland'. Issues being mainly the villainy of Sinn Fein and the British politicians who spoke to them.

ChelseaHooligans.com had 'No Surrender' as the strapline on their website and among photos of 'loyal fans' were a couple of men in parkas in front of Red Hand of Ulster flags. Chelsea had an extremist wing of their hooligans called the Headhunters – ultra-violent hooligans with right-wing connections, notorious for having drunken days out at Auschwitz for a laugh. Several English football teams had this nasty corner of fans – Leeds, West Ham, Millwall – but in the mid-1980s the National Front and British National party made a particular point of targeting Chelsea fans for recruitment and found they had a good uptake. The rampant Britishness of Ulster Loyalists also became cause of choice for this level of Chelsea fan. The Chelsea Headhunters, and right-wing fans from other English clubs, usually got up a charabanc or two to go to Belfast for the 12th of July.

The National Front constantly courted the Loyalists as a like cause; they believed Loyalists were protecting Britain from the IRA. Straightforward Unionists were appalled by this connection, just as Conservatives in England didn't see themselves as anything to do with the National Front. Some Loyalists vehemently denied this ultra-right connection even existed – but for others it was definitely all a like-minded brotherhood.

A sports journalist told me he once reported on a Chelsea v. Rangers game, a friendly, where fans of both sides joined in a rousing chorus of 'Fuck the Pope' at the start of the match.

You could hear this kind of song on the District Line on Saturday afternoons if Chelsea were playing at home. A couple of times I'd stood among beer-sweating Englishmen, listening to them sing about what should be done to Catholics, or simply the Irish.

Liverpool, Everton and Manchester United were considered 'Irish clubs'. Their hooligan 'firms' sought connection with the INLA, PIRA, RIRA, etc. They went to Dublin for Saint Patrick's day, waved tricolours occasionally – but the true Republican supported Gaelic games, so the connections had been less enthusiastically followed. And there was that left-wing aura about Republicanism that just didn't sit well with the football hooligan psyche.

There was a hinterland of Irish politics on both sides that was simply about gaining criminal wealth, bullying maintenance of local power and enjoying hatred. For the sincere political believers of either side it had always been impossible to be completely free from these elements professing the same aims and beliefs.

In East Belfast I wasn't facing tattooed Chelsea Headhunters or even big men singing, just small boys, but I still didn't want them to throw something at me. I kept walking and left them behind – then realized I was in a cul de sac. I took my street map out of my pocket to try and look as though I had a purpose for going up and down the road – being lost seemed more of a purpose than just noseying around. They were small, so I could always slap at them with the map if the worst came to the worst.

They were looking and muttering, I could see it would

crush their boyish pride to let me go past without at least shouting obscenities at me. I kept walking, feigning interest in my map, waiting for them to do their worst.

'Look at you!' one shouted ferociously. I kept walking. Look at me what, what? 'Look at you!' he yelled again. 'Pink shoes!'

They roared with laughter, although when I glanced over, the shouting one looked a bit crestfallen that this was the best he'd managed in a crisis.

I had something to eat in a café with those flat glass cups – not retro trendy, still there from the sixties. Two elderly ladies in bright blouses were taking tea at the table next to me. They didn't seem to have anything to say to each other for a long time. Then, just as I was leaving, it got interesting.

One of them suddenly said: 'All this business about the gay bishop, it's terrible. I mean that's what the Christian Church is supposed to be about, minorities and outsiders. All I can say is I'm glad my mother's dead so she doesn't have to see this kind of hypocrisy.'

The other one laughed and said, 'Well I can see you're on good form.'

I thought of ordering a second dinner, to hear what other unexpected turn the conversation would take to make me feel happy about human nature, but I had things to do.

I could have walked downhill to the right and seen the big white parliament building, Stormont. Instead I got myself all tangled up in muralled flats, far too far back down the road, looking for the site of C. S. Lewis' birthplace, formerly Dundela Villas, now Dundela Flats.

A childhood spent trying to get into wardrobes by accident had made me think this would be interesting, but there was nothing to see. A three-storey block of modern flats, with a blue plaque commemorating C. S. Lewis, 'Author and Christian Apologist'.

Lewis' grandfather had been rector of a nearby church, with a lion head door knocker; this was supposed to be the inspiration for the messianic lion, Aslan. When Lewis was eight, his mother died. The golden age before her death and the countryside of Northern Ireland were the Narnia he longed to return to, after he had been sent away to an unhappy boarding-school life in England.

Outside the public library in Holywood Road was a statue of a man by a wardrobe, commemorating Lewis. It wasn't much.

There were a few C. S. Lewis tours run by resourceful independent citizens, but it seemed to me that Belfast City Council could spend less time carping about the Anglo-Irish Agreement and more time thinking of ways to provide jobs and income from the city's neglected assets. At least a C. S. Lewis museum. The success of *Lord of the Rings* and *Harry Potter* had put the *Narnia Chronicles* next on the slate as multi-million dollar movie projects. Maybe that would inspire the Council. A C. S. Lewis theme park might provide a better prospect for kids in East Belfast than Chelsea shirts and militaristic murals.

I stomped back up the Newtownards Road, thinking how annoying it was that I was supposed to care one way or another about all the flags and murals around me, annoyed with everyone in Belfast for not getting on with the peace and realizing what brilliant gold there was to pick up in the streets.

I threw the sweat-smelling duvet into the chair at the corner of my room as I imagined I could still smell it from the floor, then realized it was probably me, cross and sweating in the heat. On television there was news that George

Best, with a new liver and a stomach full of antabuse, had started drinking again.

'Oh, for God's sake, George, what's the matter with you?' I said to the television, remembered he wasn't related to me and realized I had spent the day turning into some bossy know-all who thought she knew what everyone should be doing. Worse than that, I was slipping into a tone of thought I'd always found upsetting in books and articles about Northern Ireland. Journalists in particular, who'd spent too long in the province, seen too much and not understood enough, would descend from what had quite often been a liberal, open-minded start into a baffled, angry, 'exterminate all the brutes' attitude to Northern Ireland. Of course it tended to happen to them after too much interviewing of paramilitaries, politicians and bomb victims – not just over C. S. Lewis, unwashed bedding and George Best.

I fell asleep and woke up early, still frowning at myself.

In the stuffy dining room was a family of Americans. I ate a full Ulster breakfast, with fried bread, black puddings, two eggs, piled bacon, two sausages, potato bread, tomatoes, a different kind of bread fried . . . Even the coffee tasted lightly fried, so that was good – if the caffeine didn't get me, the extra drop of lard would do it. I eavesdropped to see why the Americans were there, but only heard them arguing about whether they had to clean the hire car before returning it.

As I'd been up so early, I'd done some reading and realized how ignorant I was. The Newtownards Road was at what was called a 'flashpoint' – adjacent to the Catholic district, Short Strand. For years there'd been toings and froings of bombing and brick-throwing. Hence the burnt-out houses. The boarded-up shops close to the dividing line. Hence the police presence this morning.

Everything seemed to be closed and I couldn't see a bus. Men in shirt sleeves and orange sashes came down a side-street, followed by a flute band in uniform. Then came some straggling women with pushchairs. I followed them. We stopped and were joined by a band of boys in decorative uniforms, more men with sashes and more women ambling along on the pavement. Among the camp followers, I noticed two teenagers with backpacks beside me. I wondered if they were tourists and where from, but they were local, they'd just brought their lunch with them. They didn't seem to be very sure what was going on.

'What's the best way to follow the march?' I asked them.

'Find one of the feeder bands and follow it to the centre of town,' one said.

The second one asked me if I was English. I said I was, as that seemed easiest. They'd just accept me and not get that unsettled look people got the instant I said I was born there, needing to know what I was before they could settle again.

'Just curious?' one asked.

'Just curious,' I said.

I asked if they knew what tune the flute band was playing. They looked awkward. They either didn't know, or wouldn't say. I drifted away from them to mingle with families waving small Union Jacks. I asked a woman how far the march would go.

'Up to Edenbury field. But that's miles. I'll just go to City Hall.'

Near City Hall everything seemed to be building up. Banners, bands and the crowd seemed less vague. More women, joined by beercan-carrying men with tattoos, Rangers shirts and shaven-headed children.

The Orangemen with their sashes all looked like

respectable shopkeepers, keeping stern faced, but slightly embarrassed by such a public display of themselves – a tough job but it had to be done. The bands seemed innocent, boy scouty. There were no big Lambeg drums – apparently these were a rarity in Belfast now. There was plenty of drumming, though. Frenzied drumming of small drums that would get anyone that way inclined worked up into fighting mood. Band after band came by, wearing what appeared to be overly decorative Scottish military uniforms, followed by banners of Ulster this and that brigade. More drumming and flute playing. It wasn't cheery music, it was music to march to – military, piped occasionally into melancholy by the flutes. It made me think of war films, men going off to battle who wouldn't come back.

There were Orange Lodges all over the world, even in West Africa, a remnant of Protestant missionary work. There were lodges in England, America and Canada. The Canadian lodge included Innu Mohawks, who were often shown in full regalia in Orange Order literature, along with pictures of Togolese and Nigerian Orangemen, to dispel any accusation that the order was racist. The Orange Order felt it was important to affirm that the order is 'a society open to all Protestants of good character, and has been a multi-racial organization for a very long time'. They were against the break-up of the United Kingdom, whether by 'European federalism, militant Irish nationalism [or] Scottish nationalism'. More fundamentally, the order stood for spirituality in society, social morality and nuclear family values: 'the rise of secular culture-based individual self-indulgence has not created the liberal society the "flower power" generation promised. Instead we have an amoral, fragmented and confused society'.

Their views on moral decline were no more out of touch with the world than the Pope's, no more alien to the amoral, fragmented and confused way I liked to live.

I'd expected to feel some anger, or some overwhelming irrational fear while watching the marches. I only felt hot and jostled. Maybe it was difficult to feel threatened by men playing flutes. I didn't quite feel like I was having fun. It was all too determined. And someone behind me shouted in a Glasgow accent: 'Kill a Catholic for Ireland!'

The two backpacking boys seemed to have caught up with me and tutted.

'That's why we never come,' one said. 'Who cares about that shite?'

'Isn't that shite part of it?'

He frowned at me. 'Not everyone thinks like that.'

The Scotsman started some bizarre jerky dance to the drum rhythms.

'Let's move along a bit,' the second boy said.

I followed them. We found ourselves pressed against a shuttered shop window by big women screaming and cheering at people they knew in a passing drum and fife band.

There was one big woman with a hairdo that would have been elfin on a smaller head but made her look like she'd gone bald and had to quickly borrow a small boy's wig. She turned and beamed at me: 'Is that an English accent?'

Before I could say it was, she grabbed my face in her hands and kissed my forehead.

'God bless you for being here!'

She turned to her friends and said, 'A wee English girl here!' I tensed, fearing all five of them would be grabbing and kissing, but the others just gave me vague smiles. Their kissy friend had quite a raspy smell of vodka about her, so perhaps they were less far gone.

A group marched past in some fancy regalia that looked like one of the camper branches of the Italian police force.

The PSNI, who barely looked as though they were in uniform at all compared to the bands, were around, but less than I expected.

'Not many police,' I said to the boys. The big ladies had moved on. We'd room to breathe. Plenty actually: it wasn't just that there was little visible police presence, the crowd wasn't as large as I'd expected.

'The police will all be further north, where there'll be trouble.'

The Catholic community of the Ardoyne had tried to stop the march going through their streets and failed. Frantic last-minute talks had gone on between community leaders, hoping to keep it peaceful.

The boys weren't going north, they'd seen enough. So had I. Wimpishly, I felt hot, sun-sickened, headachy from the noise and really didn't want to go all the way up to the Ardoyne to see if there'd be trouble.

I ducked away down a side-street full of what seemed to be an alternative festival of drunken tramps and then found myself in deserted streets, drum thuds and music receding. It had somehow become mid-afternoon. I'd no idea where the time had gone. Ashamed to say, I found the cool interior of a bland modern hotel and was grateful. No one there but me and some confused Spanish businessmen. I had food, gallons of water, still felt ill and expected I'd have to walk all the way back to East Belfast. Possibly dying of heat stroke in a gutter en route . . . But there was a cab number at reception.

'I thought there'd be no transport anywhere,' I said to the driver.

'It's just a parade,' he said. 'There isn't a war on.'

'Of course, I know. I just thought everyone had the day off.'

He looked at me in the mirror.

'Didn't you like the parade, then?'

'I got a bit hot.'

'And a bit bored?' He was about twenty with a trendy haircut.

'A bit,' I said, thinking with that hair he wouldn't be offended.

He was quiet for a long time. I didn't much feel like talking, so if he'd disappeared into offended silence, I'd have been happy to leave it like that. But he was thinking . . .

'You know, how I see it . . .' he said, 'it's like going to the park to watch some band on the bandstand, that's how I see it. What's it got to do with people our age?'

I was so pleased he thought we were the same age, I didn't want to argue, but had to point out, 'There were a lot of young people in the crowd and in the bands.'

He made a scoffing noise. 'Well, if they were in the crowd it was an excuse for a drink and if they were in the band . . .' He made a more seriously scoffing sound. 'Well, you know, there's a lot of people in Belfast still live with their mammys and don't know there's a big world out there. As soon as I get the money I'm out of here. Where are you from?'

'London.'

'Yeah, London, Manchester, you know, somewhere, anywhere that's not depressing and people have a life that's like modern, you know?'

'You don't think Belfast's catching up?'

'I want it now, not when Belfast's finally caught up. I want to start a club. You know, a friend of mine's brother has this lap-dancing place in Newcastle, makes a fortune.'

This was all getting a bit too amoral, fragmented and

confused for me. I grunted and pretended to fall asleep. He seemed to charge me a lot, but I needed to get into the quiet of the guest house and didn't quibble that funding his emigration to a life of individual self-indulgence wasn't all down to me.

I'd wanted to be open-minded, but I'd crept away from the Protestants' big day to lie down in a darkened room, watching the big day on the news. I hadn't tried nearly hard enough.

Protesters held up placards saying, 'No talk, no walk' referring to the Unionists' refusal to talk to Sinn Fein. The protesters were supervised by senior members of Sinn Fein. One senior member of Sinn Fein, picked out for a close-up by the news camera, wasn't pleased to notice he was being given this attention and moved behind some PSNI men.

Later, the police were putting up huge metal barriers to screen the returning marchers from the protesters, fearing the evening mood, with both sides fuelled by alcohol, might be less controlled.

There were stone- and bottle-throwing incidents at night but nothing like the trouble that had been predicted. It seemed to be an exercise in good PR for all concerned.

One of the afternoon's main speakers was Unionist Geoffrey Donaldson. He said that in any other country of the twenty-first century, the pageantry, music and tradition of the Orange marches would be seen as a family day out and a useful, vibrant tourist attraction. Unfortunately for him the television edit cut straight to 'a right wee bastard', a shaven-headed, vicious-looking child in a Chelsea shirt tossing a mace and marching along to the drums as if on his way to kick a few heads in.

It was reported on all channels as the most peaceful 12th of July since the Troubles began. But the Republican newspaper *An Phoblacht* complained the next day of media bias, particularly in the BBC, accusing them of completely ignoring the offensive anti-Catholic slogans chanted and the fears of Catholic families on the route, who had lived in terror of post-march attacks for thirty years.

It seemed to me that the Protestants had every right to their marches; the Catholics had every reason not to want the marches in their streets.

The news ended with talk of George Best being back on the drink.

'Ah, it's a shame,' said the newsreader. 'But what's to be done?'

Although I'd taken against her for her sharp manner and her unwashed duvet cover, the landlady was friendly over breakfast and said it was a pity I'd only stayed a couple of nights.

'I'm just passing through this time but I'll definitely be back.'

'Well there's a lot more to Belfast than you can see in a couple of days.'

'I know. I was just interested to see the marching season.'

She looked at me thoughtfully.

'It's a good day out. It's a shame people have to call it that. It's a parade, not a march. A friend and I were talking yesterday and saying it should be called the carnival season, like Rio de Janeiro.'

'That's a good idea,' I said, to keep the peace.

I did want to spend more than a couple of days in Belfast – but at any other time of year.

It was summer; seaside time.

Newcastle had been a great place to be an energetic toddler. My escapes from the back garden to the sea front were something my parents cited as early evidence of wanderlust. I thought they were more early evidence of ruthless greed, because I'd escape to an Italian ice-cream stand, insisting I could swap stones and dolls' heads for ice cream. The ice-cream man would have to oblige, while waiting for the local policeman to come by and escort me back home. The policeman didn't have to conduct a great investigation to find out where I belonged – I lived next door to him.

I recognized the Newcastle house – I knew exactly what road to turn into without reading the street sign – there it was, unchanged at the end of the cul de sac. I realized I used to cover an impressive distance on short legs to conduct my sea-front bartering. I rang the doorbell, thinking the house looked as though pleasant elderly people lived there now and might let me in for a cup of tea, in exchange for nostalgia about my life there as a child. Probably less valuable as currency than dolls' heads, but it was worth a try.

No answer. Peering round the side of the house, I could see the garden was the same simple patch of grass with a shed. I could picture where my brother's pram would be parked by the high hedge on summer afternoons. He'd been billed as 'a little brother to play with', but all he did was sleep. So he may have been to blame for the runaway, con-artist lifestyle I fell into before the age of five.

A man washing a car a few doors down was taking an interest in my snooping about. Maybe he'd ring the police-man who might still live next door. The policeman would come out, recognize me and realize I was now of an age to go to prison. He'd do me for attempted burglary, revenge for all the trips up the hill he'd had to make to return an ice-cream-stained child to stressed-out parents.

★

Oh Mary, this London's a wonderful sight,
The people all working by day and by night
They don't sow potatoes nor barley nor wheat
But there's gangs of them diggin' for gold in the street.
At least when I asked them that's what I was told
So I just took a hand at this diggin' for gold;
But for all I've found there, I might as well be
Where the mountains of Mourne sweep down to the sea.

Singer, watercolourist, storyteller and composer Percy
French has been laid claim to by Newcastle. All his papers
and memorabilia were housed in an archive in the town,
although he was born in Roscommon, buried in Lancashire,
and there were rumours the song was written about the view
of the Mournes from the Hill of Howth, Co. Dublin, on a
clear day.

But it's obvious the mountains do sweep into the sea at
Newcastle, a far more arresting and inspiring sight than some
squinty view from the Hill of Howth.

By the edge of the mountains, the stone buildings and
fishermen at work in the harbour felt like the makings of a
simple life someone would miss in gaudy, goldless London.

Old trawlers were still in use among the modern sailing
dinghies; nets were being repaired, shellfish pots stacked, and
I was sorry to see that I was too early for the *Herring Gutters'
Festival* – a four-day summer extravaganza with boat trips,
live music, clowns, mountain walks, a float parade, a wait-
ers' race and a daft raft race. I particularly liked the warning at the foot of the advertising poster: 'All times are subject
to weather and Murphy's law'.

Trippers thronged around, buying rock, ice cream, and
most of the high street seemed unmolested since the 1960s.
It was a cheap and cheerful sea front, much of it needed

a coat of paint, but Newcastle didn't have to care about this kind of surface detail — it had a long, wide yellow-sand beach running parallel to the high street, and those mountains.

I don't know if trippers of the day scattered in alarm when eccentric local inventor Harry Ferguson made his 1910 flight along the promenade in a home-made monoplane. Ferguson also invented the four-wheel drive and won a multi-million-pound law suit with the Ford Motor Company, when they tried to infringe the patents on his invention of the modern tractor. He later merged with the Canadian tractor company Harris Massey to form the still profitable Massey Ferguson Tractors. Massey, by odd coincidence, began his career with a small mechanics shop in Newcastle, Ontario.

In later life, Ferguson developed an influential interest in car and motorbike racing. On-road motorbike races were particularly popular in Northern Ireland. A triangular road race between Portstewart, Coleraine and Portrush, known as the North West, brought biking enthusiasts from all over the world.

Until his recent death at a race in Estonia, 23-times winner of the Isle of Man TT and thirteen-times winner of the North West Joey Dunlop OBE MBE was the County-Antrim-born hero of motorbike racing, personally drawing international crowds to Northern Irish roadsides. One of Harry Ferguson's campaigns had been to legalize and regulate these thrilling but very dangerous off-track races.

I liked a kind of thrill that was less likely to break my collar bones, legs, arms . . . I bought an ice cream from what I was sure was the same old 1930s Italian shop, full of young women now, who looked as though they'd have no sense of humour about a child trading in dolls' heads. The music play-ing loudly in the shop might have been intended as child friendly: the clunky comic song 'Camp Granada' . . . 'It's stopped hailing, guys are swimming, guys are sailing . . .', although the severe efficiency of the new assistants made it seem more likely the song was just on the radio, nothing to do with their intentions.

Guys were swimming and sailing. The ice cream was still worth committing crimes for. I watched a train of children on ponies waddle down the promenade, cross the main road and disappear somewhere up a side-street. Other children ran in and out of the sea with bright plastic buckets and spades; fathers built elaborate sand castles, amusing themselves and boring their children, who preferred to dig a good hole and try to fill it with sea water. A seaside resort was a dependable place to come from, the essence and purpose of it wouldn't ever really change. No wonder I'd been thrown by RAF bases in Wales and London – my father might have wanted a broader life, but Newcastle had been a very cosy, child-ideal little place to leave behind.

At the end of the town, facing the mountains, the vast Victorian Slieve Donard hotel raised the tone way above the Kiss Me Quick, candy false teeth, main sea front atmosphere. The spired hotel was built by the railway company to attract wealthy visitors to the coastal resort. Charlie Chaplin stayed there, as well as the grander citizens of Northern Ireland. With the demise of the railway and some neglectful management, the place began to fall into disrepair and slipped on to the target lists of bombers in the 1970s. The nineties brought new owners, massive reinvestment and an upsurge of fancy visitors using the adjacent Royal County Down Golf Club. A few days after my visit, President Clinton was to head for Newcastle and a game on this golf course, where local observers reported him to have a 'shocking bad temper'.

Set in acres of sea-front gardens, the hotel was named

after the Slieve Donard, highest peak of the fifteen-mile-long Mourne range, in turn named after Saint Donard, who lived in a stone hut at the top of the mountain, while trying to convert the mountain people to Christianity. Although there were walkers in stout boots trailing about the mountain paths, the Mournes were still a place for feeling contemplative and awed by nature – if not quite driven to hermity sainthood.

In a small country, it was strange to suddenly find so much remote, quiet space, but I suspected the Mournes were a magic dimension, expanding once you'd crossed into their silent territory. I wasn't alone in this feeling; C. S. Lewis drew heavily on memories of the Mourne mountains for his descriptions of Narnia.

In the eighteenth century, the coast south of Newcastle was a smugglers' landing strip, bringing in spirits, tea, silk and tobacco from the Isle of Man. The goods were then taken up through the mountains on a track called the Brandy Pad to Hilltown, the distribution centre for the contraband. Hilltown still had an excessive number of pubs, a legacy from the wild old days.

I stopped for more sea air at Kilkeel, a busy fishing harbour, piled with lobster pots. In an old stony part of town with winding streets, shops sold ornaments made from polished Mourne granite and black crystal jewellery. There had always been rumours of gold in the Mourne mountains but you'd have to mind yourself – the mountains were supposed to be full of little people and fairies who could turn nasty if you were caught taking anything away. There were turn-of-the-century reports of two-foot red-headed people, 'wild looking with scanty clothing', bothering prospectors and little troll-like men coming into settlements and chasing children.

In this district, if you put a bench outside your front door you should put it on the right, so a friendly type of creature called a Pooka might turn up for a cheerful chat and bring you good luck. If you put the bench on your left, you'd get a bad Pooka, who would tell you nothing but terrible news and maybe cause you some harm. The bad Pooka was a gobliny creature who would particularly like to sit down with strangers and newcomers, to tell them stories of dreadful things that had happened to people in the area, fortunes swindled from fine families, murders . . . Then the Pooka would just go off without saying goodbye, with no apparent purpose but to make the stranger feel they'd made a bad choice of place to land up.

The Pooka could travel. In the James Stewart film *Harvey*, the invisible six-foot rabbit who befriends Stewart is referred to as a Pooka. Some of the County Down Pookas took animal form, but I couldn't find a local story about a six-foot rabbit. Perhaps Pookas, like so many of the Irish, got to America and became what they'd always wanted to be — for people it was presidents, for Pookas it was giant white rabbits in the movies.

A friend who'd not made the journey since the nineties had warned me the roads I had to travel next, through the 'bandit country' of South Armagh, often had signs on telegraph poles saying 'Beware of the Sniper', or 'Sniper at Work'. The signs were a dark joke aimed, like the guns, at the British army or suspect strangers. I meandered down tiny roads between Newry and the border, and finally spotted a sign on a pole ahead. It had a phone number and read: 'Lose Weight Now, Ask Me How'.

'So you survived the North?' my friend Anthony asked me when I arrived at the cottage in the middle of nowhere,

County Cavan. I'd survived it very well, thank you, I told him, and I hadn't even noticed I'd crossed the border until I saw different-coloured post boxes. The little road I'd come along would probably have been blocked off at the height of the Troubles, to try and minimize lawless toing and froing – but now, not even a customs man. If only I'd thought to bring butter.

Some would say Cavan wasn't in Northern Ireland, but the former divisions of Ireland – Ulster, Munster, Leinster and Connaught – had included Donegal, Cavan and Monaghan as part of Ulster.

When Ireland was partitioned, Cavan, with its poor farming land, and nothing anybody wanted, had been given up by the British without too many tears. They'd also wanted to keep the predominantly Catholic Cavan population out of the new Ulster, to maintain a loyal Protestant majority. So the new state was three counties short of being accurately Ulster.

Cavan people had a reputation for meanness. Jokes abounded: 'How was barbed wire invented? Two Cavan men fighting over a penny.' Or more tellingly: 'In Cavan they eat their dinner in the table drawer in case anyone comes to call.'

The meanness came from a history of terrible devastation in the famine, endless struggle to make bad land pay and, until recently, as in most border counties, an inability to cash in on the Southern Irish tourist boom because of proximity to the border with the North.

These border counties were notoriously full of the more lethal elements of INLA, PIRA, RIRA . . . So I was surprised when Anthony told me I'd missed the local Orange parades.

Anthony's mother said, 'Oh yes, they have parades, they're all black around here.' Which gave me a bit of a mental double take.

I'd completely forgotten that the North was black and Protestants were black. And when we met some of my Cavan friends' relatives, they assumed if I was from the North I must be 'black'. Anthony's mother had quickly started to talk of my brother the priest.

Why the North was black and Protestants were black was one of those things there are ten, at least, opinions about. There was the obvious recent connotation of black-hearted, black-souled and all that kind of thing . . . But in the seventeenth century, the Scots in Ireland were forced to swear 'a black oath' by Charles I, to make the Scottish Church conform to the English, which led to those who took the oath being called 'Black mouths'.

To complicate matters further, there were the black Irish in general. Some think this refers to the dark colouring of many Irish people, with romantic speculation about people all round the coast being ravaged by shipwrecked Spaniards. There were shipwrecked Spaniards occasionally, but they'd have been very busy . . . Some say it refers to the dark indigenous, pre-Celtic population, therefore a look still found in certain areas of the country.

In America the 'black Irish' referred to the Catholics who arrived to escape the famine in 'black 47' – the potato blight that began the famine being referred to as the 'black blight'.

I'm not going to stick my half-black neck out and decide on an answer. Basically most of the Irish were called 'black' at some stage by someone who didn't like them.

Anthony's cousins, just south of the black North, farmed hard and supplemented their income working in a factory in Monaghan half the year. Fishing and hunting tourism was opening up in Cavan, but it was still an area where working the land was the main purpose of it. It was a place where people died with a million in the bank and lived as if they hadn't a penny, not meanness so much as deep fear of poverty. Next year could bring a bad harvest, cattle disease, factory closure, or some spill-over atrocity from the North to put off tourists.

It might have become difficult to tell where the border was, but the North and South of Ireland seemed to be growing further and further apart psychologically. People in the North, of whatever religious persuasion, always had some tale of the villainy and treachery of people in the South. People in the South always had some anecdote of a terrible experience exemplifying the bigotry and dangerousness of the North.

Happily, it seemed to have been established in the Cavan household that I wasn't dangerous.

Anthony's mother had been brought up in the Cavan countryside and slotted back into country life without a lot of panic. Anthony and I, Londoners for too long, were inclined to panic – it was so quiet at night, so dark, and creatures scrabbled around in the roof.

Anthony said we were 'plastic paddies', that is, people brought up in England who made a great deal of show-off noise about their Irish ancestry, particularly applicable to the sort of person who decided to return to their ancestry and write books about what it meant to them.

I argued that 'plastic paddies' were second generation, not people like me, who'd been born in Ireland.

'You were born in the North, in Britain. Half black and plastic,' Anthony teased me.

I said, 'You know my granny warned me. She'd say, "Southerners, they seem friendly, they smile and smile but they'd stab you in the back as soon as look at you."'

'Did she say that?'

'All the time.'

'But she married a Protestant, she was subjected to a lot of their propaganda.'

'Black propaganda?'

'Exactly.'

After this pretence of really giving a damn, we went to the pub. A great barn of a place in town, where there'd been a riot in the eighties. Local young men had got so crazed at a Samantha Fox stage show, they'd stormed the stage. Samantha Fox had been whisked away and the disappointed young men of Cavan went wild with disappointment, wrecking the place until the Garda stopped them. There wasn't a lot to do at night in Cavan.

Although we tried to spend our evenings in the Cavan cottage burning a turf fire and reading Irish novels, Anthony and I soon started fretting that we couldn't get any recognizable television programmes on RTE and some of them were in Gaelic. We flapped about helplessly when we realized the two shops in the village three miles away shut at five; and we were always having to call the farming relatives to fix water pumps, examine electrical failures, or tell us his mother was right, it was just mice in the roof, not bears.

I took to walking the roads looking for kindling sticks for the fire we'd become obsessed with. Although there was warm sunshine until ten o'clock at night, we felt the turf fire was the one authentically country lifestyle feature we'd mastered. And stick-collecting along the roads at daybreak made me feel as though I was practically ploughing fields and herding heifers.

One morning, I'd ambled about two miles from the cottage when one of the cousins drew up in his car, offering me a lift.

'I'm fine thanks, I fancied a bit of a walk.'

'What's that you've got?' He nodded at my puny fistful of twigs.

'I'm collecting sticks for the fire.'

He looked at me amazed. 'But there's fire lighters in the bucket by the door.'

'I know,' I said. 'But I like collecting sticks, it seems like a nice country thing to do.'

I knew by the way he looked at me the story would be all round the cousins before lunchtime. As soon as I said it, I realized I sounded like Penelope Keith in *The Good Life* and knew I had no idea what country life was really like in a hard-farmed place like Cavan. It didn't matter any more if I was black, green or plastic – the cousin had discovered the real truth about me. I was, as they said in the North and the South, *an eejit*.

11. What People Really Want

'So you're flying in to Derry?' Uncle Joe asked when I was on my way back to Northern Ireland at a better time for reunions and grand tours than early July. 'Well, I suppose it'll be no worse in February than it always is.'

'What's wrong with Derry?'

He laughed. 'Now your aunt, your mother and all sorts of people will tell you I've borne a grudge against the place since my schooldays there. But it seems to me it's always raining in Derry and the people are terrible whiners.'

It was raining. But the guest-house landlady who greeted me seemed an exuberant sort of person, rather than a whiner. As she swooped about with armfuls of clean white towels, she wanted to check I was only staying three nights because they had a party of fishermen booked in for the weekend.

'We're unbelievably busy for February. I mean, February in Derry? In fact this is the first quiet week we've had in a year. It's been astonishing this year.' Then she smiled confidentially. 'You know I was saying to a friend of mine that we're not used to this sort of success in Derry. Usually, things go all right for a while, then something happens and you're back to nought or below. But this last couple of years, nothing. Not even the Apprentice Boys' march turned nasty. Nothing has happened to annoy us at all and we can't handle it. I was thinking of setting up a self-help course for people in Derry called "Coping With Success" – because it's coming as a bit of a shock to us.'

Another success, although he seemed to be coping with it, was Martin McCrossan, a one-man Derry tourist development bureau. I wondered if Martin had been taller before he'd started his enterprises, because I saw his stocky, always smartly suited form, all day and long into the evening, pounding round the city walls with groups of visitors listening to his synopsis of the history.

A city-centre newsagent, Martin had noticed that foreign visitors were coming to Derry long before anyone else in town seemed aware of the gathering clumps of curious Italians, Americans . . . He met with scepticism and occasional derision when he insisted to Derry businessmen, councillors and central government officials that tourism was the future for the city. Martin went ahead, working on deals with hotels, coach-tour operators and travel agencies abroad. Despite setbacks – 'too many and too depressing to talk about' – he made his new business work. Tour groups used Derry as a base to explore the whole north-west and they were coming in from Europe, America, even Japan. The most surprising groups were the ones from the South of Ireland: 'People who live only forty miles over the border were on a tour with me last week, and it was the first time they'd ever been in the North.'

Enthusiasm was definitely one of his personal assets as a businessman. He raced out at a moment's notice to take me on a walking tour in freezing sleet. His talk was energetic, animated, as if the hundreds of years of history he recounted were something that had just happened to him that morning . . .

The walls of Derry, an exciting twenty-five foot high and thirty foot wide, were built in the seventeenth century to keep the Irish from marauding the city while it was being developed as a lucrative trading centre and seaport by a consortium of the Liverymen of London. Hence the London added to the original name Derry.

Derry derived from the Gaelic Doire, meaning 'Place of Oaks', because, presumably, there had been oaks. Martin pointed to a straggly one near a churchyard. 'I mean presumably a lot,' he said.

Martin stamped his feet and rubbed his cold hands as he told me that the arrival of the London Liverymen had been the real start of Derry's troubles. 'When people visit who don't know much about the history, I can honestly say to them that it started with English businessmen and English kings hundreds of years ago, not the civil rights movement in the sixties.'

Kings William and James had one of their big seventeenth-century run-ins around Derry. In hopes that he was en route to reclaim the British throne, Catholic King James joined with the Irish to take the city. City Governor Lundy had made up his mind to surrender, but the 30,000 Protestant residents inside the city walls thought surrender meant certain massacre. Thirteen boys apprenticed to tradesmen seized the city keys and locked the gates. A long siege began, with escalating starvation and disease inside the walls. An estimated 7,000 people died while waiting for King William's troops to save them. The siege kept James occupied and gave William time to organize an army efficient enough to win the Battle of the Boyne, securing his position as King of England. Eventually the city was relieved by Protestant forces.

The 'no surrender' slogan of the siege, which helped enable a Protestant king to rule Britain, was on Loyalist murals all over Northern Ireland. And Lundy, the governor who'd have let the Catholics in, was burnt in effigy every year.

The Apprentice Boys of today, an organization of local

Protestant businessmen, paraded in August to commemorate their seventeenth-century suffering and the subsequent defeat of the Catholics. This parade was always an occasion that provoked riot and rampage at the height of the Troubles. But now, after constant negotiation, the annual Apprentice Boys' march was held 'tactfully'.

'Oh, it's all been negotiated in the minutest detail,' Martin told me. 'They don't wave the British flags in certain places, they don't play certain tunes in certain places, they don't bang the drums when they're passing along the walls that overlook the Catholic estates of the Bogside. It's been minutely negotiated.'

We overlooked the Bogside, and he pointed out 'Free Derry Corner', where there remained the gable end of a house that had marked the temporary end of British juris-diction when the barricades went up in the 1960s. A picture of the wall reading 'You are now entering Free Derry' was a favourite on postcards of the city.

Free Derry Corner wasn't the mural that interested Martin the most. He pointed out a mauve and purple affair on the side of a house facing the city walls. It featured a little girl who'd been shot dead in cross-fire.

'Everything in the picture is symbolic. There's a lot of purple to symbolize mourning. And there's a picture of a rifle pointing down as if to say all people in Ireland should put down the gun. And there, beside the little girl, is a butterfly. You might ask why is it plain purple and not all the beautiful colours a butterfly should be? The artist says it's because when there is peace and people can flourish in their true beauty, then he'll come back and paint in the true butterfly colours.'

Just as I was thinking the mural was the most mawkish, saccharine monstrosity, I was shifted towards a thought that

I might not be a very nice person. Martin pointed to where the father of the little girl still came to stand every day, the corner where his child was killed. 'He stands, prays and hopes to remind people of the need to put down the gun.'

The girl would have been about the same age as me now. Her father had been mourning her for decades. My snobbery about the artistic quality of the girl's memorial turned sour inside me.

To a large extent the gun had been put down in Derry. There were no more scuttling manoeuvres of armed men across the bridge, no more barricades in the Bogside and no reason why a family cavalcade would be reluctant to drive through the streets on their way to a seaside holiday.

Derry was really the size of a market town, not a city, so the surprise was that there was a building left standing after decades of close-fought battles. And after centuries of determined domination, the other surprise was that the Protestant community had largely abandoned the city. Most Protestants now lived on the other side of the river Foyle, in a district known as Waterside. Always a better end of town than Bogside, Waterside had expanded and the significant Protestant population in central Derry had shrunk down to what my guest-house landlady described as 'their sad little Fountain estate'.

There were Protestants who were more than sad about their eventual surrender of Derry to Catholic control. As soon as the term 'ethnic cleansing' became available, some used it to describe what had happened in Derry. Then the term was bandied about all over Northern Ireland, by both sides, to describe the way people were violently driven out of their homes during the Troubles because they were the wrong religion for the area. But even at the most murderous times in the last thirty years Northern Ireland hadn't really let go of sanity and set out to massacre the other side. When the British army was in the country, there were arguments that there would be a bloodbath without them. It didn't happen; for all the people full of hate there must always have been enough people trying to keep life possible in the country.

Martin and I could look down on the Fountain estate from the high city walls. Soulless, hurried architecture, as on most of the estates that ringed the city. Unlike most, this flew tattered Union Jacks, and had red, white and blue kerb-stones.

'It looks very tired,' I said, 'very bashed about.'

'Oh, it is bashed about,' Martin said, 'but the majority of the people in there are old now. Lived in there all their lives. Why should they cross the river?'

To make his point, a bent old lady shuffled up a street with her shopping in a string bag.

'They just want to be left alone,' Martin said. Then he pointed further along, to a high wire fence running all down one side of the Fountain estate, separating it from the Catholic estates.

'That's the peace wall. You'll see the improvement, it's wire, it's transparent. A few years ago that was solid metal sheets, but now they can manage to look at each other.' He sighed. 'But I don't know if you saw a local paper today. Petrol bombs were thrown over from the Fountain last night. No one was hurt, but it's so stupid, and it probably won't have been anyone actually from the Fountain.'

'What, there are flying pickets of petrol bombers now?'

'God, I hope not.' Martin smiled and held up his hand as he took a brief call on his mobile phone. I'd first spoken to him on his mobile and thought he might be a bit scary he was so abrupt. But he was just a man in a hurry, running golfing tours, coach tours and executive excursion packages to the beauty spots of the north-west – while personally conducting his walking tours, and keeping an eye on the newsagent's.

Whatever fast-talking dealing he had to do on the phone was soon over and he was back to looking at the wire-mesh peace line with me.

'You get youngsters from the Catholic side pestering and throwing petrol bombs too, as if they need to bother with one wee estate left behind. Last night, though . . . What I think is it's youngsters from over the Waterside. Youngsters who know nothing about what people on the Fountain have been through but they get a few beers in them and think all this is a sport. It's a local equivalent of football hooliganism.'

Because the city walls hadn't been breached in the siege, Derry had been nicknamed the Maiden City. But Martin suggested there were other reasons: 'Can you see that big building over there? That's one of the last of Derry's shirt factories. Because of the linen industry in Ireland and because it had the port for export, Derry was the place for shirt-making. Women would come from all round to Derry for work. Consequently there are at least ten women for every man in Derry.' He beamed. 'Which was great when I was young because no matter how ugly you were, you could always get a girlfriend.'

I said I'd heard Derry men could be quite mollycoddled, with all this excessive female attention for the very least of them.

'Excessive female attention?' He laughed. 'Don't we all wish. Have you seen how the women go around in this city? In packs, talking to each other nineteen to the dozen and God help a man who tried to interrupt. They've always had the money and they've no time to be coddling any fool of a man.'

It was true. Derry women of all ages bustled around the shops in gangs. All with determinedly styled hair and all seeming to talk at once, as they converged ravening on sales or teashops. Men ambled alone, wary; men waited in cars to collect their wives, or stood shuffling and smoking outside dress shops – and any complaining about the length of their wait was ignored as their finally emerging wife would wave to a friend across the road and engage in hectic talk about whatever it was the women of Derry were always talking about.

Derry was full of brand new shopping complexes; work in them had replaced shirt-making for younger women. There were building jobs for the men putting these things up, but then what, I wondered.

'There's still a lot of unemployment,' Martin said. 'Derry's developing, but we still need our own IT industries, that kind of thing. And more tourism of course.'

New fancy hotels in the city and cheap flights to Derry City airport from London were making him hopeful.

'Although the airport does need to expand. There's opposition because it would expand only by disturbing farmers who've been on the land round there for generations, but, well, you saw it, it's just tiny at the moment, but developing it right could really open up the west of Ireland. Hopefully we'll find a compromise with the farmers.'

The landlady had told me she loved the new cheap flight busyness at the airport. 'We've always felt very cut off here in Derry. Psychologically cut off as well as physically. Cut off from the rest of Northern Ireland as well as the mainland.'

Derry was full of people from Donegal, particularly

youngsters from the countryside. They came over in the evenings to roar up and down the new clubs and bars of the Strand Road. There was a hope of a further boom in this cross-border socializing, as the ban on smoking in Southern Irish bars was enforced.

'Who knows,' the landlady said, with a glint of hope, 'we could become a den of iniquity.'

'A sort of tobacco Amsterdam?'

'It would be better than some of the things we've been.'

A freezing rain was coming down on Martin and me. We seemed to have circled the walls but he was still telling me something about them and my ears were too cold to listen properly any more. I was wrapped in all kinds of layers but I worried that Martin, in just his smart suit, was going to have to put all his enterprises on hold as he recovered from pneumonia.

'Shall we have a coffee break?' I suggested.

'Good timing.' Martin set off at a pace I had to skip to keep up with. 'We can warm up and have a good chat before my next tour.'

We passed the front of the Guildhall. This housed the city council and currently the Saville Inquiry, or as it was known locally, the Bloody Sunday Inquiry.

When the Troubles had erupted in the late sixties and civil rights marches were suppressed by the predominantly Protestant police forces, it was the subsequent rioting and barricading that led to the arrival of the British army. There were further civil rights protests, ending on a Sunday when British troops shot dead thirteen demonstrators. The four-year-long Saville Inquiry into the events of that Sunday was ending the week I was in Derry.

'You should pop in there,' Martin suggested briskly as we

passed. 'I'd like to have had more time for it myself but they say it's very interesting.'

As we went into the welcome steam and smoke of the coffee bar, Martin gestured to a burly man at the counter.

'Well, there now, you've missed nothing by coming in here. There's one of Derry's most famous monuments getting his breakfast.'

It was Ivan Cooper, the civil rights leader who'd led the march on Bloody Sunday. Ivan Cooper, who had recently been the central character in a television drama about Bloody Sunday.

'I saw him on telly last month,' I said as Martin and I took our seats, accepting Ivan's offer to buy our coffees.

'With Nesbitt playing him? He's not a bad actor, Nesbitt, is he, but do you see any resemblance?'

Ivan didn't look at all like the actor James Nesbitt who'd played his younger self.

'She was saying Nesbitt's better looking,' Martin teased, as Ivan joined us with the tray.

'Old age creeps up on you,' Ivan said. 'I'm sure I looked just like him only a couple of weeks ago.'

I didn't know what sort of presence the actor James Nesbitt had, but Ivan had waves of it. He wore broad, bold pinstripe and braces – a big George Melly style of a man, visible down a crowded street for hundreds of yards around. He was a successful businessman and politician. The sort of man you'd imagine would be seen comfortably through life by sheer force of personality, but . . .

'Have they done you at the inquiry?' Martin asked.

'They've done me. I was crucified,' Ivan said, acceptingly.

Ivan, in case you didn't see him on television, played by Nesbitt, or as himself in the news thirty years ago, was a Protestant. He had attempted, as SDLP member for Mid

Derry, to argue with the governing Protestant Unionists for reforms to help Catholics have equal rights to a say in local government and a chance at access to public housing. Arguing didn't work.

Along with fellow SDLP men John Hume and Hugh Logue, Ivan had joined a sit-down protest to prevent British army vehicles heading into the Bogside. They'd been arrested and on their subsequent release there was further rioting, with the army attempting to quell the violence. The little girl in the mural Martin had shown me, Annette McGavigan, was shot during these riots, caught in cross-fire by a British soldier's bullet. More violence erupted in the Bogside and Creggan estates; the army tried to break down barricades. Internment of Catholics increased. A soldier was shot as he fired CS gas into the Creggan. More army incursions, more street violence.

There was a march on the British army base at Magilligan. The troops in the base fired on the crowd with CS gas and rubber bullets. John Hume, who'd been on the march with Ivan Cooper, described the soldiers as 'beating, brutalizing and terrorizing the demonstrators'.

Nevertheless, another march for civil rights was planned in Derry. This time people were killed and lawyers were talking to witnesses decades later in the Guildhall about what exactly happened – and Ivan Cooper, crucified, was trying to have his breakfast. A bacon sandwich and a pile of crisps.

'I know what you're going to say.' He looked at me.

'Cholesterol?' I suggested.

He laughed. 'You can say that all you like, but at my time of life, I'm past saving.'

Martin told Ivan what I was doing, coming back to find my roots and writing about them. Ivan looked unimpressed but asked me where my roots were. I explained there was a bit of Belfast and a bit of Strabane, although everyone had left Strabane and moved now . . . I mentioned the tiny place near Portadown where some of my relatives lived. Ivan looked surprised and said, 'That's a very Loyalist area.'

I said I didn't know about that, but my Catholic family had lived round there for years and survived.

'Yes,' he said, suddenly immensely irritated. 'That's what people don't realize about Northern Ireland, especially in rural areas, people have lived side by side happily for years. Particularly in rural areas, people sharing farm equipment and helping each other out. People can get along just fine.'

All said as if I'd been the one who'd implied the opposite.

Still, I made allowances for his recent crucifixion and his generosity to Martin.

'I wouldn't do it for anyone but Martin,' he said, 'but he does a tour by special arrangement where people can walk the history of the civil rights movement, meet me and have what happened explained to them. Martin deserves support for what he's trying to do.'

Martin's phone was ringing. Apologetically, he said he had to meet a tour group.

'I'll leave you two to chat.'

He gave me a pile of leaflets about his tours and told me to phone him any time, constantly if I liked, if I had any questions.

Left alone with me, Ivan was uneasy. He made small talk about how many cousins I had, what they did. I tried to ask him about the tours he did with Martin. I was curious to know what he told people. Curious to know what it felt like to be a live local monument. But my attempts at a tactful lead into his soul were way too obvious for Ivan.

'You've misunderstood. Sometimes I let him bring select

informed groups to have a chat with me, that's all. I'll have to go now.'

He went very rapidly. Busy man under constant mental siege. And far too fly to give an impromptu interview to the likes of me.

I hesitated about going into the Saville Inquiry. Bloody Sunday had been pawed over by writers, journalists, film-makers . . . Part of me didn't want to go into the inquiry because then I'd have to say I'd been and get sucked into having an opinion about it all.

'I'll come with you,' Sally, my new friend from the Creggan, told me. 'It's nearly over and I've never been there myself.'

In her fifties now, Sally had lived around the Bogside and Creggan all her life.

'There were times in the seventies when I just wouldn't go down the town for weeks. We didn't have these kind of nice shops then, but even so . . . I'd get what I needed at the corner shop. Things will never go back to the way they were. People went through things that we're only just hearing about. A woman I've known for years had a cup of coffee with me last week and said she'd decided to tell me she was a Protestant. I said that was fine by me. She said she'd been terrified living in our estate for years. Only her own husband knew. She'd go up to visit her Protestant relatives in secret and they'd never come down here. Now she feels terrible that she did that, you know, denied them. I said to her people would have accepted it if they'd known. She told me I was forgetting how it used to be. Maybe I am forgetting. A case of wanting to, you know.'

My new friend Sally was so warm and open, she didn't feel new, but I'd only just met her. Gerard, from the shop near me in London, was her brother. When I'd told Gerard I'd be passing through Derry but didn't know anyone there, he phoned Sally immediately and told her to save me from a lonely visit. She did.

Typical Derry woman, Sally's progress through town was somewhat slow, always having to talk to the next clump of women in her path.

Outside the Guildhall she introduced me to one of the families who'd been campaigning for a full inquiry since the shooting of their son, over thirty years ago. Along with other families bereaved that Sunday, they went into the Guildhall every day and gathered at lunch breaks in the Bloody Sunday Centre over the road. This campaign centre had a room for family members to recuperate and talk in; it had an exhibition about the campaign and a slide show reconstructing the events of Bloody Sunday. It had the feeling of a chapel of rest and seeped with sadness.

The woman I was introduced to just nodded politely when Sally excitedly told her I was writing a book. I didn't know what to ask this tightly held woman. She asked me, 'Will you include this?'

I said I hoped I could.

She nodded again. We stood on the steps in the rain. I didn't know if the woman wanted to leave or not.

'It's taken a long time to get here,' Sally said to her.

'I'm pleased to see it's all being conducted with such decorum,' she replied. 'We've all given our evidence, the families, and had a thank you letter. So I'm reassured that they feel we conducted ourselves with decorum.'

It seemed an odd thing to say.

'Well, good luck to you. I wish you success in your endeavours,' she said to me, as she went with her family across the rainy Guildhall Square.

'This has been her whole life since, you know,' Sally said. 'Campaigning for this.'

Over dinner the previous night Sally had told me about another friend whose husband had been killed on Bloody Sunday. 'Then her son, named after the husband, was killed in a car accident a few years ago. That poor woman.' Sally reflected. 'She describes herself now as dead inside.'

So many people stranded in pain in the wake of the Troubles. In a culture that had no habit of forgetting.

Sally's husband, Dan, said, 'The trouble with us here is we're obsessed with the past.'

'Haven't people said that about the Irish for hundreds of years?' I asked him.

Dan made a face. 'You wonder what the hell they all did on day one when they hadn't got a past. Sat around and waited for day two so they'd have something behind them to go on about.'

Dan had recently survived major surgery. 'The miracle man', his family called him. And the experience had left him determined to see nothing but the seasides and lakes of life.

He certainly wouldn't be going down to the Saville Inquiry. 'For one thing, it's all steps up to the public gallery. That's no good for me. And for another thing . . .' He shrugged and went back to serving dinner.

Most of the population of Derry had not been anywhere near the public gallery of the Saville Inquiry. There had been spluttering from Unionist leaders about this . . . They'd used words like ingratitude. Maybe cynicism was more appropriate. There'd been inquiries before and there'd been no squeak of an admission of fault – why would this one be different? Or was it common sense. If, as the guest-house landlady said, the population of Derry was struggling to cope with success, why would they want to look back to the point where the population, on all sides, had abjectly failed?

The Guildhall's rich stained-glass windows had been restored after bomb damage to them in 1972. They told the story of Derry's history in coloured light, making the interior of the red-brick building seem surprisingly bright and cheerful.

'It's such a lovely building,' Sally said as we went up the broad oak staircases.

I'd always seen the Guildhall on the horizon as the landmark of Derry, as we'd driven through to Buncrana. The wide, solid stone bridge we'd crossed had gone. There was a harshly modern double-decker bridge in its place; it looked like a car transporter lorry and felt very precarious to drive across.

'Oh, just look,' Sally said, gathering her coat round her as we gazed down from the Guildhall public gallery. 'It's like Houston mission control.'

The floor of the Guildhall was crammed with people at computer screens. There were banks of recording equipment, cameras, relay equipment; there were giant screens to show enlarged forms of the evidence being examined to the family and public galleries.

'It's cost millions,' Sally whispered. 'When you think that every person down there is some kind of lawyer.'

Dozens of people down there – lawyers, clerks, technicians . . .

A lawyer with the tone of a particularly nasty public school headmaster was cross-examining a man who'd been vaguely in the IRA at the time of Bloody Sunday. The lawyer upped the level of intimidating sneer in his voice; the witness was intimidated.

The witness had admitted he had a stone in his hand when he was at the barricades. Then, when the soldiers started firing, he'd fired at the soldiers.

'You fired? So you had more than a stone?'

'No, I fired the stone.'

'Were the soldiers firing stones?'

'No, they had guns.'

'So did you then, you had a gun, when you fired?'

'No, I had a stone and I threw it.'

'You said fired not threw.'

'I meant I fired the stone.'

'Fire a stone?' the lawyer sneered. 'Surely one fires a gun not a stone.'

'You can fire a gun or a stone in my way of thinking.' The witness had begun to stammer.

'Can you?'

'Yes. I'd say fire a stone.'

'Yes, yes, so you've said,' the lawyer snapped at him, then sat down, a contemptuous expression on his flushed face as if to say, 'Look at these people, they can't even speak English.'

This kind of bullying went on and on. Money and cruel expertise defending the attitude that the people in the Bogside were liars, had always been liars and not one British soldier had done the impossible and panicked in a crowd.

After a tea break we came back to hear a witness on the stand talking about Ivan Cooper, which felt a bit odd. The witness was an IRA man who'd been subpoenaed to appear and granted immunity from prosecution. A surprise addition to the witness list, he was the man who'd actually been in charge of the IRA at the time of Bloody Sunday – everyone had always thought it was Martin McGuinness. But no, it had been this now quite old man, referred to as PIRA 24. He said he'd ordered the IRA not to carry weapons on that Sunday and they'd moved any weapons they had out of the city, as they expected the soldiers would raid houses after the march.

The public gallery began to fill. Word had got round and a lot of people were curious to see who PIRA 24 was. He was small, skinny and nervy. From further remarks it sounded as though he was too proud to admit that he'd been losing control to tougher elements at the time of Bloody Sunday. This was a key thing I noticed with all the IRA witnesses – they didn't want to admit to doing anything, but didn't want to admit to not being a force to be reckoned with since way back when.

PIRA 24 was also denying a conversation with Ivan Cooper in which Ivan had asked him for assurances. He said he'd warned Ivan that the situation might get out of control, something Ivan had apparently denied.

He was cross-examined about his relationship with Cooper. Of course, they knew each other well. 'Derry's a village,' he said.

More questions about the command structure of the IRA at the time. A lawyer representing Martin McGuinness got to his feet objecting to something that might compromise his client. Heaven forbid Mr McGuinness be distressed by the proceedings in any way. There were discussions about geography, how people couldn't have been in places they'd been said to be . . . I began to wonder if Saville was on medication, he was constantly calm and constantly appeared to be listening carefully to endless repetition and verbal blind alleys.

It wouldn't end in Derry that week. Crates of evidence were going to be taken away and expertly examined for months.

I don't think anyone will ever know who fired the first shot. No one is going to tell the truth, or remember accurately. There was no forensic evidence to show that gunfire had come from the Bogside. There was something dubious

about there being a claim to justifiable panic among the
paratroopers – for one thing, if it had been more than a
couple of soldiers losing their heads, wouldn't more people
have been killed? There were conspiracy theories that the
IRA saw the whole civil rights movement as an opportunity to gain themselves mass support. And they'd manipulated the situation toward violence, to isolate the Catholics
into needing them. But the Catholic civil rights movement
had erupted when vociferous demands for civil rights were
being made all over America and Europe. With Derry being
a 'village' it was easy for a grass-roots movement to spread.
And how would the IRA have manipulated the Protestant
police forces to brutally suppress peaceful demonstrations?

The conspiracy theory running the other way was that
the British government wanted to do something drastic to
end the civil disorder and send the Catholics quaking back
to their slums. They'd already been drastic, beating and
imprisoning the civilian population without trial. Would they
have thought they could get away with just killing people?

There were lots of theories, lots of opinions.

Gerard from my corner shop in London said, 'I was there
at that time. Nobody was even talking about the IRA, they
were an irrelevance, barely functioning at the time. We were
interested in our rights. We were interested in people like
Bernadette Devlin. She was brave. A lot of people took against
her just because she was a wee girl with a big mouth,
Northern Ireland was old-fashioned like that. But she used
words well. We wanted some basic rights and that's what she
was articulate about. You should have seen the house my
family were brought up in, a crumbling, overcrowded slum.
Things were so bad for Catholics that when the American
troops left their bases in Derry after World War Two, people
rushed to live in their old prefab buildings. Things were no

better by the sixties. We were the majority, but the Unionists didn't want us in the city and that meant giving us nothing. That's what we wanted something done about. That's all.'

Under cross-examination, PIRA 24 was becoming increasingly vague and evasive. To me it didn't matter what he'd done; British citizens were shot dead by British soldiers. 'We didn't start it' seemed to be the army's line of defence and it was pretty pathetic. Millions of British tax-payers' money were being spent, my money was being spent, arguing over something that shouldn't have been done, whatever the reason. If soldiers didn't do their job properly, they should have been punished decades ago, not protected in a pantomime of counter-accusation.

What struck me as not decorous about the witnesses – IRA, army, whoever – and their lawyers was that no one on any side was going to say to the poor woman on the steps, 'It was my fault. And I'm really sorry.'

I listened to the inquiry for hours – Sally came and went. She had things to do and people to see about town. As the cross-examination of PIRA 24 was coming to an end, she slipped in beside me with a bag of shopping.

'My wee grandchildren's school usually have their end-of-term concerts in this room,' she whispered, as she settled herself to keep me company again. 'Up there on the stage where the recording equipment is. It'll be nice when all this is over and we can have the Guildhall back to ourselves.'

12. The Men of Crossmaglen

It was a card-playing night for Uncle Joe and Aunt Helen.

'Have fun,' I said, as they went out, shortly after ten at night.

'Whether it's fun or not is immaterial,' my uncle said. 'It's our work and it has to be done.'

I don't know how they managed this work, this night shift. Aunt Helen had been childminding and baking at Veronica's all day. Uncle Joe had played golf, visited a sick friend, been to a credit union meeting and had a long hour discussing credit unions and the state of the world with his niece.

Uncle Joe believed that a little bit of thrift went a long way. He felt that, culturally, Catholics hadn't been encouraged to aim high or have confidence in themselves as entrepreneurs. But building savings and a small line of credit enabled people with small means to make small steps forward.

'It's not master of the universe stuff, but credit unions handle money in language people not accustomed to organizing money understand.'

He had always encouraged people to join and was a long-trusted founder member of his local branch.

Credit unions were simple financial co-operatives, owned and controlled by the members. The credit union movement was believed to have started in Lancashire in the nineteenth century. Usually they were formed by people who worked together, were in the same church or lived in a small community. Uncle Joe's was a community credit union.

People saved their money in a credit union and could take out loans at reasonable rates. The main difference between a credit union and a bank was that these organizations were non-profit-making. They were made up of people who knew each other, or could give references for each other. There were forms to fill in, but the union members would know the person as well as the bald facts on the form.

'When you look at the old ledgers you see why a credit union's needed. My favourite was an old boy who'd written under the question "How long employed?" "Since birth".'

Credit union members would know how well educated someone was, would have heard that someone had been ill, or would understand that someone had fallen behind on repayments because they had been recently bereaved. Modern banks, with all the boxes to be ticked before they'd make a loan, particularly didn't understand rural life. Credit unions didn't expect borrowers to fit a computer profile.

'Another favourite of mine was a man who applied for "money to buy calf". And then you see a couple of weeks later that he hadn't quite thought the investment through, because he applies for "money to buy hay for calf".'

Uncle Joe said the difficulty with credit unions was gauging the right size for them to be. If they were too small, there wasn't enough money in the pot. If they were too large, they became unmanageable and faceless.

'But it's not just me and my pals with a drawer full of used fivers, you understand. All the money is kept in a bank and we're properly insured.'

Even in the bad years of the Troubles they'd only had one robbery. Suspected to be a gang of Loyalist youths who knew a local man had just sold his lorry and would be making a deposit. They stole the money from the office before it went over to the bank.

'Luckily the sensible woman in the office at the time just handed over, said goodbye and locked the door behind them as they left.'

Generally, among all levels of paramilitary groups and sectarian gangs, it was considered beneath contempt to rob a credit union. The bank yes, but never the credit union, even in the worst of times.

The worst of times around Portadown were in the eighties, years when my uncle thought all sanity had gone and life might become impossible for his family.

'That was when they started a seemingly indiscriminate killing of Catholics. I thought about leaving then, sort of thought about it. I'd always have the cars outside at night with their tanks at least half full, just in case. And we had money saved in a Southern bank. It was there because we were thinking of buying a place in Donegal anyway, but it was there for an emergency too. But we survived. It's still dangerous for the young ones, but no one's coming after an old bugger like me now. I've always kept to my ways, going out and about whatever time of night I felt like it, but at least now my friends and associates aren't all to be found shut in with a baseball bat behind the door when I come calling at some perfectly reasonable hour, like midnight.'

I wasn't planning to succumb to the household ways and be roaming around the countryside after midnight, but my cousin Paul arrived home for the weekend and took me out to a very raucous pub.

'We'll only stay here a while, because the crowd gets younger later and it'll get too loud to talk.'

Paul was always considered a quiet one in the family but when he did talk, he usually made the funniest or cleverest remark of the night. He had some kind of career to do with higher mathematics and computers, so complicated you needed to be as clever as he was to understand even the job description. It took him all over the world, but luckily for me he was home. He'd walked in the door with fistfuls of broadsheet newspapers that looked as though he'd devoured them. It wasn't just at maths he was clever; he'd absorb information from newspapers and life around him, distil it and give you an insight on the world you couldn't have arrived at in a thousand years of thinking.

Our next stop was at some friends of his who lived in the Garvaghy Road, the beleaguered Catholic area of Portadown. His friends didn't seem too beleaguered, more concerned that Paul had brought enough beer with him. We started talking about my return to my roots. His friend Brendan said, 'I'd a mate over from Australia last year, he was talking to my grandad about his family name and how he thought his ancestors came from this part of Ireland. "Ancestors?" my grandad said. "People round here are fuckin' grateful if they know who their da is."'

There were long arrangements to be made about a trip to see Liverpool play at home, then we were off again. In the taxi, Paul was getting a string of text messages from a girlfriend.

'I think I messed this up with a phone call I made the other night on my way back from the pub. They should put a warning on mobile phones for people like me: "Don't drink and dial".'

We went over to visit Cousin Veronica and John. I'd no idea what time it was by this stage, their children, the under-cousins, were all in bed, and I envied them. I was teased for being tired and startled out of a near doze by Veronica's shrieking disbelief that she had a cousin who'd never seen a Gaelic football match.

'You just have to go,' Paul said, 'or you'll never under-stand half your conversations with this family.'

Not all the family.

'I'm very disappointed in you,' Mikey said as Paul, Veronica, Jack and Jack's friend Dermot and I set off the next day. 'I thought, at last, someone who won't want to talk about football. But . . .' He shook his head and kicked at the ground in a non-sporting fashion.

'I have to see a match, Mikey. I won't necessarily start talking about it.'

'You will,' he said. 'They've pulled you into their evil cult.'

'Do your homework,' Veronica told him.

He slouched out of view in the way only a fifteen-year-old can slouch.

'You wouldn't believe this car was nearly new,' Veronica complained as we drove down the lane from their long, low house. The size of people's houses in rural Northern Ireland was phenomenal. Quite often people built their own houses, chipping in their labour to help a friendly builder. Once, financial necessity drove this, but these days it was more often simply how people chose to spend their money. Home and family were important – the family might not turn out how you wanted, but at least the house could come close to your dreams.

Cars were another important thing to spend money on. I saw more new cars on the road than there were in the fanciest streets of London – maybe fancy London had less to prove.

Veronica's nearly new car had suffered already because they lived among John's farming relatives: 'The old farmers just see a new car and think, "That looks roomy, I could get a sheep in that."'

'Tell her about the old car,' Jack piped up.

'Oh, we had an old thing that would have lasted out the year with normal use, but John's uncle flagged him down and said, "Quick, there's three maggoty sheep in the field." You probably don't know this, but if you've got a sheep with maggot you have to rush it back to the farm for dipping. So John and the uncle shoved the three sheep in the boot, with their heads looking out at the road behind. John and the uncle fell into some deep conversation, probably about the price of sheep, and next thing John looks in the rear-view mirror – no sheep. They thought they must have jumped out, but when he stopped, he saw there was no boot in the car. The weight of the sheep on the rusty boot floor had made it drop right out. They turned back, thinking the sheep would have no more maggot problem because they'd be decapitated, but there they were. Sitting in the road on the floor of the boot.' She sighed. 'So when we got this car, I said to John, no sheep, no hay, no nothing – this is a car for family only. The evening I brought it back, I was so pleased, you know, "Look at my shiny new car." Well, I don't know if he was looking out the window with binoculars, or if he'd planted a bug in our kitchen, because next thing, the uncle was there at the door saying, "Veronica, lend me the keys, I've a lamb has to be picked up." Three hours later, he brought the car back, filthy, with a dent in the side and a cracked wing mirror.'

Jack tutted. 'Mum, you should have said no.'

'And have him talk about me the way he'd talk about me? I'd rather end up walking.'

'The problem of geriatric joy-riding in rural Ireland,' Paul said. 'Be sure and put that in the book.'

'Vandalism by sheep,' Jack said.

We slowed down to pass a group of men at the side of the winding road.

'There's something you'll only see round here,' Veronica said. 'Road bowls.'

Road bowls was pretty self-explanatory. Players had to get a twenty-eight ounce iron ball along a couple of miles of bendy country road in as few shots as possible.

'What happens if they hit a car?'

'Do you see many cars?' Jack asked.

'Hitting a car, or a person, to give you a good angle round a bend is probably OK,' Paul said.

'There's a skill to it,' Veronica said, waving to the men. 'You have to know to throw short just before a corner and there's a special cornering technique of getting a spin on it. There's some sort of rule about staying in the road boundaries but not much else. The main point of it is betting. They bet hundreds on it.'

It looked like a very pleasant way to spend a Sunday.

Road bowls was hundreds of years old. It used to be played in the north of England and all over Ireland. Now, outside of Armagh, the only other place the game was played was Cork. It had completely died out in England – except in Essex, where Irish workers at Ford had reintroduced the game.

The hills down through South Armagh were pretty, rocky and occasionally flashed with yellow gorse bushes. We were going to see Armagh play at home in Crossmaglen. There was no question of me taking an interest in any other team.

'Tyrone have been doing quite well,' Paul explained, 'but they're said to play a very skilful game, which to Armagh means they play like a bunch of jessies. Whereas Armagh . . .' He grimaced. 'They play a sort of Rollerball-style game.'

'They play a very physical game,' Veronica corrected him. 'If that Tyrone player had his groin in front of someone's fist last week, why wasn't he looking where he was going?'

Gaelic football was an amateur game. A star player would be back at work on Monday and did his training in his spare time. If there was a long period of training, say before the championships, they'd take it out of their own holidays. Costs of strip and travel were met by the fund-raising activities of club supporters. As players had to come from the county they played for, most people supporting them knew them, so involvement was intensely personal. Especially for Veronica and John, who spent a lot of time organizing community games. John had trained many championship players as juniors.

'It's not like soccer,' Veronica said. 'It's a real family thing. Both sets of supporters mix in the stand. People always take their kids, even if they're a nuisance. Do you remember, Jack, when you were a nuisance?'

Jack sighed heavily. 'She always goes on about this. I was five.'

'I'd thought he was right by me but I realized as I took my seat in the stands he wasn't there. I couldn't see him. A man beside me asked what was wrong and I said my child had gone missing. Within minutes the word went all round the stands that a child was missing. The match was due to start but an announcement was made – they wouldn't start until a missing child had been found. Regardless that this was a really big important match . . . A few minutes later a couple of Armagh players brought Jack out – he'd darted off and found his way in to talk to the players. So that's the kind of community atmosphere you get. Mind you, there's another part to the tale. A month later, I was organizing a minibus trip of kids to go to a match in another part of the country. One of the fathers turned out to be the man who'd been in the stand next to me. He said, "So it's you taking charge of my son on this trip. Tell me, can I be sure you'll not lose him?"'

'I was five then,' Jack reiterated. 'She always has to go on about that story.'

Crossmaglen had a large market square – trading had been the town's mainstay in the late nineteenth and early twentieth century. Horse-trading and agricultural markets still went on, but the reputation of Crossmaglen as the heart of IRA country had overshadowed the earlier reputation men of the town had for being astute dealers. There were songs about the 'Dalin Men of Crossmaglen', who not only traded livestock, grain and animal feed, but also second-hand clothes and exotic goods, such as citrus fruit, that they'd buy up on trips to England. They'd work in England for a while to get a stake, then return to Crossmaglen with whatever they'd spotted as missing in the marketplace.

Another faded reputation was for linen thread lace-making. In 1895 a Miss Harris, who sounded like a friend of Miss Bamford, had opened an agency to sell lace and a school to teach local girls the craft. The lace was sold to stores in London, Belfast and Dublin, and by 1930, over 200 local girls made their living making lace. Then the genteel cottage industry started by Miss Harris was taken over by a large firm in nearby Cullaville. This firm didn't pay the workers in cash; they paid with a ticket, usable only in the company shop for groceries, hardware and drapery. Some of the lacemakers rebelled and traded independently with city stores or dressmakers, but by World War Two, lace-making had almost vanished from Crossmaglen.

Tricolours, signs on lampposts saying 'Brits Out' or just 'IRA' told you that lace-making was unlikely to make a comeback as the town's preoccupation in the near future. There were boards outside churches with a Roll of Honour – lists of names of Volunteers who'd died in the Troubles.

It was disturbing to see the number of people from the IRA alone who'd been killed in South Armagh.

We deliberated outside a shop selling Gaelic football shirts. Jack and Dermot collected the shirts from all teams and there was a shirt in the shop window from some team that neither of them had.

'But the shop's shut, so there's a tragedy,' Veronica said.

Conversation turned to their new collecting craze, soccer shirts. Veronica teased them all the way up to the grounds for supporting Manchester United.

'You'll grow out of it,' she told them.

'I don't know anything about soccer,' I said, 'but even I know only girls support Manchester United.'

Jack looked hurt for a moment then said sombrely, 'Well, like you said, you don't know anything.'

Passing into the ground through turnstiles, we could choose to pay in euros or sterling; this close to the border either would do.

We positioned ourselves well, just under the shelter of the centre field stand. The stands held about 200 people, waving and greeting – all the Armagh supporters knew each other. The Armagh supporters mingled cheerfully with the blue-shirted supporters of Laois. There were probably more women and children present than men.

'Laois is a small county,' Veronica said, 'so they're a bit disadvantaged in their choice of players.'

Paul said Laois, pronounced Leesh, had originally been named Queen's County in honour of Mary Tudor and was renamed in 1922.

'So their team supporters could shout for the Queen's but they tend not to.'

'Why not?' Jack wanted to know.

'That'll teach you,' Veronica said to Paul, who suddenly needed to go and buy us all coffee and sweets.

It was a cold day, misty. Behind the grounds were some bleak-looking houses with cameras mounted on top. Behind them, a horizon of mountains hung with low grey clouds. Slapped up beside the ground was a massive, dark-green, steel-clad army post with a high observation tower. It was the kind of grim presence I'd forgotten about feeling in Northern Ireland. But in Crossmaglen there it still was, the dark weight of the war.

Beneath the observation tower, the football supporters went about their business, buying sweets and coffee and hoping the rain wouldn't come off the hills at a slant because they hadn't got their kids far enough back in the covered stand.

'Ask me anything you don't know,' Jack said.

'Have you not been to a football match before?' Dermot looked awed such ignorance could exist.

'She lives in London,' Jack said.

Dermot looked even more awed. 'Are you English?'

'I was born here,' I said, not wanting the child to associate me with all the dark metal beside us.

'She's my mum's cousin,' Jack said impatiently. 'She's writing a book.'

'A book about football?' Dermot asked hopefully.

Jack laughed. 'That would be a short book. No. She's writing about everything interesting.'

Dermot nodded, as if he knew exactly what this meant.

Paul came back and pointed to the dark cloudy mountains. 'Doesn't it feel like the start of a film about the Troubles? You know, some kind of sectarian thriller. It gets more like that. Just before the match starts, the people stand

and sing the "Soldier's Song", under the shadow of the big army post. What you'll miss is the shot of the army helicopters hovering ominously over the mountains in the mist but you'll get the feel of it.'

It was a weird feeling. I straggled as we all stood to sing, I sort of knew the tune but . . . Some people seemed to know some of the words, but an old woman behind me belted out every syllable of every verse. Most people put their hands on their hearts. The voices drifted up towards the army observation towers, as they must have done for decades, more melancholic than defiant.

> . . . out yonder waits the Saxon foe,
> So chant a soldier's song,
> Soldiers are we
> Whose lives are pledged to Ireland . . .

The clouds rolled lower on the mountains, darker. I felt a well of emotion, realized how easy it would be to hand your life over to these moments of fellow feeling. If you were lonely, unemployed, unhappy . . . Surrounded by people telling you that the way to be part of it was to be part of it. The romantic sadness of dying for your country had welcoming comfort.

But for me it was an emotional moment that passed. I'd had the same feeling at rock concerts and funerals.

Gaelic football was very fast, very exciting to watch. It was most like Aussie rules football, or like rugby without all the hold-ups of the scrum − and the players tended to be less bashed to ugliness. They were young and tall. They wore black leather gloves to protect their hands when passing, which made them look very cool. Otherwise it was the usual sort of game − running up and down, touching down or kicking goals. I could see Armagh were going to win it, but Laois were just good enough to make it interesting. When Laois looked like getting a bit too interesting, Armagh became more physical. Right in front of me, just out of the linesman's eyeline, an Armagh player punched an opponent who thought he might run after the ball – wallop in the face. Then on the far side, an elbow to the stomach. It was carnage. One in ten incidents of 'physical play' were apprehended, no one was sent off, and I was the only person in the stands gasping.

'They're stricter when it gets nearer the championship,' Paul said. 'But at this level they just get on with it. People like to see a manly game.'

I didn't think I'd start wanting to play, but I was surprised how much I enjoyed the match. It just kept going, none of the stopping and starting involved in soccer. Possibly because of the loose attitude to punching.

Armagh won but Laois had put up a respectable show. We all filed out satisfied. We thought we'd lost a child, but Jack knew Dermot well and tracked him down at a hamburger stall.

I told Paul he'd been right about the atmospheric moment at the start of the match, it felt emotional and it felt like I'd lived through it before in some film.

'What they don't tell you is how much money the army pay to be there. Armagh's training field was where they have that fortress thing. The club took them to court wanting them out of there. To try and keep the peace in the meantime, the army make a massive compensation payment to the club. They don't call it rent, but that's what it is really. It's a legal dispute that neither side will settle. So Armagh are the best-funded club in the league.'

'She's not claiming she saw punching again, is she?'

Veronica asked, catching up to us. 'She doesn't understand the game, she doesn't know what she saw.'

'We're talking politics,' Paul said.

'Stop when you get in my car,' Veronica said. 'I don't want to hear it.'

'Compensation,' Paul continued, 'that's big money here. People injured, house damaged, car blown up. They can get criminal compensation and things like that. There's people all over the country got money out of the army for posts on their land, vehicles passing over their land scaring the livestock . . . Northern Ireland is full of lawyers now.'

Veronica made an exaggerated yawn. 'Oh, Paul, tell her about something else.'

'Look,' Jack said, 'a Chinese restaurant.'

'A Chinese restaurant in Crossmaglen,' Veronica said. 'Now there's progress.'

Back at my uncle and aunt's, progress was being made on my aunt's long-expressed wish to have the front room re-decorated. A man was in measuring things, one of many friends of the family.

'There was a time I'd have done this kind of thing myself,' my uncle said. 'But the old ticker might not stand it. And if I'm to die before my time, I'd prefer it to be in a nobler cause than wallpapering.'

He was sent away to read. My aunt did what she liked to do, find out if people had something to tell you that you wouldn't have expected.

'My niece is visiting here,' she said to the papering man. 'What would you think would be interesting for her to see?'

'Interesting? She should go to the South.'

'You don't think there's anything in the North?'

'Fermanagh. People go to Fermanagh and look at the lakes.'

'What about round here, though?'

'There's nothing round here. Only work.'

People did work hard, and had done for centuries. One of the things to see around Northern Ireland was stately homes, dozens of grand houses built by people who'd arrived to put the Irish to work with varying degrees of kindness. February wasn't the season for viewing these manor houses, castles and fine abodes, mostly run by the National Trust these days and closed over winter. I was slightly relieved, as there was only so much of furniture and oil paintings I could find riveting.

A project to set the Irish to work with a degree of kindness was the mill village of Bessbrook, founded in 1845 by John Grubb Richardson, a Quaker linen manufacturer.

The village was built around two greens, the houses all matched – black and white with slate roofs. The village had schools, shops, a dispensary – but no pub and no pawnshop, these being considered undesirable by the Quaker landlord. One of the first model villages, Bessbrook was the inspiration for the Cadbury Garden Village near Birmingham.

'They all have peculiar latches on their doors,' Uncle Joe told me. 'So I noticed when I went up there canvassing for the Alliance party. I never knocked on a door that had the same type of fixings. They'd all designed their own, with some bit of metal from the mill; animals, names, faces, mythological beasts, all manner of outlandish imaginings of door fixings.'

The Alliance party that had led him to encounter these outlandish imaginings of door fixings had become a fairly enfeebled movement. Founded with the main aim of making politics without sectarianism, they'd attracted their greatest following when violence was at its height, people drawn to their message of communication and an end to bloodshed.

'One of the main reasons I'd say the Alliance faded was that we knew we were against sectarianism, but what the rest of our politics should be we never really agreed on.'

I thought he was being hard on the party he'd worked for, because none of the parties who now had power seemed to do anything that wasn't about sectarianism – whether trying to end it or continue it. And the Alliance didn't have the power to stop violence – because they were never responsible for creating it.

The founder of Bessbrook decided it would have no police station, as the community would be so contented it would have no crime. This was a fine ideal when there was work at the mill and religion was just about God. When the Bessbrook mill closed, men of the town travelled by minibus to work in Kingsmills. This was at the time when Loyalist murder squads were picking off Catholics they considered political. The IRA wanted to take some striking revenge to stop the killings. They halted the Bessbrook minibus and asked the ten Protestants from Bessbrook if there was a Catholic on the bus. The workers thought the hooded gunmen were Loyalists and said there was no Catholic. The gunmen insisted they'd heard there was a Catholic on the bus. The Protestant workers wouldn't give him up. The gunmen said in that case they'd kill everyone. Thinking he was saving his passengers, the driver admitted he was a Catholic. The gunmen pulled him to one side and shot all the Protestant workers.

Decades on, Bessbrook was as pretty as a postcard but felt tense. Walking into a shop, I had the feeling you get when you're staying with friends and you walk into a room, everyone stops talking, and you just know a massive argument's been going on. You're a guest, so everyone makes polite conversation – or in my case showed me the road I needed to get out of town – but you know there's something . . .

'Of course you're lost,' a woman in the shop told me. 'People take down signposts, or turn them around.'

'Why do they do that?'

'Oh, all part of it, you know, the carry-on.'

I sensed the people in the shop relax when I left; they didn't like to see people they didn't know.

I drove over to Keady, where there was supposed to be an old mill and information centre about the linen industry. I found a solid red-brick building with a huge water wheel attached to it. In one part of the building there was a restaurant. Round the other side there was construction work going on.

I asked one of the half-dozen workmen, 'Is there an old mill information centre round here?'

All six stopped work and looked at me. With slow amusement, the nearest said, 'You know, I think that's what we're building.'

'There,' his sidekick grinned at me, 'you wanted information and now you have it.'

The signposting problem made it hard to find my next place of interest, Scarva. This may have been because of the 'carry-on', or because I was getting blinded by a sudden snow blizzard.

Scarva was, eventually, small, quaint and quiet. In Scarva on the 12th of July each year there was a famous sham fight between King James and King William, with everyone dressed up in costumes of the day. King Billy wins, King James runs away, everyone takes off their costumes until next year and has a nice cup of tea. It should have been a silly

Sealed Knot type of day out, if the events re-enacted weren't making people kill each other hundreds of years later.

In a small park, Scarva had a recently garlanded First World War memorial. Around 15,000 Northern Irish Protestants died in World War One. Five thousand were killed or wounded on the first day of July 1916, at Thiepval Wood. Commemorations coincided with the marching season and were a more touching reminder of what Protestants loyal to Britain felt than commemorations of King Billy. These men had died for Britain, in living memory, a long way from home.

At least as many Catholics, mostly from the South, died in the First World War, but memory of them became unfashionable with the rise of Irish nationalism. The Protestants were always proud of what they did. In such a small country, those thousands dead meant there were few Protestant families who didn't lose someone for Britain.

In World War Two, Southern Ireland was neutral, although thousands of men from there joined up to fight Nazism. Twenty-three thousand recruits joined from the North, Protestant and Catholic. In 1941 Belfast was heavily bombed – on the 15th of April, 745 people were killed in German raids on Belfast in one night. On the 4th of May 1941, over 3,000 homes were destroyed and the shipyards were devastated by an incendiary attack. The bombing went on; the city had no air-raid shelters, citizens fled to the countryside. My father was evacuated to Tipperary, after a German bomb exploded at the end of his street. Northern Ireland went through what the rest of Britain went through.

Uncle Joe said to me, 'When you see Protestants at a Remembrance Day ceremony you feel very moved. You see them differently. Hurt and betrayed all the time. They didn't get a country as a compensation for falling out with the

English; they didn't fall out with the English but get treated like a nuisance and old stick–in–the–muds while the Shinners are suddenly the darling boys of Westminster.'

Their loyalty had been kicked in the teeth by the English for hundreds of years. It baffled me. 'I don't get them. Why can't they just accept that they're Irish? I don't get why they don't hate the English more than anyone.'

'Ah, a lot of them do now. That makes them all the more stubborn that they're not going to bugger off into the sunset with Gerry Adams. But there's nothing fashionable about them, and there's no glory here for Blair that lies in their direction.'

I realized wishing the Protestants would just give over and get on with being Irish wasn't about me going to Crossmaglen and finding I was a Republican at heart – it was a typically contemporary English point of view. I'd come to Northern Ireland to find my roots and discovered I was Tony Blair, which was more than disconcerting.

13. Proud to Be a Prod

'Is that the price of a pen? That can't be right. No one has bought a pen for a while, I didn't realize they'd gone up to that price.' The lady with very bottle-blonde hair stared at the biro I'd handed her. 'Twenty pence? I'd think ten pence for an ordinary old biro like that, wouldn't you, dear? I'd charge you ten but it's my son's shop and I suppose he knows what he's doing.'

Overpriced or not, the small, old-fashioned shops of Sandy Row seemed to sell everything – furniture, sewing machines, home-made bread – and there was a shop selling flutes, books about flutes, flute lesson books, flute carrying cases . . . I pushed the door, but a man walking past said, 'He's closed the week, dear. A family crisis.'

I wandered around a bit more, delaying getting back to my hotel room with the biro, which would mean I was in for the night and writing. Maybe there was something else I needed to buy . . . No, I had my new pen and had to get to work with it. I really meant to . . . Then I discovered a latch on my hotel window was broken and I could distract myself doing something that must have become almost illegal in modern hotels – fling the window right open.

In a city of harsh-worded graffiti and stern murals, I was surprised by the graffiti I could see if I took a good lean out of my window: 'Happy 40th Joyce from all off the family'.

Perhaps if pens were still only ten pence, people in Sandy Row would spell better.

If I leant right out of the window and craned my neck, I could see the more typical slogan 'You Are Now Entering Loyalist Sandy Row'. I could also see the Napoleon face of Cave Hill, the Boyne Bridge and the exotic pagoda roof of the Whitehall Tobacco Factory.

I knew tobacco had been one of Belfast's boom industries in the nineteenth century, and thought it would be gone now, along with the shipyards that built the *Titanic*. But the sweet tobacco smell wafting from the factory contradicted heavily bolted doors and shuttered windows.

I had to go out again to investigate.

In Belfast, buildings that looked closed could be merely guarding against breakage. Whitehall's had 170 windows shattered when a bomb exploded in the nearby Europa hotel, but otherwise they'd kept a low profile and only lost two days' production to the Troubles, quietly continuing a successful trade.

In 1810, brothers George and John Murray had a small grocery store down near the Belfast docks. Their most frequent customers were sailors buying tobacco. The brothers decided they wouldn't make their fortune in the shop, but they might in tobacco. They built up a tobacco business, finally creating a best-seller in 1862, with Murray's Mellow Mixture. Pipe-smokers were a conservative crowd, so introducing a product that caused brand-switching was a real triumph.

In the twentieth century the company's best-sellers were the range of Erinmore mixes. The main Erinmore mix had a blend so secret only one senior person in the company knew the recipe. New tobaccos were being created all the time. Experiments had been made with exotic curry flavourings, or fruits, like kiwi and lychee. One of the company's professed aims in the present anti-smoking climate was to create tobaccos that weren't unpleasant to the non-smoker; chemists worked away to create what the company press officer called 'wife-friendly aromas'.

The factory smelt friendly to me and had the endearing, wayward eccentricity that seemed to go with pipe-smoking. The building had its pagoda-style roofing, amid square castle turrets, with flashes of gold mosaic and patterned brickwork on the exterior walls. I've always thought cigarettes were just something to smoke, but a pipe was a sign of character – and a hobby. There was all the tapping out of the bowl to do, the cleaning and scraping with special tools. Then there was the decision to be made about what kind of pipe – short, long, straight, curved. There were the different kinds of fancy woods to choose from, the scents and textures of different tobaccos . . . Never mind wife-friendly aromas, I was starting to consider smoking a pipe myself. Wasn't it time chic handbag pipes for ladies were investigated? Long thin ones for the evening, bright coloured ones for the beach . . . There was something about the manly atmosphere of Murray's factory that told me, despite only losing two days' production to the Troubles, they'd rather burn their premises to the ground than hear my schemes for the 'lady pipe'.

Staying on the edge of Sandy Row seemed a good idea, because I wanted to make a better attempt to understand the parts of the population that were, as the nuns at my school used to dismissively call every other religion, non-Catholic.

The big blank chain hotel was surprisingly cheap, this close to central Belfast. The cement seemed barely dry, it smelt of drains, but there was a very welcoming, red-faced, sweat-drenched man roaming the corridors with a trolley; he seemed to keep the hundreds of rooms spotlessly clean all by himself. His helpfulness made me feel as though I was in a little family-run B & B, without that awkward sensation of being in someone else's house.

I didn't understand why the cheap hotel was even cheaper at the weekend – until the weekend came.

Belfast had a young population, and after dark, a blast of night clubs throbbed around the city. Dublin might have established itself as one of Europe's party cities, but much cheaper Belfast was catching up. Stag and hen parties travelled from the South of Ireland, flew in from Liverpool, Essex, Manchester, Newcastle . . . Teenagers who looked barely old enough to leave school left their homes to get completely plastered in Belfast.

My hotel filled with girls in nine-inch heels and two-inch clothes, clanking up to their rooms with bottles of vodka, Bacardi . . . I could hear them through the walls shouting, 'Come on, Cerise, let's get bladdered and then meet the others downstairs for a drink!'

Girls like Cerise and friends teetered around the streets, holding on to each other, leaning against walls, shrieking, waving blown-up condoms, and there always seemed to be one at the heart of the pack in a bridal veil, vomiting in a gutter. Still, it was fun for them and all new income for Belfast . . .

I took a less philosophical view of them when they came screaming back to the hotel at five in the morning, accompanied by some boys who kept shouting that they were from Manchester, in case all of Ireland hadn't heard them the first time . . . It took them an hour to realize the girls had no interest in anything but shrieking giggles about how many bruises they'd acquired falling over at various locations in Belfast. The boys then abandoned making heavy hints about sex and were happy to shout about the more important matter of how much they'd had to drink themselves. Finally, the boys left, the girls crashed about in the bathroom, screamed a receding chorus and went silent. Possibly they'd all died on the bathroom floor. I didn't care.

Don't think I didn't take my revenge on them. I got up at a quarter to seven, put the television on as loud as it would go, sang, showered like a rowdy herd of bison and slammed my door behind me.

I'd had an interesting night out myself. Mine had probably not damaged my liver in any way but it had spun my head around.

Very conveniently for me, a play called *Protestants* was having its opening night a few hundred yards down the road.

The play was directed by a young Catholic woman, married to a Protestant. She'd wanted to go back to the simple core of Protestant belief, hoping to understand Protestant identity in a way that reached way beyond the small, distorting confines of Northern Ireland. The director already had a West End transfer with a play about snooker player Alex Higgins; troubling herself with Protestant theology wasn't something she was doing to make her name. As she said in the after-show discussion, 'I could have done the play about Protestants that everyone would have expected to come out of Northern Ireland and had a controversial hit − but that would have been so lazy, and everyone in the audience would go out feeling they'd got exactly what they expected and could have written it themselves. You know the play I mean, you can see it in your heads now.'

A lone actor played a range of characters; a Catholic-hating Glasgow football hooligan, a Cromwellian soldier from Cork, an American snake-charming fundamentalist . . . Somewhere in all this was a Protestant from Armagh, remembering his grandfather's preparations for the Orange parades, tending his garden and wondering what his heritage was, beyond the carefully brushed bowler and lovingly ironed orange sash.

All these types had a clever tilt to their character that made me understand, if only for a moment, their point of view. The tilts also gave them resonance. That Cromwell's loyal soldier was Irish took the story of Cromwell's massacres away from the familiar 'look what the bad English did to Ireland'. And reminded of constant internal betrayals in Ireland, convoluted contradictions . . .

At the core of the play was Martin Luther himself, seeking a simple loving relationship between man and God – without wealth, hierarchy or politics to intervene in this spiritual relationship. Luther concluded that each person had a responsibility to create this relationship for themselves, protesting against anything they felt corrupted it – responsible for this relationship in how they thought, lived and prayed. True Protestantism was a very grown-up religion.

Most of the mesmerized audience stayed for the opening-night discussion. Among invited guests was the Moderator of the Presbyterian Church of Northern Ireland, an elderly bearded man, who professed himself baffled for a while by the play's abstract structure and that he'd been very 'put off by the f'ing and blinding' but he conceded: 'In the end I saw what you were getting at, although to my mind you could have got at it by a more straightforward route. The Glasgow hooligan talks of a culture of "every man for himself", there is that danger in our religion. Individualism can be seen as a licence for anarchy. There still have to be structures – family, moral responsibility. Luther was saying man's relationship with God is individual, but not presumptuously self-indulgent. And the play reminded us of how much, in this province, frippery and unnecessary trappings of so-called tradition have been attached to what is a simple religion.'

A young man at the back, with trendy hair and what looked like very expensive designer clothes, put his hand up to speak and beamed when it was his turn. 'I have to say the play made me proud to be a Prod. And I'm a Catholic.'

Much laughter round the room. I agreed with him. Judging Protestantism by the Northern Irish trappings of Loyalist paramilitaries and Unionist belligerence was like judging Catholicism by the Magdalene Sisters and the Vatican bank.

The Catholic proud Prod concluded, 'I liked being made to remember that the word "protest" is in there and a protesting conscience can belong to anyone. I liked the play making me understand something I've always felt excluded from – what on earth it is that most of my neighbours believe in. What they believe is simple and moving, I didn't know that. And it's modern, about seeking God. Seeking for yourself, that's very modern. I didn't know about that.'

I had the same ignorance about Protestantism. However long you've been away, you know you're a Northern Irish Catholic when you hesitate writing the word Protestant, because you think it has a 'd' in it.

A man in front of me asked why there had been no mention of the Bible in the play, as the Bible was such an important part of Protestant worship. The director said, 'I didn't want to put the Bible on stage, as many would feel that was blasphemy.'

The man was then introduced to the audience. A Unionist politician from City Hall. He asked where else the play was going.

'We've had invites from community groups in Protestant areas. We've also had an inquiry from a Catholic community centre in the Ardoyne. If it turns out they really want it up there I think it would be very interesting.'

The Unionist politician then asked, almost rhetorically, why Protestants were so under-represented in the arts.

The director replied, 'I don't know. There are Protestants in the arts, lots of them but they tend to be . . . well, very few of them are Unionists.'

The politician said nothing. There was a mumble from some of the audience, but no one offered a contradiction.

Everyone left in ebullient mood, for different reasons, some feeling vindicated, others, like me, feeling educated.

The play really needed to be compulsory viewing for Catholics who couldn't see the woods for Paisley and Chelsea Headhunters.

There was definitely a shifting mood in Belfast – a Unionist politician had come out to see a play by a wee Catholic girl about his religion. And he'd wanted the audience to know he was there.

His question about the lack of Protestants in the arts was probably one he could have answered himself, if he'd thought further about the history of his religion in the city.

Belfast had put in a bid to be European City of Culture 2008. This would have meant a massive injection of cash into the city; it could have been on the map for a whole new range of reasons. Being City of Culture changed Glasgow completely – or certainly changed its reputation. Belfast's bid wasn't even shortlisted. Liverpool won the prize – so it almost went to an Irish city.

The remnant of the Troubles came quite low on the list of reasons given for the bid's failure. The main reason given was that Belfast had no culture. This provoked fury among Belfast artists, partly because most artistic endeavours were from people of Catholic backgrounds. But for a capital city,

Belfast had very few theatres, concert halls, major art galleries, artistic education establishments . . .

From early on, Belfast culture was dominated by a Protestant way of life that had no time for the arts. Belfast grew up as a port and an industrial city. Making money and praying gratitude to God were the reason things were built in Belfast. And until the latter half of the twentieth century, the Catholics had no say in anything as important as the city's cultural development.

As well as rumblings about the influence of a generalized English racism about Northern Ireland, there were two other things that made the artists of Belfast dissatisfied about the failure of the City of Culture bid; they believed that fear of resurgence of the Troubles had played a larger part than the judges would admit. And they felt Belfast's Unionist Council, without a history of interest in the arts, hadn't pulled many stops out to back the bid.

The Unionists were running the city the way history had made them run it and they hadn't grasped the fact that the arts were a business, attracting business, as much as the grand old trades of linen, tobacco and shipbuilding.

Between 1880 and 1925, one in ten Belfast men worked for the Harland and Wolff shipyards. The value of this business was one of the reasons why Northern Ireland had remained immensely important to Britain. Harland and Wolff became an emblem of Protestant pride and Catholic resentment. Yet the owner, Edward Harland, had begun with a determined anti-discrimination policy. After Protestant workers rioted in protest about Catholic workers coming in from the South in 1864, Harland had threatened to close down the yard and relocate. But by 1872, when rioting broke out again during the Home Rule debates, Harland, now Mayor of Belfast and against Home Rule, gave up on his stand against discrimination, and let the intimidated Catholic workers drift away. Many Catholic ship workers emigrated. Although a handful remained, shipyard jobs tended to be passed on through family connections, so by the twentieth century, Harland and Wolff had a reputation for only employing Protestants.

Indirectly, the shipyards did provide Belfast with some of its more influential Protestant artists, although these artists didn't live in Belfast any more, and certainly hadn't been influencing how the city was run. Van Morrison's father worked at Harland and Wolff. It gave him enough salary to spare to buy the blues and jazz records that he played around the house – not everybody in the shipyards grew up hearing the Old Orange Flute. Those who did, like James Galway, went off round the world and did things with a flute no one in a marching band had ever thought of.

Little by little, through the latter half of the twentieth century, Harland and Wolff closed down. The shipyards went through a long period of neglect, rusting and collapsing. But recently they were being reconsidered, viewed as historical monuments.

Visible from far across Belfast are two giant yellow harbour cranes, nicknamed Samson and Goliath. These had been given a conservation order, to be lovingly oiled and painted, or whatever it was big cranes needed to be kept in a contented old age. Other harbour areas were slated for redevelopment, or had been developed – the massive Odyssey complex, with a concert hall, a Hard Rock Café and bars, had been up and running since the millennium.

One of the waitresses from the Hard Rock Café was on the little boat trip I took round the shipyards, along with a gathering of her relatives from Canada. The chatty guide told us the history of the yards, while urging the boat-driver to get further away from the Sea Cat ferry to Holyhead which was about to set off and swamp us with its wake.

There was still passenger and cargo shipping in Belfast, but this had been moved away from the city centre, since the construction of the Lagan Weir in 1994. This barrier meant the level of water in the city could be controlled to allow for residential development, pleasure boating and the construction of new bridges across the old shipyard complex.

The biggest development plan was for the Titanic Quarter, with housing, shops and a maritime museum. The boat's guide thought it was ridiculous that Belfast of all places had no maritime museum.

'But there's been a lot of time wasted over the last thirty years.'

He pointed out where Queen's University Science Park was being developed in the former shipyards. 'It's appropriate it's there, as the engineering and scientific innovation that went into Belfast's ships was cutting-edge at the time.'

Belfast became a great port in the eighteenth century despite obvious drawbacks: the river Lagan and the Lough weren't deep enough or wide enough for major shipping. Huge engineering works were undertaken to dig out the waterways and the land on which the shipyards began was entirely man-made.

A sailor's grandson, James Pirrie, returned from a brief emigration to Quebec and drove the political machinery of the city into action to keep the harbour growth going and make more provision for shipbuilding. The industry began to struggle toward success.

Harland, who'd worked for the great shipbuilder Robert Stephenson, came over from Newcastle to be manager of the Hicks shipyard in the mid-nineteenth century. He cut wages and pushed men to a higher standard of work – work he inspected personally and minutely. Harland could see the shipyard had enormous potential. He could also see that Hicks' business was failing through bad management.

Harland was connected by marriage to the Schwabes, a family of Hamburg merchants. They were originally Jewish but had converted to Lutheranism. The Schwabes had various shipping interests in London. They were related to Gustav Wolff, a Jewish engineer. Harland took on Wolff as an assistant and head of the drawing office in 1857. By 1858 Harland had bought the yard from Hicks. In 1861, Wolff, bringing considerable family capital with him, was made a partner.

Harland and Wolff made radical changes to ship design and changed business practice. As shipbuilders they put up all the initial costs but would then get a commission on the finished product from the shipping lines. Most major shipping lines became tied in to this circle of obligation to Harland and Wolff, including the White Star Line, which shipped emigrants to America. Entrepreneurial James Pirrie was invited to join the company to help secure these convoluted deals with shipping lines and to give the company political clout.

Three times Harland and Wolff built 'the largest ship in the world'; in 1889 the *Teutonic* at 10,000 tons; in 1899 the *Oceanic* at 17,000 tons; and the ill-fated *Titanic* in 1911, which displaced an unprecedented 76,500 tons.

Pirrie pioneered the idea of ocean liners as floating hotels. Cabinet-making, linen-finishing, glassworks – all these crafts as well as related industries benefited from the need to fit out the liners to the highest standards. He recognized oil as the fuel of the future and had diesel engines manufactured for the company in Glasgow. There were also Harland and Wolff yards in Glasgow. The close ties between Glasgow and Belfast that still exist today were developed through the shipyards. Workers would move from one yard to another depending on where the bulk of the labour was needed.

Eventually, Pirrie was left in control of the company. He was an extravagant, ambitious and very peculiar man. When the *Titanic* sank, Pirrie had already brought Harland and Wolff to the verge of ruin with his bizarre and secretive business practices.

The *Titanic*, intended to compete with Cunard's new large liners the *Lusitania* and the *Mauretania*, had been Pirrie's attempt to reassert his White Star Line's supremacy of the waves. The *Titanic* would be the biggest, most luxurious liner ever constructed. Pirrie had much of the interior modelled to replicate the designs of his own lavish homes in England, where he constantly entertained and courted influential figures of the day. His book-keeping might have been chaotic, but his ambition was ferociously single-minded.

When the *Titanic* was being built, it was considered a lucky ship. Only two workers died building the ship, a statistic well above average in this hazardous line of work. There's no truth in the story that the ship was considered cursed from the start because the hull number 390904, when read backwards with narrowed eyes, could read NO POPE. For a largely Protestant workforce, this would have been seen as a good omen.

According to the standards of the time, there were no design faults in the *Titanic*. Subsequent ship design added more watertight safety features. And these later ships had the advantage of a North Atlantic patrol being set up, to chart the position of icebergs after the *Titanic* disaster.

The *Titanic* didn't have enough lifeboats but it had more than were required by the Board of Trade regulations of the time. There were no crew drills about what to do in the case of a major emergency. The ship took over two hours to sink and people were reported to have remained calm, yet there was massive confusion, with lifeboats leaving near-empty and men refusing to leave until all the women and children were safe. Lifeboats that could have picked up survivors seen in the water didn't go back because escaping passengers were afraid they'd be swamped by the slowly sinking ship. The *Titanic* disaster was worse than it should have been because of incompetence and strange, unnecessary, stubborn courage in some, alongside cowardice in others.

Pirrie had intended to be on board on the maiden voyage of the *Titanic* but was recovering from a prostate operation. One of the other owners, Bruce Ismay, was on board, and survived. Derek Mahon's poem, 'Bruce Ismay's Soliloquy' speculates on the shipbuilder's lonely, guilt-ridden life after the disaster.

Pirrie struggled on, selling off shares in the company. Eventually, he died of pneumonia at sea, in a bid to find new orders for his yard in Argentina. He died on a ship built by another Belfast yard.

Pirrie left no will but massive personal debt and a collection of annual business reports that on examination turned out to be half incomprehensible and half invention. A man who could be cruelly whimsical with employees and wantonly dishonest with associates, he nevertheless was remembered ambivalently. He was also sentimentally generous, charming and inspirational.

Building military ships and mail boats kept the company going after Pirrie's demise. Short's aircraft factory used many of the former shipyard engineers and workers, creating a new source of employment for East Belfast. Although Short's was very successful, it didn't dominate the drive and psyche of the city the way shipbuilding had.

There was a sense our little boat making its tour of the old shipyards was puttering around the remains of a lost city, once inhabited by giants. Huge dock walls and locks soared above us . . . The guide on the boat was telling us Belfast hoped to develop an IT industry to rival the success of this new industry in Southern Ireland.

'But I don't know,' he sighed. 'I've a cousin writes computer programs. Great money, but what is it? Lines of numbers in the air. We used to make great big things everyone could see. All over the world, I guarantee, people would rather be making big things they can see and touch.'

One of the Canadian tourists said they had no shipbuilding these days either. 'It's a shame,' he added. 'It's a job with grandeur.'

'Exactly,' said the guide. 'Exactly.'

The affable boat tour men had plans of the *Titanic* for sale. They were also selling, with authentication certificates, small rectangular wooden boards, made into key rings. Every man who worked at Harland and Wolff had to have a board, a sort of clocking-in card. It had his number on it and if he didn't have it to hand in at the end of the week, he wouldn't get paid. The boatmen had found thousands of these lying on the ground and saved them. 'There were probably thousands more that were ploughed into the ground but we thought they were great, each one of these belonged to a man who worked hard making a bit of Belfast history.'

Shipbuilding and dock work was dangerous and cited as one of the reasons why Belfast developed a high standard in medicine. The guide on our boat tour said more men died building ships than had ever died in the Troubles. Pirrie, as Mayor of Belfast in 1896, started a campaign to build a modern hospital in Belfast. He set up a fund for what was to become the Royal Victoria Hospital, although he eventually funded most of it himself.

★

Panels from the *Britannic*, the *Titanic's* sister ship, decorated the upstairs room of one of Belfast's most famous bars, the Crown Liquor Saloon. The Crown was known for fine Guinness, oysters and fast-moving bowtied barmen. The tiles, stucco and paintings all over the inside almost rivalled the decorations in City Hall.

When I walked past the bar I thought there was a fight going on outside, but the bouncers were trying to stop a very fat, very drunk man from reeling into the traffic.

'I need to get across the road.'

'Not now you don't – will you wait!'

In an exact replica of the Crown bar, James Mason had hidden out in the 1947 film *Odd Man Out.* James Mason's dying IRA man staggered out into the streets to face further fatal torments. The staggering fat man met a better end and was escorted to a pelican crossing by the bouncers, then manoeuvred into a taxi.

'He knows where he lives, get him out of here, will ye, we've no time for this.'

The bouncers went back to their doorway and I continued on my way to a concert being held outside City Hall. This was a massive event on an outdoor stage built across the hall's entrance gates.

People formed orderly queues around the block, people of all ages. A couple in their sixties in front of me said they didn't care who was playing, they simply wanted to enjoy the fact that such a huge public event could happen in Central Belfast with no hint that there'd be disruption.

The PSNI were obviously so confident there'd be no disruption they'd lent a number of their water cannon to the Dublin police. While the concert in Belfast passed off peacefully, Dublin had riots. They were hosting celebrations to welcome new countries to the European Union, but it wasn't going well. The Dublin rioters seemed to be a mixed bag of disaffected youth looking to pass the time, and anti-globalization protesters from all around Britain. An even more depressing element among the protesters were straight-forward local xenophobes objecting to the money that would go to poor Eastern European countries joining the union. Countries in exactly the state of disrepair Eire had been in before they joined Europe.

It felt darkly pleasing that Dublin, for so long Cinderella to Belfast's ugly sister, was having a bad night for a change, while Belfast was quiet and dull. The concert had been given the Father Tedesque name 'A Beautiful Night' – this didn't bode well for the music content. There were some inter-national stars, but there were also choirs of schoolchildren, vaguely famous Northern Irish singers and boy bands from Dublin massacring Van Morrison songs. As a man in his thirties behind me in the crowd said, 'How can they have the nerve to do that in Van's home town?'

I muttered agreement and wondered, 'Why couldn't they get him here?'

The man laughed. 'I expect he looked at who else was on the bill and then heard it was to be called "A Beautiful Night" and told them to f off.'

Despite the disappointing line-up, the crowds ambled home contented to have an enormous outdoor event in the city pass off so gently.

Not so gently, the Manchester revellers in my hotel crashed home around five and began another hour or so of noctur-nal squealing.

The next morning feeling headachy and underslept, I went to a Presbyterian church. My granny and my mother would have been more mortified that I was wearing jeans than by the defection. Just like Catholics, Protestants dressed up for church.

Everything inside was plainer than most Catholic churches – no shiny stuff, no fancy robes, no incense. There was a lot of Bible. There was a cross but slightly rambling sermon.

I forced myself to engage properly and stop mentally fidgeting. I felt no more uncomfortable than I always felt in a church service – likely to do the wrong thing and not quite understanding what I was supposed to feel. At least I wasn't being asked to contemplate the complex notion of transubstantiation – a Catholic service could send my brain into perplexed overload with that one. The Presbyterian service was much more down to earth and straightforward.

I'd never liked the idea that every Catholic was supposed to believe and feel the same things. But in the Protestant service I didn't have any greater sense that it was my individual relationship with the almighty that mattered. I was in a large group of people who were all supposed to feel the same thing about God, morality and using leisure time constructively – the theme of the main sermon, I think. A poor ability to concentrate for over five minutes could be the real root of my problem with organized religion.

Still, at least I had discovered an unbiased inclination to mentally drift and fidget on both sides of the religious divide.

Outside the church I started sneezing and feeling ill. I was sure the damp plaster in my hotel had given me some kind of bronchitis. I had some newly discovered relatives to meet up with and worried that giving them my germs would be a bad way to introduce myself.

I don't know what kind of relatives these were – the children of my grandfather's cousin? Way beyond under-cousins into the outer realms of cousinage.

Mark and Sam were Protestants from Lurgan, living in Omagh and Fermanagh respectively. They were a few years older than me, one was a businessman, one was in show-business – this is how they'd have defined themselves, rather than by religion.

They lived within miles of my Catholic relatives but they didn't know them. These were Caulfields who were barely related to me; how would they know they were related by marriage to the other half of my family? Mark did believe that most people in Northern Ireland were related anyway.

'It's such a small country without much immigration. What's that thing about six degrees of separation? In Northern Ireland you've probably only got the two.'

They thought it was funny I was staying on Sandy Row.

'It was cheap,' I said.

'I can imagine,' Sam said, looking at the concrete tower I'd condemned myself to. 'And I'm sure it wasn't here a fortnight ago.'

We went for a drink in the upstairs bar of the Europa – I have a very forgiving nature.

We talked about how many Caulfields there were, although none of them closely related to our dwindling branch. We plotted to storm and squat Dublin's Municipal Gallery and discussed what we knew of my grandfather. They'd heard there had been some rift between my grandfather and some of their grandparents' generation. They didn't think it was about him marrying a Catholic: 'People had very complicated opinions back then. I heard they didn't like it that he'd joined the British army. Not because it was British, but because it was the army. Their religion would have been against that.'

'And against gambling?'

'Did he gamble?'

'There was a rumour.'

'They wouldn't have liked that. But they were only cousins. How well do you know all your cousins?'

'Some hardly at all. But I have a lot.'

'You see, unless you make the effort it can be very hard to keep track,' Sam said. 'I only met your father a few years ago. I just didn't know he existed before then. But our side of the family must have taken your grandfather back into the fold. He was buried with them.'

'I went down there but there's no headstone.'

'That's the Ebeneezer Tabernacle for you,' Mark laughed. 'But then I was with Presbyterians at school who weren't allowed birthdays. What a nightmare. Imagine. No cake, no presents your whole life.'

I was glad to find my distant Protestant relatives had very comprehensible things in their heads. Whatever falling out there'd been in previous generations because my grandfather had been a soldier, a gambler, married to a Catholic . . . It seemed that was all just ancient strangeness to the three of us.

They didn't talk about the Troubles, or politics, or history in the active, engaged and vociferously interested way my mother's family did.

I wondered if being Protestant, successful and middle-class was almost as good as moving to England for protecting you from the situation.

But towards the end of the evening, talking about what I thought I'd be writing, Mark said wistfully, 'I suppose you'd have a thin book without the politics. I'm so sick of it. There's such beautiful countryside. Do you know anything about fishing? There's great fishing in Northern Ireland. My children live in Scotland now. It has a very similar kind of scenery, so I won't miss that. I see nothing else keeping me here, really.'

★

People were leaving; people were staying. Mrs Khan was definitely staying.

Mrs Khan lived in the Malone Road district of Belfast, a mixed peaceful area for the moneyed of all religions, perhaps a little more Catholic than not. There was supposedly a Malone Road accent I remembered my cousins imitating – a refined pseudo-English accent. The district had very big houses, big gardens and a green wealth of roadside trees.

Mrs Khan's husband was a consultant cardiologist, a typical Malone Road occupation. They'd lived in Belfast for eighteen years and, as she said, 'We live here, our children live here. Where are we going? We're not going anywhere. We live here.'

I'd arrived at Mrs Khan's doorstep sneezing. She'd opened the door and sneezed.

'I am so sorry, if I'd known how to contact you I'd have rearranged our meeting.' She sniffed. 'I have a flu, and I'm not thinking straight. Please come in, I hope I can give you a sensible interview and I hope you won't catch anything.'

My damp plaster chill had turned into a feverish shaky type of proper plague. I sneezed and told her I was already getting flu, so not to worry.

Pretty, small and slight, Mrs Khan nodded as I explained about my book.

'That's good,' she said. 'People always think this is a homogeneous community, just the two religions, but it's not like that.'

She told me that not only had she been in Belfast eighteen years, her children were now professional people working in the city. She ran the Al Nisa organization, a support network for Muslim women in Northern Ireland.

'The Muslim population of Northern Ireland has a small recent percentage of asylum-seekers, mostly we are established and professionals – medical professionals in particular – who have been paying taxes for years, not living on compensation or giros.' She stopped, sneezed and looked at me sharply.

'Do you mind me asking what community you are from?'

'Mixed, brought up in England.'

She nodded, as if making detailed mental notes about that.

'Anyway . . . Yes, the population also has students and business people, people in retail, IT, that kind of thing. The Muslim community has certainly been well established for thirty years, but records go back at least seventy years. My husband has been researching this and thinks the history is longer, sailors, traders – Muslims around and about Northern Ireland for hundreds of years.'

I asked her if she thought the situation had changed recently.

'Yes. Sudden and recent change. A man stopped his car last week. I mean stopped on purpose, backed up in the street and started screaming names at me, telling me to go home. I said, "This is my home!" But I ran into the nearest office block because I didn't know how crazy he was. This wasn't some kid, that's what really disturbed me, it was a middle-aged man.' She had her own accent with occasional words sounding very Northern Irish. 'Usually it's kids. I don't know how they bring them up here. They've been brought up on both sides hearing about their rights all the time. Their rights but not their responsibilities. I have rights too, I have the right to go about my business and no one is going to stop me doing that.'

She spoke of Muslim households suddenly having to live in fear of stones, or petrol bombs through the window. Young men attacked by gangs, women pushed and spat at.

'Where has this come from? This isn't about September

the 11th, this started before that. Getting worse now, but it started in the nineties.'

'Where do you think it's coming from?' I asked her. 'Is it bitter individuals, or . . .'

She cut across determinedly. 'Oh no. It's orchestrated. It's orchestrated for various reasons by different kinds of para-military gangs. It gains them popularity with these bitter indi-viduals you're talking about, but it's orchestrated. Oh dear, all this negative talk. Let me show you something positive.'

She handed me glossy brochures for her women's organ-ization.

'The original idea was for Muslim women not to feel isolated in a new country. To have our own place to meet. To go to organizations like the police and medical services in a positive way and tell them about our way of life. We go into schools with exhibitions about Muslim culture. We're trying to get a better media profile, not just bad news about attacks. I'd like to see our festivals reported, maybe a docu-mentary about the Muslim contribution. We have events with other women's groups to learn about each other. And a lot of what we do is just fun.'

She showed me a long list of classes from Arabic and Qu'ranic classes, to keep fit and car maintenance. There were training courses in fostering, childminding, computers . . . There were group outings to the seaside and historical sites around Northern Ireland.

'If there are no more questions, I have to go now, as we are having one of our social gatherings today and I'm running a bit late. This flu has made me all over the place.'

If she was this tough and together when she felt she was all over the place, I was sorry for the person who crossed her when she was going full strength.

★

Belfast wasn't the only part of Northern Ireland where attitudes to ethnic minorities had changed. In Portadown shops and the town's indoor market had been run by Indian families for decades. There had always been feeble jokes about how no one minded them because they weren't Catholics or Protestants. Most of the Asian families around Portadown had come to Northern Ireland after being expelled from Uganda. They'd chosen Northern Ireland to avoid some of the anti-Ugandan Asian fuss going on in mainland Britain – and because they felt they knew Ireland, having been brought up Catholics, attending Catholic schools run by Irish nuns and priests.

It was their race not their religion that had caused the recent stoning of their shops on Saturday nights, usually by gangs of Loyalist youths.

My mother said she couldn't believe this had started: 'I remember being really shocked when I came to England and heard racist remarks – I was proud we'd had none of that, whatever else was wrong with us, we never had that. There were Chinese and Indians in Northern Ireland long before even the Asians in Portadown. There's Indian families in Derry were there since I was a child. They had shops, clothes shops. I think they started coming over after the Second World War.'

Sally in Derry told me she definitely remembered Indians appearing in the city in the late forties and fifties. 'I remember running out to stare at this Indian man on a bicycle with a big box strapped to it. I'd never seen the like. And they came into the poor, poor areas like the Bogside selling things, which was amazing for a start, but then they were offering to let people buy things at a few pence a week. I'm afraid we used to call them the darkies – you'd put a bit of money aside each week that you had to give to the darkie for something. No one had ever trusted poor Bogside Catholics with credit before. They were a godsend. Now they've shops, their children and their children have grown up here. What else do they have to do to be Northern Irish?'

The Jewish area of Belfast was near Thorndale Avenue, a little further along the Antrim road. This was a very old community. Not only was Wolff, of Harland and Wolff, Jewish, the Mayor of Belfast in 1899, Sir Otto Jaffe, was also Jewish. The Jaffe family first came from Hamburg in the 1840s to trade in linen, and along with several other Jewish families had successfully established themselves in the Belfast linen trade within a decade. The Jaffe family built a synagogue in Great Victoria Street. Fleeing pogroms in Central Europe, more Jews arrived in Belfast and another synagogue was opened by the Jaffe family, near the Antrim Road. During World War Two a children's hostel was opened for orphaned Jewish children in North Belfast. There were over 1,500 Jews living in Northern Ireland after World War Two; now there were less than 200. This community had found itself suddenly under attack. Extreme Loyalists with their 'little Britain' attitudes were suspected of most attacks on ethnic minorities. But in the case of the Jewish community, their attackers were believed to be Republican extremists, expressing their support for Palestine.

Traditionally the Jews had been businessmen, gravitating to the mainstream in society, therefore they'd grown closer to the Protestant community. The Republican identification with the Palestinians and the flying of the Palestinian flag on Republican estates led to some Protestants identifying themselves with Israel and the flag of Israel began flying on Loyalist estates. The Jewish community's spokesman described himself as 'bemused' by this.

The shifts from sectarianism to racism were a sad betrayal

of Belfast's past, the city port that had refused to let slave ships come in. The Protestant community had been very strongly against slavery. The ships weren't allowed in, and many Protestant churches agitated to stop any contact with the trade.

Although Belfast didn't trade slaves, they did trade with slave plantations in the West Indies, provisioning plantations with food and beer, and cheap Belfast linen was used to clothe the slaves. Meat-packing and fish-salting for this export trade became lucrative, with consequent benefits for fishing and agriculture. Belfast's sugar-refining industry was built on imports from slave plantations.

The United Irishmen called for a boycott of sugar products and one of their founders, Thomas Russell, said, 'On every lump of sugar I see a drop of blood.'

Russell's lover, Protestant philanthropist, political activist and feminist Mary Ann McCracken, was a committed abolitionist and constantly tried to rally more commitment to the anti-slavery movement in Belfast.

In 1789 former slave Equiano spoke in Belfast against slavery. He was warmly welcomed, particularly by Quakers and non-conformists. Catholics were suspicious of the anti-slavery movement, mainly because Protestants were so centrally involved. And because the leaders of the Catholic Church were very conservative, particularly those who'd done well for themselves in America, exemplified by John Hughes, the Tyrone-born Bishop of New York, who said an abolitionist was 'an anti-hanging man, women's rights man, an infidel frequently, bigoted Protestant always, a socialist, a red republican, a fanatical teetotaller'.

A busy man who managed all that.

Slave trading in Britain officially ended in 1833 but American abolitionists wanted to keep pressure coming from

Britain. In 1845, another former slave, Frederick Douglas, gave a lecture tour in Britain. In Ireland he was warmly welcomed by committed Catholic abolitionist Daniel O'Connell. At the death of O'Connell, Douglas said, 'The cause of the American slave, not less the cause of his country, had met a great loss.'

Douglas was a religious Protestant himself and under the wing of Belfast Protestant abolitionists he gave seven lectures in the city that were rapturously received.

On his return to America, Frederick Douglas remained interested in Irish issues, particularly the increasing racism among Irish immigrants to the USA, speaking of this with disappointment: 'Perhaps no class of our fellow citizens has carried this prejudice against colour to a point more extreme and dangerous than have our Catholic Irish fellow citizens, and yet no people on the face of the earth have been more relentlessly persecuted and oppressed on account of race and religion than have this same Irish people.'

In the African Cultural Centre near the university, May, the tired Belfast woman running the office, had similar tales to Mrs Khan's. Some of the African community had been there a long time – medical professionals, civil servants, academics and businessmen. Some Africans had chosen Northern Ireland out of curiosity, some had been posted there from the British mainland, some had married into the country. There were students and an increasing number of nurses. Again, attacks were on the increase. Most of the African community had moved to South Belfast and the University district, not to be among Catholics or Protestants, but to be out of areas where people were poor, unemployed and looking for someone to blame.

'There's a lot of envy. People in public housing see Africans buying houses. They don't understand that the Africans are working three jobs to pay those mortgages. We don't have that kind of enterprise here. We're stuck in a benefit culture. It's such a shame the way things are going here, but the government doesn't govern. It has tantrums about the peace talks and doesn't do anything about getting people back to work and rebuilding areas that the Troubles have wrecked. A lot of Northern Irish people have got so stuck they need energizing and leading. They're not getting it and they don't understand when they see immigrants getting on.'

I thought she was being a bit hard on her own. 'But isn't there a class thing? A lot of immigrants are educated professional people, way ahead of the people on sink estates around Belfast.'

'But immigrants will scrub floors, even if they're doctors, to get on,' she argued.

I knew this was true. But people in Northern Ireland had become very discouraged from being enterprising, because of historical prejudice in the case of Catholics. Or the thwarting of entrepreneurial schemes by violence in everybody's case. Immigrants arriving hopeful and energized were meeting a lot of battered-down, worn-out people.

May showed me exhibition materials the organization had been taking into schools. Mostly it concerned the anti-slavery movement.

'It's something from the past to be proud of, and the children are so interested. We also do a music and dancing show. Actually one of the dancers brings her baby at the moment. The kids go wild about the baby. Imagine, schools out in the country, white white Irish children, they don't get to see Africans let alone talk to them. Oh yes, schools of all denominations. Maybe they'll grow up less narrow-minded and envious.'

I suggested that, historically, successful immigrants were always resented, anywhere.

'Maybe. Just because something's always happened doesn't make it right. People in Ireland are too fond of things that have always happened.' She shrugged. 'Sorry, I've had a lot of upsetting things to deal with this week. If you were here another week I could take you out to the schools with us. Show you something positive.'

I nodded and sneezed. The lady with the baby was due to arrive, so I didn't want to give it my germs. I walked back towards Sandy Row, seeing fewer and fewer non-Caucasian faces.

There was a scattering of police in Sandy Row, protecting a solemn Salvation Army march up the road – slow, sedate and melancholic in the evening sun.

My hotel was quiet, the hen parties and stag parties had checked out. The friendly cleaning man stopped me in the corridor, telling me someone had left some aspirin behind in the next room if I wanted them. And there were plenty more tissues if I needed more.

'You poor love, imagine being so sick in a strange place.'

It was dawning on me that it was a strange place, to me.

I had thought Morrissey's anthem of the plastic paddy, 'Irish Blood, English Heart,' was the wrong way round. I only had a bit of English blood and romantically assumed I had an Irish heart.

If I wanted to come back to Northern Ireland, plentiful and welcoming family regardless, I'd have to make a huge leap of heart and mental effort to feel at home. Being a Catholic, or a Protestant, Irish or English meant nothing. I lived in London – every street full of different-coloured faces, every tube stop with a different culture. London was as vast and anonymous as a new continent – every day, if you wanted, you could re-create yourself. Or you could live in a community you'd chosen, not inherited. Being accustomed to all that, taking all that for granted had rubbed into me so much, like Flann O'Brien's bicycle, it had become part of my identity. I'd immigrated and I wasn't going anywhere.

14. Definitions of Success

Uncle Eamon set off down the cliff path ahead of us. 'What we'll do is take a wee dander round the headland and see how we get on.'

Outer-cousin Mark might have been exaggerating when he said most people in Northern Ireland were related, but a lot of the population did seem to be related to me.

I'd come up to the seaside resort of Portrush to clear the germs out of my head and to have some quiet time out of Belfast. I'd walked into a hotel dining room and there were my uncle Eamon and aunt Sarah. They'd whisked themselves away for a peaceful weekend break. They didn't seem too disappointed to have the peace broken into by a stray niece.

Sarah teased me, asking if I'd come up to Portrush for a sneak visit to Kelly's night club, a notorious den of drugs and badness. I told her how I'd managed to have enough of Northern Irish nightlife just lying in my hotel bed in Belfast.

Despite Kelly's and a few other brash clubs and bars, Portrush remained a subdued resort town. The headland, jutting into the Atlantic, had unspoilt, sweeping views of waves crashing on rocks and the grassy cliff tops were crawled by bird-watchers managing to find quiet for their hobby.

After our dander round Portrush headland, we drove on to the wide beach at Portstewart, a handy and permitted way to avoid parking. Range Rovers and fine family saloons were lined up on the sand; prosperous-looking people ran about with children, kites and dogs. Portstewart felt like a Malone Road of a beach, although it wasn't as grand as it had been. The railway company weren't allowed to build a station at sedate Portstewart for fear it would attract 'vulgar people' to the town. These days, vulgar people without their own transport could get a bus.

We waited on the beach for the sunset. It was something of a non-event, even though there was a sculpture near the boating pool with a plaque announcing that the song 'Red Sails in the Sunset' had been inspired by a Portstewart sunset.

Uncle Eamon said they'd just come up to Portrush to 'foughter about'. This spelling doesn't capture the pronunciation. This word has far more unscriptable syllables. Foughtering could be pleasant, akin to pottering but with a wistful edge, or it could be bad: you could foughter away your time when you should be doing your work, as I knew too well.

While foughtering and dandering, Eamon, Sarah and I reminisced about Sion Mills.

'It was such a good place to grow up, a real country childhood,' Eamon said, happy at the mere thought of it. 'I'd get up in the mornings and be off up the fields and into the woods. There were hazel trees there, I could make bow and arrows out of those and hunt things. Look for things to hunt anyway.'

I told them about my attempts to live a country life, collecting sticks for the fire in Cavan and ending up sounding like a crazy Margo from *The Good Life*.

Eamon smiled, indulgently avuncular in my defence. 'Well those farmers would be only just removed from the generation that did have to collect sticks for the fire. My mother and Mary Eliza used to go out for long walks by the river, chatting away and collecting sticks. Mind you, when the firelighters came in, my mother would still go for the walks, because it was Mary Eliza's social life. I remember her saying,

"I'm run off my feet but if I don't take Mary Eliza out to get sticks she'll be so disappointed." Poor Mary Eliza.'

We sighed sadly over Mary Eliza for a few moments.

Sarah laughed. 'So there you are, if you ever feel down about life, at least you've got more than a walk collecting sticks to look forward to.'

Eamon remembered me singing to the hens. 'I thought you were a strange sort of child. I thought it must be being transplanted had done it to you.'

Of course, Uncle Eamon thought transplanting was what had done for George Best and Alex Higgins, as well as his hen-serenading niece. Not that he was against transplanting, you just had to know there'd be consequences. All his children had been born in central Africa, while he'd taught in a school for ten years. It had taken them a long time to adjust to Northern Irish life, where your skin became pale and school teachers didn't have servants.

'It was peculiar for them, but they didn't take to an unnatural relationship with poultry.'

'I really believed I would be the one to make Granny's ship come in.'

'She'd have had a long wait for a ship to come in on her egg money,' Eamon sighed. 'She went to the pictures a lot, you know, anything American. I think that's where she got the idea there'd be a ship to come in.'

I thought she had made a ship come in — hadn't everyone done very well for themselves?

'Oh, determined . . .' He smiled. 'She thought anyone related to her could be anything they wanted.'

I left Eamon and Sarah to their dandering early next morning. I had a Sunday evening mission in Portadown and wanted to see as much as possible on the way down there.

Of no interest to me, Portstewart and Portrush were surrounded by championship golf courses. More interesting was Limavady, where the Ross sisters had lived. They did nothing spectacular, except in 1851 Jane Ross noted down a piece of music played by an itinerant fiddler. It became the unofficial Irish national anthem: 'The Londonderry Air'/'Danny Boy'.

There were no glens and mountainsides on the road I passed through towards Derry; this was strange flat land known locally as 'the levels'. These former marshes were below sea level, and had been kept drained by pumps for flax-growing, now they were used for market gardening. In World War Two, the wide, flat surfaces were used as aerodromes and present-day Derry City airport was at the edge of 'the levels'. Continuing the aeronautical theme, further along the levels was Ballyarnet field, where Amelia Earhart landed after her solo transatlantic flight.

In Derry, Sally's family greeted me for Sunday lunch as if I'd just flown the Atlantic myself. There was a crowd of Sally's relatives around the table, new names and faces coming thick and fast. One familiar face was Sally's husband, Dan. He cross-examined me about what was going into my book and as he served the main course he said, 'Well, it won't be any kind of book if it doesn't include the gravy you're having with this roast beef. I made this gravy and I want it properly recorded for posterity.'

On hearing I'd been back to Strabane, Sally's brother Liam reminisced about the most frightening man who ever lived in that town: 'I couldn't tell you his real name but everyone called him Gandhi, because in the summer he wore just a sack around him tied with string. He was some poor man with no legs, but he'd great strong arms and he'd move himself along on this contraption like a skateboard . . .'

I couldn't stop myself: 'Leatherarse,' I interrupted, making grandchildren splutter and take more interest in the conversation. 'My mother told me he was the most frightening man ever lived in Strabane.'

'And she called him Leatherarse?'

'Because he was always dragging himself along, one of her brothers said he must have a leather arse, so that's what they called him.'

'He was a terrible, bad-tempered creature. If you caught his eye he'd swear blue murder and throw something at you.'

My mother's tales of Leatherarse had been vivid: 'Apparently he'd lie in wait for children, then scoot out silently, so he'd be suddenly there, at eye level with them, and make a terrible screaming noise to freak them out.'

'Where does he live?' a nervous grandchild inquired.

'Oh, poor Leatherarse will be long dead,' Dan reassured her. 'I expect children had teased the poor crittur and that was his revenge.'

'He had a goat cart as well,' I remembered. 'On a Sunday he'd get dressed up and ride around the town on a little cart pulled by a goat.'

'No? A goat cart. I wish I'd seen that,' Liam laughed. 'Did he get very far?'

'I don't know.'

'Well.' Dan raised his glass. 'He might not have got far but he certainly made his mark: here we are all talking about him fifty years later. Here's to Leatherarse, world famous in Strabane.'

'Leatherarse!' a child shouted.

'Please,' Dan said sternly. 'Mister Leatherarse to you.'

Apparently poor Mister Leatherarse had lost his legs in an accident working on the railways in Canada. This led to a drift in the conversation toward the topic of emigration. No one had sad tales of leg loss to report, but it was a wistful topic all the same.

Derry had been a major port for the twentieth-century 'suitcase brigade', heading away from northwestern Ireland. Dan said he hardly saw his father as a child, he spent so long working in England.

'At least he'd keep coming home with the bacon,' Liam said. 'There was nothing sadder than the Irish hanging around England who'd never made it and felt ashamed to go home.'

'That was terrible,' Sally said. 'They went on their own, the men. That's what was wrong with the Irish. Other people brought the whole family, so they didn't come to that sort of end.'

'Well it makes sense,' Dan smiled. 'Men should not be trusted to go anywhere on their own, and it's a good thing those days are over.'

Their son, who'd just moved back from London to Donegal, thought it still went on to a certain extent.

'There was this couple I knew when I was working in London, nice enough. Where I moved to is their home town in Donegal. When they came back they'd a big flash car I didn't remember them having in London. Turns out they'd hired it to put on a show for their trip home. What sort of bollocks is that? There's still that mind set, that you can't come home without making a big blow of yourself.'

After much hugging, as if I was off to seek my fortune, never to be seen again, I had to leave them. I raced to Portadown, hopefully not making a big blow of myself on arrival in an average-looking hire car.

Under-cousin Mikey was disappointed I only had an average hire car this time, no secret panels, no surprise springing meal trays.

'Oh, that thing. I hope they burnt it,' Aunt Helen said.

Everyone had gathered round the wide-screen television in John and Veronica's house for a Sunday evening event that had become as sacred to family life in Northern Ireland as any kind of church-going. Sally's grandchildren had been fretting about it over lunch, although they had hours and hours to spare they wanted to go straight home after pudding to be on time.

In my family, it was Uncle Joe who was fretting the most. He'd had the calendar circled for months and been impatient since breakfast.

The holy event was a television show called *Little School Around the Corner*. Cameras went to a different primary school in Northern Ireland every week, interviewing the children about their school. Children sang, danced, played instruments, recited . . . Sometimes there was footage of a sporting triumph. This week, one of Siobhan's children was at the featured school; we'd see her singing in the choir.

Tension mounted as the programme time drew nearer. John flapped about with curtains to eliminate glare, Veronica fiddled with video controls, and Uncle Joe puffed so intently on his pipe I thought he might swallow it, set fire to his innards and miss seeing one of his precious grandchildren's moment of glory.

There were other children talking, other children dancing, other children singing solos – but finally, the choir.

No one watched for brief glimpses of our girl at the back of the choir with more rapt attention than Uncle Joe. He hadn't set fire to his innards but he was lit up with happiness. There he was, surrounded by family, watching family, having brought all of them safely through to happy lives. If they did need someone to teach a course on 'Coping with Success in Northern Ireland', Uncle Joe was the contented man to talk to.

Less contented, possibly suffering a little spasm of green-eyed monsters, Mikey complained to me when the programme finished.

'It's very unsophisticated, isn't it?'

'A great idea, though.'

'A great idea? I thought you worked in television? I'd say its days are numbered.'

'It'll run for ever,' I said.

'Oh, maybe here,' Mikey said disdainfully. 'But they won't sell it round the world.'

'They'll sell the format,' I said. 'A programme like that works anywhere.'

'Anywhere? I don't think so.'

'Annie's travelled all round the world,' Veronica told him, with a sly wink at me. 'Annie, don't they have a version of *Little School Around the Corner* everywhere?'

'Everywhere.'

'Everywhere?' Mikey still wasn't having it. 'I don't believe you. Have you seen it for yourself?'

'She's been everywhere,' Veronica said. 'Of course she's seen it.'

'Afghanistan? Have you seen it in Afghanistan?'

'Yes.'

'Really?'

'Yes, they've got it. *Little School Around the Corner in Kabul.*'

A pause, then laughter erupted. Mikey stared at me reproachfully.

'Oh, you. *Little School Around the Corner in Kabul.* You're as silly as . . . How could anyone ever take you seriously?'

Being taken seriously, even by myself, wasn't something I was used to. Intermittently in Northern Ireland it bothered me. I'd hear about tragedies and think, I'm too ill informed and far too flippant to take all this on. Bookshops in Northern Ireland had banks of military analysis, political memoirs, IRA men's memoirs, UDA men's memoirs, victims' memoirs, historical analysis, religious analysis, sociological, psychological . . . So many serious people had written about Northern Ireland, I worried my foughtering about the country would be worse than some kind of jeans-in-church type of sacrilege; it would simply be consistent insensitivity. But life in the country was not homogeneous – there was no more room on the bookshelves for seriousness. There was no law that said only Northern Ireland's sadness and darkness could be recorded eternally. There were other things. And enough light to make the dark places seem even sadder.

'Weren't you here before?' the boatman asked as he helped me down the steps.

'I did the other tour last week.'

'The *Titanic* tour? And you're back again? Well that's good. We must have acquitted ourselves well.'

The little boat that toured the harbour had alternate days when it went in the opposite direction, up the Lagan to Stranmillis.

As the boatman fiddled with ropes and canvas flaps, a different guide came on board.

'The other fellah loves boats and ships, this is your man for the river history,' the boatman explained as he made the introductions. 'Each to his own.'

Three families came on board next, all from Northern Ireland with assorted sizes of children. A thin, quiet man I'd assumed was another customer was introduced to us: 'This is our friend who's a quick sketch artist and caricaturist. He works so quickly and quietly, you won't know he's drawing you. But if you like what he's done, he only charges three pounds for the sketches and you can sort yourselves out with him at the end.'

I gave the thin, nervous man a warning look. If he thought I'd like to see what a caricaturist did to my aquiline nose, he had better think again . . . He wasn't new to the job – he knew his best bet was drawing the children and he left adults who might be touchy well alone.

The boat set off, this time away from the harbour. The guide told us the colossal value of the flats opposite the Waterfront Hall.

'Anyone who bought into property along the Lagan early on, they're laughing now. The penthouses over there are worth 450,000 pounds each.'

The Lagan banks had several apartment complexes, with river-view balconies and roof gardens – the guide knew the current value of all of them.

'The river was a different place before the weir. The banks were all stinking mud at low tide. And the shore was lined with warehouses and factories, but now people have more access to the river, it's become part of city life.'

He pointed out a big dye works still in operation.

'With all the development going on, the land that factory's on is worth a fortune. They could make a profit if they relocated, but I expect they're holding out for an even bigger price rise.'

As well as prices, he knew every inch of the river. As he pointed out new bars and trendy warehouse conversions he told us what had been there before.

'That was flour, that was meat-packing . . . Over there used to be an abattoir. Life's got easier for the members of Queen's University rowing club since it closed down. They used to have to row through slicks of blood and bits of . . . I apologize, children present.'

He handed round photographs, showing an old ferry boat that had run across the river, pointing out where the landing stage had been.

'They're thinking of bringing it back, with some kind of animal-shaped boat as a bit of fun for the kids in summer.'

Beside another luxury development of flats was what looked like a giant rubbish tip. The flats behind it were painted with UFF at every gable end.

'It's only April, but they've started to build the bonfire for the 11th of July. The locals have to live with it looking like a tip head, but it's going to be a massive bonfire. If you like that kind of thing.'

On the opposite bank, near the Ormeau Road, was a mural of a No Entry sign, with a silhouetted figure of an Orangeman inside the circle. The guide pointed away from it: 'Look a few houses along, there's a more unusual type of mural, some student group have been putting these up.'

It was a white square with lower case black writing, all run together: 'howcanquantumgravityhelpexplaintheorigin- oftheuniverse?'

Once we'd all deciphered it, the guide grinned. 'It could still be religious, but it makes a change.'

We were handed more old photographs of former factories where there were little parks now. A whole swathe of the bank had been designated a wildlife conservation area.

'There's water birds coming back, fish in the river. Industry was good for the coffers but it created stink and filth.'

As we came to the attractive wooden boat sheds of Queen's rowing club, he said Errol Flynn had done some rowing there. 'His father taught at Queen's, so people had to lock up their daughters whenever Errol came to visit.'

Beside some more increasingly valuable flats was a small jetty.

'Now there's a sad story about that jetty. We had the idea

it would be a great idea to run a commuters' river bus service from here down to the centre of town. We began with five loyal customers, and ended with the same five loyal customers. Those five loved it; we'd give them coffee and newspapers in the morning and a glass of wine in the evening. They swore by the service and we all became the best of friends. But after a few months, we had to face the sad fact that no more than five were ever coming. There was weeping and hugging and wine flowed at the party afterwards but we had to face reality.'

They'd been downhearted for a while, then couldn't believe their luck when someone made a film about the *Titanic*. They called up their mate, who knew the shipyards like his own soul, and they were off again, part of the flotilla of determined individuals who made Northern Ireland unexpected, hopeful and workable.

The boat meandered on, up to the pretty enclave of buildings around Stranmillis weir.

'The plan is to shift that weir and widen the channel, so boats can go all the way up to Lough Neagh. There'll be holiday homes, pleasure-boat cruises galore, swimming areas, one big long waterfront resort stretching for miles from central Belfast. Queen's University and Trinity are going to have an annual boat race to rival Oxford and Cambridge. This river will be alive, lit along the banks, advertised by the tourist board . . . As you can imagine, we're very cheerful about that. We've struggled away with our idea that a boat had to be an idea, and now we're thinking we'll soon get a second boat, maybe a third.'

He beamed and jumped down from an upturned crate he'd been using as a stage to deliver his history lesson.

'We'll turn back now. I'll keep quiet, put on some music and let you enjoy the river in peace.'

He put on a gentle piece of Mozart. The sun sparkled on the water, blossom–laden trees trailed the banks and the music wafted away into near blue skies. Rowers outside Queen's were taking to the water and the boatmen murmured to each other contentedly, two boats soon, maybe three . . . Even the smallest of the children on board settled to a mood of dreamy detachment as we chugged home. Through the Mozart another tune came into my head: 'It's stopped hailing, guys are swimming, guys are sailing . . .' And little boats, if not ships, were coming in.